German Actors
of the
Eighteenth and
Nineteenth
Centuries

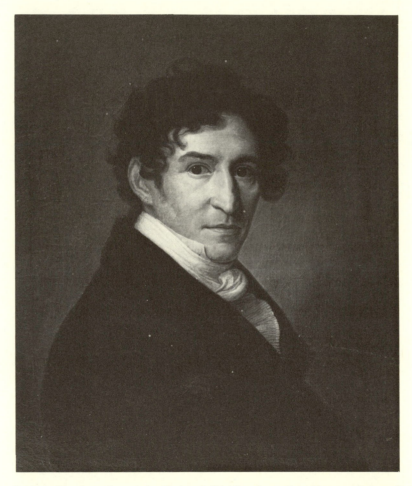

Ludwig Devrient. Portrait by Christoph Wohlin. Reproduced by permission of Theatermuseum der Universität zu Köln.

German Actors of the Eighteenth and Nineteenth Centuries

Idealism,
Romanticism,
and Realism

SIMON WILLIAMS

Contributions in Drama and Theatre Studies, Number 12

Greenwood Press
Westport, Connecticut • London, England

Library of Congress Cataloging in Publication Data

Williams, Simon.
  German actors of the eighteenth and nineteenth
centuries.

  (Contributions in drama and theatre studies, ISSN
0163-3821 ; no. 12)
    Includes bibliographical references and index.
    1. Actors—Germany. 2. Theater—Germany—History—
18th century. 3. Theater—Germany—History—19th
century. I. Title. II. Series.
PN2657.W5 1985   792'.028'0922   84-6524
ISBN 0-313-24365-4 (lib. bdg.)

Library of Congress Catalog Card Number: 84-6524
ISBN: 0-313-24365-4
ISSN: 0163-3821

First published in 1985

Greenwood Press
A division of Congressional Information Service, Inc.
88 Post Road West, Westport, Connecticut 06881

Printed in the United States of America

10 9 8 7 6 5 4 3 2 1

To my mother and father,
Cynan and Sheila Williams

CONTENTS

ILLUSTRATIONS

PREFACE

The recent revival of interest in the eighteenth- and nineteenth-century theatre seems, on the whole, to have left the German theatre aside. While there are one or two excellent general surveys, in contrast to the Anglo-American and some other national European theatre traditions, few specific thematic studies on the German theatre have appeared. Even in Germany, scholarship on the eighteenth and nineteenth centuries, while not nonexistent, is surprisingly small. This book represents a partial attempt to fill the vacuum. The actors whose careers are described and discussed in it were all highly prominent in the theatre of their day, enjoying national, and, toward the end of the nineteenth century, international reputations, equivalent to those of actors in other countries, such as David Garrick, Frédérick Lemaître, Rachel, Tommaso Salvini, and Henry Irving. Their work also helped to define the duality of idealism and realism that vitalized the development of acting in Germany to the beginning of the twentieth century.

Naturally there are many to be thanked for making this project a reality. I would like to thank *Theatre Research International* and *Shakespeare Survey* for their permission to adapt material from articles I published under their auspices. In my research, I was given invaluable help by the excellent staffs of archives in West Germany and Austria. In particular, I would like to thank Dr Roswitha Flatz of the Theatre Museum of the University of Cologne, Dr Eckehart Nölle of the Munich Theatre Museum, Frau Helga Haas of the Walter Unruh Archive in Berlin, the indefatigable staff of the Theatre Collection in the Nationalbibliothek in Vienna, and members of the dramaturgical section of the Vienna Burgtheater, all of whom offered valuable help and advice. I am also grateful for the permission to reproduce materials from their archives. My travels were made possible by a generous grant from the Humanities Research Grants Committee of Cornell University.

Special thanks are due my colleagues at Cornell and elsewhere for many interesting and informative discussions I have had with them on the history of acting. I am especially indebted to my patient students, who have so often been the first recipients of the information provided in this book. Above all, I must acknowledge the constant support and never-failing encouragement of my wife Euzetta, who has always been my most exacting and perceptive critic.

Santa Barbara
October, 1984

German Actors
of the
Eighteenth and
Nineteenth
Centuries

Chapter 1

THE RISE OF THE GERMAN ACTOR, 1700–1778

Actors have never been among the most respected members of society, but rarely has their profession stood so low in public esteem as in Germany during most of the eighteenth century. There were some theatres offering regular employment, attached to courts of the various principalities that composed the patchwork of German-speaking Europe. These, however, were occupied exclusively by French companies, whose performances of opera and tragic drama, in French of course, were presented as models of a highly developed culture that native German citizens could hardly hope to attain. Meanwhile, German actors were forced to earn their living on the road, travelling from one town to another, suffering the hostility of local inhabitants, who were intensely wary of all itinerant folk, and the persecution of Lutheran ministers, who accused actors of "wild masquerades" and "beastliness"[1] and general anti-Christian behavior.

There may have been some truth in this suspicion. Forced to live constantly on the borderline between bare subsistence and absolute penury, actors stayed in the humblest of lodgings, generally the more sordid taverns. Such living conditions were hardly conducive to fostering a respectable domesticity. Drunkenness, both on- and off-stage, was common, and fights would frequently break out between members of a troupe, often leading to arrests by the watch and several nights in jail. Sexual promiscuity was widespread in the profession, and there was considerable justification for the traditional prejudice that linked acting with prostitution. Indeed, the unconstrained behavior and moral laxity described by Goethe in *Wilhelm Meisters Lehrjahre (Wilhelm Meister's Apprenticeship*—1795) were probably typical of the theatrical profession.

Naturally, no settled family of any social class would encourage its offspring to take up the theatre for a living. It is, therefore, impossible to speculate accurately on the origins of actors. Some were born into the theatre and took to the boards as it was the only occupation they knew; others came to it as nothing else was open to them. Few made a clear choice to act as an alternative to other employment. In general, the appearance of an actor on stage was indicative of failure in some other walk of life, of an unfortunate crisis in private affairs, or of a peculiar retardation in personality. It was a lowly life. "Ruined students formed the aristocracy of the profession," wrote Eduard Devrient.[2] Like the army, the theatre absorbed those who were down on their luck, destitute, or whose lives were, in some way or other, broken.

Performance conditions for the travelling troupes were most rudimentary. Stages would be set up wherever space was available, on temporary wooden structures in market-places or outside city walls, in larger towns in ballrooms or other sizeable chambers in taverns or town halls. Permanent theatres for the troupes were unheard of until the second half of the century. Consequently actors never had a locale that would allow them opportunity to create an attractive scenic environment. Anyway, the appalling conditions of the roads, frequently deeply rutted mud, meant that they could travel only with the barest essentials of props and costumes. Even when a longer stay in one of the larger cities might have allowed them to accrue some capital to spend on improving the appearance of the stage, most of their profits would be eaten up by the payment of debts, especially those acquired through travel. Further expenses came through compulsory donations to the poorhouse or prison, often mandated in the conditions by which local authorities allowed the troupes to perform.

In the early decades of the century the repertoire was, not surprisingly, of little artistic merit. It was composed mainly of broad, often graphically obscene farces, improvised in a manner inherited from the *commedia dell' Arte,* and of *Haupt- und Staatsaktionen.* These plays were a degenerate form of the English tragedies brought over to Germany a good century before by travelling actors from London. They dramatized crudely the deeds of ancient heroes or of famous rulers from more recent times. They were episodic in structure; in their recreation of great political transactions and battles they reduced historic personages to little more than strutting marionettes, who let forth tumid tirades. The serious action of the play would be doubled with a farcical action in which figures such as Harlequin, or Hanswurst as he came to be known in Germany, capered around grotesquely. Their buffoonery and ribald conversation undercut the seriousness of the main action and provided a necessary ingredient of rowdiness to the proceedings. It was a vigorous but undisciplined theatre in which everything was for momentary effect, in which the wildest improbabilities and incongruities were happily accepted by the audience. Of stylistic unity there was nothing.

Political events, astonishing, great deeds by renowned or mythical heroes and kings, the bloodiest horrors next to the most affected, fine speeches of princes and princesses, and the most impertinent pranks of buffoons, conjuring tricks and transformations, dreams and apparitions, heaven and hell in the oddest combination with solemn allegorical-didactic figures, intermezzi, ballets, choruses, arias, illuminations and fireworks, these were the ingredients of these *Haupt- und Staatsaktionen.*[3]

Such was the fare offered on most German stages during the first half of the eighteenth century.

Then something quite remarkable happened. During the 1770s, throughout German-speaking Europe, the travellers suddenly found a home. Theatres, several of which received a high degree of subsidy from royal patrons, came to be founded, staffed by companies of German-speaking actors performing German-language plays. In the following fifty years, the German theatre was transformed. By the end of the 1820s, over sixty-five theatres, ranging from court institutions to fully commercial establishments, were in regular operation. Germany suddenly enjoyed a network of provincial theatres that was unequalled in Europe, that outranked the theatres of both France and Great Britain in variety of repertoire and social esteem. Such rapid development was unprecedented in the history of Western theatre.

This transformation was not, of course, unanticipated. During the theatre's years on the road, ambitions had frequently been expressed for its acceptance as an institution of national significance. These ambitions referred principally to two overriding political and intellectual concerns of the time. First, as the century progressed, the theatre increasingly came to be regarded as a means of aiding substantially in the creation of a national culture. The political fragmentation of Germany had hindered the development of a specifically national art and way of life; in contrast to the centralized nation-states of Europe, Germany was a backwater. But theatre, a public art in a public place, might help create the national identity that was being sought—might, by the sheer communality of the event, create recognition for works of German origin. Aligned to this nationalist preoccupation was the felt need to educate the common man. In a theatre that was properly administered and staffed, the audience might be able to witness plays that were morally improving and that increased their awareness of how people in spheres of life different from their own behaved and thought. It could expand their knowledge and increase their sensitivity, while the actor, who ideally should be possessed of education and social graces, could provide models of conduct from which the spectators could benefit.

THE LEIPZIG SCHOOL

Given the deplorable lack of education common to the acting profession, such ambitions were not realized easily. Nevertheless, even early in the eighteenth century, some progress had been made toward creating theatre with a repertoire slightly more refined than the *Haupt- und Staatsaktionen* and with a style of acting more sophisticated than the prevalent bombast and gross farce. This had occurred first through the efforts of Johannes Velten (1640-1693?), whose troupe had enjoyed some court patronage in Dresden between 1685 and 1693. Here, in addition to *Haupt- und Staatsaktionen*, adaptations of Pierre Corneille, Jean Racine, and Jean-Baptiste Molière had been performed. But this had little impact on the immediate development of German theatre. A more lasting influence was exercised by Caroline Neuber (1697-1760), who, with her husband Johann (1697-1759), managed a troupe of actors that toured the towns of Saxony and the northern German states between 1727 and 1739. They had considerable success in performing adaptations of French tragedy and comedy. This new repertoire had been formed under the guidance of Johann Christoph Gottsched (1700-1766), the luminary of the Leipzig literati, a group of writers and scholars who were attempting to introduce a higher cultural tone into German life. Through the Neuber troupe, Gottsched hoped to fulfil some of this ambition.

Gottsched wished to see a theatre purged of improvisation and of the excesses and stylistic disorder of the *Haupt- und Staatsaktionen*. As a basic requirement, he expected the actor to be able to read, so as to study the role until he or she felt the emotions of the character to be portrayed. Then the actor should discover a method whereby these emotions could be communicated to the audience so that they too felt them. This was not to be achieved by mere imitation of living models. Rather the actor, who must have studied the technique of ancient orators, should master every means available to give words the fullest and most deliberate impact. Everything had to be carefully planned, and the actor be the soul of gravity.

For as long as he speaks quietly and collectedly, the speaker must hold [his head] in proper fashion, upright and still.... But when his speech becomes somewhat lively, then nature teaches us that in expressing affirmation and denial, doubt and wonder, sadness and joy, speech can be given certain emphasis by movement of the head. If this always happens only in a distinctly serious and manly fashion, then no one can be censorious. Excessive shaking of the head must, of course, be avoided as a ridiculous nuisance.[4]

In his writings on the art of public speaking, which he identified with acting, Gottsched explored in detail the various gestures, movements, and vocal modulations that can be used to give strength and body to speech.

Whether the Neuber troupe succeeded fully in realizing Gottsched's classical oratory on stage is to be doubted. Their failure might have been due partly to their own lack of expertise, partly to contradictions in Gottsched's view of theatre. Theoretically, he argued, the actor need only follow "nature," but the material he urged the Neubers to represent on the public stage was highly artificial, French tragedy as performed at the German courts. This, in its turn, was a debased imitation of tragedy as performed at the Comédie Française. The plays staged by the Neubers were set in an idealized, heroic world, and, as a complement to this, actors wore voluminous costumes and weighty headgear, which meant that all gesture was restricted and codified into rigidity. Hands could never be placed below the waist, while each movement had to be slow and deliberate in order not to agitate the feathers on the head or to disorder the heavy drapery. As a result, the actors failed to achieve "the gracefulness of undulating movement, the sublimity of good manners, the grandeur of passionate gesticulation" (Reden-Esbeck, 73), but were "affected and outwardly exaggerated," with agitated hands and sawing arms, travestying an acting style that was probably itself a travesty. To make matters worse, the heavy alexandrines of the verse they spoke, with their banal end-rhymes, were delivered with "a repetitive modulation, a sing-song monotony." Nevertheless, whatever the failings of the "Leipzig school" of acting, as it came to be known, for the first time some uniformity and discipline had been imposed on the German actor.

A further contradiction in Gottsched's thinking on the theatre lay in his views of its nature and purpose. On the one hand, he espoused a naive view of the stage as a literal reflection of life, but on the other he claimed a high moral purpose for it that militated against his theoretical naturalism. In practice the moral view won out. The theatre, Gottsched argued, should be a pulpit from which the audience should be intimidated into leading a better way of life. Tragedy, "an important action concerning high-ranking persons" (Gottsched IX/2, 494), should arouse in the spectators an admiration for their betters. From this they learn how to be worthy citizens. Theatre "is a school of patience and wisdom, a preparation for affliction, an incitement to virtue, a chastisement of vice." The audience should retire home from its presentations, "more sensible, more prudent, and more steadfast."

Given the severe charge laid upon them, it is surprising how well received the Neuber troupe was when it brought the new theatre to its audiences. No doubt this transfer of court culture onto the public stage had considerable novelty value, but it was more likely sheer determination that carried the troupe through, especially as audiences began to drop off during the 1730s. They were also hindered by the lack of good tragedies, though Gottsched's wooden play *Der sterbende Cato (The Dying Cato*—1731) was surprisingly popular. Often the actors were forced back onto more undemanding material, though this too was more refined than the old farce. Caroline Neuber, once she escaped the straitjacket of high tragedy, was a graceful and flexible actress, whose performances of the roles of Molière, Jean-François Regnard, Philippe Destouches, and Ludvig Holberg contributed to the gradual exclusion of improvisation from comedy. This exclusion was symbolically proclaimed in Leipzig in 1737 when Harlequin was banished from the stage in a formal ceremony, though it is doubtful whether he stayed in permanent exile, as a 1738 playbill of *Dr Johann Faust* indicates that Harlequin's successor, Hanswurst, was highly prominent in the action. It was difficult to suppress the energies of this older theatre; in fact Goethe, in his draft for *Wilhelm Meister's Apprenticeship*, has Caroline Neuber appear in the guise of Mme de Retti to deplore the passing of the improvised comedy. With it went much vitality and an opportunity for the actors to exercise their imagination, unimpeded by a text.

The Neubers and Gottsched parted company in 1739, due to disagreements over the conduct of their affairs and Caroline's doubts over the viability of Gottsched's reforms. From then on, she sank into increasing obscurity. After her death, her body was refused public burial by the church, which insisted it could only be placed in consecrated ground if the coffin was passed over the wall at night. But despite this sad decline, the Gottsched-Neuber partnership had done much for the theatre. The repertoire had been regularized and plays with some claim to artistic standards introduced. The Leipzig school of acting, although stiff and mannered, imposed uniformity on performance and gave a discipline to the actors that eventually allowed them to adopt a more systematic approach to realizing their roles on stage. Moreover, Caroline's care for the moral welfare of her troupe members, all unmarried actresses living under her strict care, contributed minimally to a rise in the social status of the profession.

A greater impetus to this rise in stature came from the requirement that all actors had to read. In an age of wide illiteracy, this was to give the profession a quasi-scholastic prestige. Not only was reading important, but the actor also had to develop prodigious powers of memory as, due to the relatively small potential audience in each town, plays were changed each day. A travelling troupe would have to have a repertoire of between 100 and 150 plays and, as no one could be allowed time off, actors would be expected to appear in any one of these at a few hours' notice. This posed no problems in the days of improvisation, but with the advent of the learned, "literary" drama, the actor was expected to memorize well over a hundred different roles at any given time. So success on stage came increasingly to depend as much upon mental capacities as upon strength of voice, ability to perform acrobatics, or skill in playing the buffoon. As the century progressed, some form of education became a prerequisite for the actor.

The Neubers also helped in the formation of the *Fach* system. *Fach* means both the recurring types of character out of which plays' casts were composed and the type of actor who was most suited by physique and vocal quality to play a given character-type. As most plays were written with types in mind or were read by the troupe with an eye to type-casting, it was crucial that each troupe constitute a cross section of types from contemporary plays. As the formality of the Leipzig school was suited more to the representation of type than to the unfolding of inner states of being, the Neubers helped consolidate the practice of type-casting. In accordance with the demands of French tragedy, most troupes through to the end of the eighteenth century would possess actors skilled in the following *Fächer*: among the men, Tragic Hero and Lover, Older Hero and Tyrant, Confidant, Second Lover, and Leader of the Bodyguard; among the women, Tragic Mother and Queen, Lover, and Confidante. These eight actors were sufficient to perform most tragedies, with smaller roles played by minor actors. Comedy required a greater variety: two male and two female Lovers, the affectionate Father, the comic Father, the Chevalier, two comic Old Folk, two Intriguers, the "First French Servant" (male), and the Soubrette. As actors appeared in both tragedy and comedy, the average size of a troupe was between fifteen and eighteen people, taking into account bit-part actors and technical staff. Later in the century, the *Fach* system developed a bewildering number of subdivisions, but until well into the nineteenth century the practice continued of hiring actors according to their suitability for stock-types, and they would train themselves according to the needs of these types. Despite protests by both actors and management that this practice of hiring and casting was against the interests of a vital theatre, it maintained a tenacious hold, especially as it enabled individual members to claim a monopoly on certain sorts of role. Furthermore, for all but the most enterprising of actors, the system gave them a comfortable niche and a status within the troupe and in the eyes of the public.

THE THEATRE AS A HUMANIZING INFLUENCE

If ambitious actors in Neuber's time were still poor imitators of an aristocratic culture, in the middle decades of the century they found material to perform that was more congenial to them and to the evolution of an idea of theatre that gave their profession its own legitimacy.

The Neuber troupe was taken over by Johann Schönemann (1704-1782), who, in his turn, came under Gottsched's influence. By the early 1750s, it would appear that the *Haupt- und Staatsaktionen* had been eradicated from Schönemann's repertoire, and though it lingered on in the troupes of Heinrich Koch (1703-1775) and Carl Theodore Döbbelin (1727-1793), by the 1770s it had disappeared entirely, to the regret, it must be noted, of some who missed its spontaneity and grotesque humor.[5] In its place were either adaptations from the French or plays constructed according to French models, most notably those of Johann Elias Schlegel, the "German Racine." But plays dramatizing conflicts particular to the life of the ascendant middle classes were beginning to appear on stage, especially in the troupe of the most successful of mid-century actor-managers, Konrad Ernst Ackermann (1712-1771). This new bourgeois drama was first evident in translations of plays by Pierre-Claude de La Chaussée and George Lillo, but it was quickly naturalized, above all by Gotthold Ephraim Lessing. Lessing's sympathetic, dramatically interesting characters from contemporary life and his dialogue, which was strikingly realistic in contrast to the verse of the "literary" drama, enabled the actor to present character studies with far greater subtlety than had previously been possible. Furthermore, his plays and the numerous realistic genre-studies of German life by various dramatists that followed meant that the stage could function effectively as a mirror for the time, rather than as a distorted reflection of an alien society.

Aligned to the rise of the bourgeois drama were the ever more clearly heard demands for a subsidized theatre that would cultivate a distinctly national drama and serve as a means of educating and refining the sensitivities and manners of audiences. The "national theatre" theme was first fully expounded by J. E. Schlegel, who had seen the founding of such an institution in Copenhagen in 1748. His views on the social function of theatre, which influenced several of those who would later be involved in founding standing theatres in Germany, were bound by the constrictive mentality characteristic of a time that identified art with moral improvement. Schlegel's prescription was, however, less draconian than Gottsched's, as he put more trust in the audience's perceptive powers. Theatre, he argued, appeals to the intelligence and teaches not as an authoritarian pedant, "but as a man who instructs through social intercourse and always guards against revealing that this is his intent."[6] The lessons offered by the theatre are, therefore, hidden, and audiences need to use their powers of cognition to discover them. However, this is not made too difficult for them, as theatre does not present "human character-types and passions" in an undifferentiated state as in everyday life. Instead, it isolates them.

Such a representation separates a subject from the accidental circumstances with which the original is mixed. Nature does not show us the hypocrite, the jealous man, the gambler, the misanthrope in the same light as does the theatre. Here their character is quite simple, without any mixture of other virtues and vices. In nature one thing is always mingled with many other things, and to seek it out in unfamiliar circumstances always requires initially that meditation, which, in a play, the author has already undertaken for us. (Schlegel, 567)

Theatre heightens the individual's awareness of the human condition by clarifying it and, through the play's action, it encourages the spectators to judge the characters they have observed. In this relatively unpretentious way, if plays are carefully designed to refine the spectators' sensitivity and to strengthen their moral outlook, the theatre can become a true "school of morals," working toward the creation of an ever-improving, just, and civilized society.

Crucial to Schlegel's conception of theatre is trust in the audience's perceptions and in the playwright's and actor's abilities to guide those perceptions. His humanely idealistic vision of theatre was more fully developed by Lessing, whose collection of critical essays *Hamburgische Dramaturgie* (*Hamburg Dramaturgy*—1769) was the only enduring product of an attempt to set up a national theatre in Hamburg in 1767. Lessing, as dramaturg of the theatre, wrote on several themes, on the weaknesses of French neo-classical tragedy, on the quality of Shakespeare's plays, not then in the repertoire, on the nature of acting, and on the purpose of theatre. Lessing argued that the playwright does not write to pontificate to audiences but out of a wish "to enlighten and better the populace, not to confirm it in its prejudices or in its vulgar way of thinking."[7] Theatre can expand human consciousness, elevate and broaden each person's knowledge of life. As it also encourages clarity of vision, it must itself be a model of clarity. Nothing on stage must be confusing. "Everything must be clear for the spectator. He is intimate with each person, he knows everything that happens, everything that has happened" (Lessing, 281). Any attempt to mystify the audience by tension, a fault Lessing claims of the French drama, is little more than "pleasing childish curiosity" (Lessing, 282) and, therefore, is a denial of people's right to foretell for themselves the play's conclusion. Theatre not only improves morals, it exercises the intellect.

Lessing's view of theatre, characteristic of the thought of the Enlightenment, presupposes humans as rational beings, controlling their own destinies. They can do this because they have a purpose in life. "Acting with purpose is what raises mankind above lesser creatures" (Lessing, 208). The best theatre also has a purpose. "Inventing with purpose, imitating with purpose, is what distinguishes the genius from the petty artists who only invent to invent, imitate to imitate" (Lessing, 208). That purpose is not only "to teach us what to do or to refrain from . . . to acquaint us with the characteristics of good and evil, of the proper and the ridiculous" (Lessing, 209), but it is also to demonstrate how nothing in the world is unresolved, all is in agreement. "We are entitled to require harmony and purpose in all characters the poet forms or creates . . . nothing in the characters must be contradictory; they must remain always uniform, always like themselves" (Lessing, 207). Lessing defined as genius the ability to see this inner consistency. But genius is also an active force that can lead individuals toward understanding the world, so regulating their conduct within it, as "genius . . . engages our powers of desire and abhorrence with such objects as deserve their attention, and always places these objects in their true light, so that no false light tempts us to desire what we should abhor and abhor what we should desire" (Lessing, 209). The end of theatre, defined through an extensive reinterpretation of Aristotle, resides not in rejecting whatever is morally abhorrent, but in understanding and extending to it our compassion. Theatre arouses our capacity to "share all kinds of suffering" (Lessing, 420), and makes us aware that such suffering can also occur to us. In this way, it creates a sense of kinship among human beings, and so can be used to the lofty purpose of unifying the human race in common understanding.

These ideals, expressed, it must be noted, in no systematic pattern, rejected the high classical theatre envisaged by Gottsched. They also had resonant social implications. No longer should serious theatre be the exclusive preserve of the aristocratic courts, nor of those who perpetuated the court theatre on the public stage. Instead its domain was the public stage re-formed to more humanitarian ends. The theatre, Lessing argued, is no place to engage audience loyalty for political causes, for "our sympathy needs an individual object, and a state is far too abstract an idea for our sentiments" (Lessing, 83). In order to hold the audience's attention, the playwright must fasten upon character, "not so that we learn what this or that particular man has done, but what every man of a certain character would do under certain given circumstances" (Lessing, 120). This understanding could not come about through drama dealing with eminent personages merely because they are eminent. "The misfortune of those whose circumstances come closest to our own must naturally penetrate our souls most deeply, and if we feel pity for kings, then we feel with them because they are human beings, not kings'' (Lessing, 83). While the German theatre was not to grow under conditions as democratic as those implicitly envisioned by Lessing, in the years ahead the ideals he expressed were to remain a potent force.

Implicit too in this reformulation of the theatre to humane purposes was a charge to the actor. As the realizer on stage of a drama that guides people to greater knowledge of themselves and the world around them, the actor should be as informed and as sensitive as the playwright. The actor too should possess the "genius" that shows purpose in human conduct and reveals the essential harmony of the human condition. But to achieve this it was necessary to abandon the grandiose gestures and vainglorious poses of the Leipzig school, as they gave no opportunity to explore the inner feelings and thoughts of characters. Rather than master a code of oratory, the actor had to come closer to the character portrayed.

The movement toward a comparatively "realistic" theatre raised two fundamental questions. How far should the actor identify with the role assumed on stage? With what right can acting be described as an independent art? As the credibility of rhetorical acting had been declining throughout Europe in the middle decades of the century, many theoreticians had addressed themselves to these questions, and, although no definitive answers could be given, the actor progressively came to be seen as a mimetic artist who represented average rather than exceptional humanity. Lessing, with his knowledge of European languages, was closely involved in the discussion. The formation of his ideas, occurring in reaction to the Leipzig school, came about through wide reading. Although he recognized the value of advocates of rhetorical acting, such as Luigi Riccoboni, he was more directly influenced by those who conceived of acting as a realistic art. Remond de Saint-Albine in *Le comédien* (*The Actor*—1747) argued that the actor must surrender to the role and then instinctively allow the passions felt to form the appropriate gestures and movements of the assumed character. More influential yet on Lessing's thought was *L'art du théâtre* (*The Art of Theatre*—1750) by Francesco Riccoboni, which Lessing translated soon after its publication in France. Riccoboni tended to take a midway position between his father's view of the actor as a rhetorician and those who asserted the emotions of the characters should be felt and reproduced. Complete identification with the character in the role was impossible, claimed Riccoboni, as no actor can adapt to all emotional changes a character goes through in the course of the play's action; all but the most skilled would become confused and lose themselves. Instead, while recognizing the strength of those feelings that impel the character, the actor must abstract them and enlarge them. Even though the stage presents the illusion of real life, it is not actually real life, so the actor must present on-stage life in broader strokes. In that way it is possible to penetrate the audience's feelings and draw their attention toward the character. Lessing had also read the occasional writings of Diderot on the actor. However, the Frenchman had not yet written his famous theory of the actor as a cold observer of character, *La paradoxe du comédien* (*The Paradox of Acting*—1773), but still subscribed to a theory of affective acting similar to Saint-Albine's. Nevertheless, Diderot's call for a drama in which dialogue was not wordy was partly in the interests of the actor developing as an independent artist who would use gesture as a more powerful expressive means than words.

While the thought of these writers had been reflected in Lessing's occasional writings, he learned most, he claimed, not from any theoretician, but from his close cooperation in Hamburg with the leading German actor of the time, Konrad Ekhof.

KONRAD EKHOF

Like most actors of the day, Ekhof's origins were obscure. Born in 1720 in Hamburg into a soldier's family, he managed to acquire sufficient education to be appointed to clerical posts in Hamburg, then in Schwerin. But his theatrical ambitions prevailed over considerations of financial security, so late in 1739 he joined Schönemann's troupe, newly constituted after the departure of the Neubers. He first appeared on stage in Racine's *Mithridate* in January 1740, in company with two other novitiates to the theatre, Konrad Ackermann and Sophie Schröder (1714-1792). These two soon left the troupe, but Ekhof stayed with it for the next seventeen years, travelling unceasingly around the towns of northern Germany. During these years, he became the troupe's leading actor, developing a passionate interest in the social status of actors and in their claim to be recognized as a "free artist." In 1753 this resulted in his founding an "academy," composed of the troupe's principal actors, in which the repertoire, the nature of acting, and the honor of the profession were earnestly discussed. But, after meeting regularly for thirteen months, the "academy" disbanded, an event that foreshadowed a decline in the troupe's fortunes. When Schönemann left to take up horse dealing in 1757, Ekhof also departed.

The troupe was taken over by Heinrich Koch, who persuaded Ekhof to rejoin, but it was not a happy partnership. Ekhof had a meditative, even solemn temperament that accorded ill with Koch's rather flashy personality. In particular, Ekhof deplored Koch's habit of inserting comic interludes between the acts of serious plays, a residue of the *Haupt- und Staatsaktionen*. All the same, the two stayed together until 1764, when Ekhof left to join the now-famous Ackermann troupe, presently in Hannover. The following years were his best. Acting with accomplished colleagues, with a varied repertoire that included much bourgeois drama, he acquired a national reputation. In 1767, when Ackermann temporarily withdrew from managing the troupe, Ekhof was the leading actor of the Hamburg national theatre, where he found in Lessing an ideal critic and colleague.

After the demise of the Hamburg project, Ekhof took to the road once more, first with Ackermann, then with Abel Seyler (1730-1800). As Hamburg had shown the financial difficulties involved in establishing a standing theatre without patronage, in 1771 Seyler's troupe gladly accepted an invitation from the duchess of Saxe-Weimar to occupy the court theatre in Weimar. Ekhof's respite from the hardships of travel might have been short-lived, as the castle, which housed the theatre, burned down in 1774, but, on the duchess's recommendation, he and the troupe were invited to the neighboring city of Gotha by Duke Ernst of Gotha. From then until his death in 1778, Ekhof was director of the first fully subsidized court theatre with a German-language repertoire. When he died, he was the preeminent actor of his time. In the words of his pupil J. H. F. Müller,

[Ekhof] is unquestionably the best German actor. As long as I have known the theatre, I have found none to equal him. His sonorous delivery, the truth, the beautified nature, the gifted qualities that this worthy man brings to his acting, transport everyone who sees him for the first time.[8]

Physically Ekhof was unsuited to his calling (see Figure 1). He was distinctly unprepossessing in appearance, "small, with hunched shoulders, with an angular, bony frame that was especially apparent in his strongly protruding kneebones: a plebeian figure" (Ed. Devrient, *Ges-*

1. Konrad Ekhof. Engraving by F. Müller, from portrait by A. Graff. Reproduced by permission of Theatermuseum der Universität zu Köln.

chichte I, 308). In youth he was unsuited to be Tragic Hero and Lover, and in middle age the Older Hero and Tyrant, as the exaggerated gestures of the Leipzig school, which initially he had to master, appeared ridiculous when he practiced them. To make matters worse, he found it impossible to deliver alexandrines in the appropriately repetitive, rythmical manner. If he were to succeed on stage, unusual means had to be found.

Necessity as much as anything must have driven Ekhof to foster a method of acting that would bring the inner life of the character to the fore and divert attention from his physical deficiencies. So, while his colleagues in the Schönemann troupe were still sawing the air with their arms, he used less pronounced gestures, adopted a more relaxed posture, and articulated his words in a more subdued manner. By 1749 he was already being singled out by spectators for his natural acting, and some years later, when the bourgeois drama was finding its way into the troupe's repertoire,[9] such acting was beginning to become standard for the troupe as a whole. Later, both with Ackermann, himself a robust, unmannered actor, and Seyler, Ekhof continued to wean his fellow actors from the Leipzig style. Grandiose gestures gave way to quieter, more individual and selective gestures, while sing-song monotony subsided into speech that was closer to the flow and rhythm of everyday conversation. Actors were now closer to flesh-and-blood beings than to marionettes, and their representation of character appeared to be invested with the spontaneity of real life.

An important function of the Schönemann Academy was to discuss the relationship between the stage and nature, by which, in the thinking of the time, was meant social conduct. "The art of acting," Ekhof stated, "is to imitate nature through art and to come so near to her that probabilities must be taken for truths, or bygone events be so naturally represented that it seems as if they are happening now for the first time."[10] Ekhof was, however, fully aware that this could not be achieved solely by the actor abandoning himself to the role, as if the stage were a substitute for real life. Although he and the academy never systematized their approaches to the characters they played, Ekhof was keenly conscious of acting as a strategy, that creating the illusion of reality was an artificial process. Acting, he posited, needed a "grammar" that would allow its practitioners "to see to the root cause of everything," that would provide them with a methodology and earn for the actor "the name of a free artist" (Kindermann, 21).

Although Ekhof never wrote this grammar, his practice both as an actor and, in Gotha, as a trainer of actors, contributed toward substantiating some basic principles. He had some respect for the French, but found it necessary "to separate their failings from their beauties" (Kindermann, 40). Such failings lay primarily in their tendency to overdecorate, so that flamboyance served to obscure the emotion or thought rather than reveal it. Simplicity was the key to successful acting, as through this the actor had direct access to the emotions of the audience, and the audience in return could identify with the character rather than wonder at it. With Ekhof a bond of sympathy was established between stage and audience. "A tear I have extorted from a sympathetic heart, a smile I have forced from a meditative man, I have always considered an unmistakeable touchstone; therefore I do not deny my pleasure . . . when I conjure forth tears in [the audience's] eyes"[11]

But while Ekhof practiced simplicity on stage, this did not lead to the reduction of character to one or two primary emotions. Perhaps the most impressive aspect of his acting was its fullness. Contemporaries wrote constantly about how easily he could change from one character to another, completely altering his voice and physiognomy to suit the new character. As he was master of "all the sounds and tones of passion,"[12] he was able to reveal "all aspects and folds of the heart." The variety and compass of his mimetic skills meant that he was happiest with relatively underwritten dramas such as Lessing's, in which the dialogue indicated a distinct subtext, allowing the actor, in Ekhof's words, "to plunge deeply into the sea of human thoughts and passions" (Barthel, 55). The freedom offered by Lessing accounts for Ekhof's seemingly perverse judgment on Shakespeare, whose plays were beginning to appear on German stages during his final years at Gotha. He said, "They will utterly spoil our actors. Everyone who speaks [Shakespeare's] splendidly powerful language, has nothing else to do except say it. The rapture Shakespeare excites makes everything easy for the actor."[13] History was to prove Ekhof wrong, as Shakespeare did challenge actors, but for one whose life had been devoted to refining the art of acting and establishing its primacy on the stage, his view of Shakespeare as a rival is understandable.

But while the combination of simple expression with complexity of inner feeling explains Ekhof's success in the bourgeois drama, it does not fully account for the hold he exercised over his audiences. In all the roles he played, with the exception of low comedy, a certain gravity gave aura to his stage presence. In some degree this could be attributed to his rich and sonorous voice, universally acclaimed for its quiet power and harmony of diction. It was an ideal instrument, through which Ekhof could exhibit his delicate sense of rhythm, while it served him well in indicating shifts of mood within the character. Even Friedrich

Schröder, his most persistent critic, denied neither his ability to invest "the clumsiest alexandrines with suppleness,"[14] nor the fire and melody of his voice, which gave life to the dullest and most trivial of passages. But an even more compelling quality in Ekhof's acting was one that is less easy to define, though crucial in the development of German acting, namely, his ability to give stature to the most everyday characters and to extract from their individual experience a more general meaning.

Lessing wrote in the *Hamburg Dramaturgy* about how theatre centers the audience's attention on character, not because the individual alone is of interest, but because the dramatic character's action tells us "what every man of a certain character would do under certain given circumstances" (Lessing, 120). Consequently, the actor must not merely imitate human beings and create a distinctly individual personality on stage but must also be able to generalize, giving the character a more symbolical stature. Ekhof provided Lessing with a model for such acting.

If given the choice between the intuitive actor who feels with the character and the technical actor who feels nothing but has a finely developed mimetic and vocal ability, Lessing would have chosen the latter. The intuitive actor, he rationalized, is dependent on moods, so performances from night to night can easily be inconsistent. The technical actor is not only more reliable but unconsciously is able to acquire much of the feeling of the intuitive actor so the emotions portrayed "will react upon the body and bring about those changes that do not depend entirely on our will. . . . [Such an actor will feel] without understanding in the least why he should do so" (Lessing, 21). While Lessing did not find Ekhof so uncomprehending as this paradigmatic, technical actor, the interdependency between external stimulus through technique and inner feeling was clearly a hallmark of his acting. The effect achieved by the mixture of the two, Lessing described as the mingling of "composure and a certain coldness" with "fire and a certain enthusiasm" (Lessing, 22), establishing a tension between a marmorial exterior and the suggestion of profound thought or emotional ferment within the character. This tension did not only give Ekhof the freedom to select and control those "involuntary changes of the body, whose existence alone allows us to believe reliably in inner feeling" (Lessing, 21), it also allowed him to judge when the character could be removed from the mere imitation of humanity in order for the performance to acquire a more symbolic status. At such moments, "the soul suddenly collects itself to throw a reflective glance upon itself or its surroundings"

(Lessing, 23). To achieve such an effect, Ekhof, with discernible pre-
meditation, adopted gestures that called attention to themselves, briefly
releasing the character from the illusion of which it was a part. It was
in this way, Lessing argued, that "moral statements should be spoken
in passionate situations" (Lessing, 23), for then they appear to be both
a natural expression of the character and statements that have application
beyond the specific world of the play. The special strength of Ekhof's
acting lay in the harmony with which he managed this transfer from
one level of meaning to the other.

Both Lessing and, as we have seen, Ekhof were concerned to define
how acting is a "free art," how the actor can make in the theatre a
contribution specifically his own. With the advent of the literary drama,
the actor was in danger of becoming solely the servant of the playwright,
who could dominate the actorial imagination. Certainly, by giving body
to the characters, the actor invests the text with life and can improve
upon the playwright for, as Lessing wrote, "he must think with the
poet at all times, even think for him in places where the poet has shown
himself to be human" (Lessing, 6). The actor can complete whatever
is incomplete, make adequate whatever is inadequate. But an even more
important dimension of the actor's "free art" is its function as guarantor
of the ideal harmony that should be theatre. While this resides partly
in successful transitions between individual and symbolic levels of
meaning, it also comprises two other aspects of acting demonstrated by
Ekhof. One is the revelation of harmony in character. Ekhof could show
widely various facets of personality in his characters, but he was also
able to demonstrate how contradictory facets could coexist within one
and the same person to form a unity. This was the reason for his success
with enigmatic figures such as Tellheim in *Minna von Barnhelm* and
Odoardo in *Emilia Galotti,* his most famous role, in which, through
carefully selected gestures, repeated at different times in different dramatic contexts, he managed to reconcile credibly the conflicting impulses of loyalty to his monarch and his desire to revenge himself upon
him and his minions. Along with this revelation of inner harmony of
character, Ekhof was able to create an external harmony that served to
mediate between the audience and any harshness or violence within the
action. This was achieved by his maintaining a demeanor that never
disturbed those who saw him. He was always completely polished, so
fulfilling Lessing's dictum that "neither our eyes nor our ears are to be
offended, and only when all is avoided that can be unpleasing to them

in the expression of violent passion can [acting] be smooth and polished'' (Lessing, 25). Through Ekhof the actor's art consisted in sustaining the pleasant illusion of the stage as another reality.

His contemporaries often compared Ekhof to the English actor David
Garrick, but the parallel is not entirely convincing; it may have been
used to give the German theatre a lustre that at the time it did not fully
deserve. There were probably marked differences between them. While
Garrick played comic and tragic roles with lightness, Ekhof was more
ponderous; while Garrick was unusually versatile, playing over a wide
variety of genres and, to use the German term, *Fächer*, Ekhof was
more limited. He was, for example, poor in comedies of manners, as
he spoke with too heavy an emphasis, failing to realize the wit of the
dialogue. Furthermore, a peculiarly vain streak in his character prompted
him to play the young Tragic Hero and Lover even in his Gotha days,
which aroused considerable ridicule. But he introduced into acting a
discipline different from that of the Leipzig school and into a stylistically
rigid theatre a welcome quality of warmth. Perhaps more accurate foreign parallels might be the Irish Charles Macklin or the French Michel
Baron.

Brief mention must be made of Ekhof's efforts on behalf of the social
position of the actor. Due to his lowly origins, Ekhof felt much pride
when he was accepted on the fringes of the literary and professional
worlds of Hamburg, Leipzig, and other cities in which he played. But
throughout his life he was plagued by poverty, a condition bewailed by
a local critic in Lübeck who, on seeing the Seyler troupe in 1770, was
appalled that ''this man who sets in motion in our hearts the noblest
sentiments, this well-bred bourgeois . . . this righteous man, must seek
his living from town to town like the lowliest actor of farces.''[15] Despite
a life of constant deprivation, Ekhof worked hard for his profession.
Many deliberations of the Schönemann Academy were devoted to dis-
cussing the state of the profession and, as an essential corollary, the
moral and personal qualities that actors should display. Good actors,
Ekhof claimed, ''must read and write, have a good memory, an ability
to learn, an inexhaustible energy to become ever more complete, and
the strength not to be influenced by adulatory praise, by pride, or by
unreasonable censure'' (Kindermann, 39-40). Much to Ekhof's distaste,
the academy was eventually disbanded due to the very vices of indifference, rivalry, and intrigue that he chastised. No doubt the actors also
rebelled against his pedantic manner and the extreme measures he took

in attempting to force respectability upon them. These are recorded in various rules that range from the alarmingly necessary—''No actor or actress shall come on stage with soiled clothes, spotted stockings, or dirty face and hands'' (Kindermann, 36)—to the somewhat snobbish—''The manager shall hire no actor who is not of honorable descent'' (Kindermann, 36)—to the downright proscriptive—''Each actor and actress shall apply himself to an ordered and reasonable life and be especially careful to avoid all opportunities of quarrelling, fighting, or engaging in other licentiousness'' (Kindermann, 36). Only in his final years at Gotha did Ekhof manage to found a company whose members, despite their low salaries, could settle into lives that were models of bourgeois rectitude.

Ekhof well deserves the title widely applied to him, ''the father of German acting.''[16] His career helped elevate the theatre in the public eye, but, more importantly, in his acting he appeared to combine two tendencies in a way that few actors would equal in future years. He was both a *genialische Schauspieler*—an intuitive actor, noted for warmth and seeming spontaneity in performance—and a *denkende Schauspieler*—a ''thinking,'' technical actor who gave the feeling of acting premeditively after long study of the role. No doubt this reconciliation of apparently irreconcileable opposites arose partly from contemporary writers who did not fully recognize the distinction that later came to be drawn between intuitive and technical acting. This was only to evolve clearly as a result of the actorial practice and critical cogitation of the next generation. Although these two types of actor were rarely exemplified in one person, throughout the nineteenth century the perception of a polarity between the types governed both the actors' ideas of their own work and critical discussions of that work.

The purpose of this book is to examine the careers of major actors whose practice contributed to the definition of this polarity. Tentatively the polarity lies, on the purely actorial level, between ''intuition'' and ''technique,'' between the actor who seems to respond moment by moment to the role and fellow actors' characters and the actor who has the whole role and accompanying gestures, intonations, and movements worked out beforehand. As will be seen, this implies a polarity between the actor who represents character as creature to unconscious forces—the romantic and later the realist actor—and one who presents images of the human being as a harmonious creation, as one who is completely master of all emotions—the ''idealist'' actor, who presents ideal images of man. On a broader cultural level the polarity can be seen as between the romantic and classical phases of human experience. Consequently, in the theatre, as in other artistic fields, it became the object of critical and practical interest toward the end of the eighteenth century, as a result of the romantic reaction against the rationalism of the preceding era. Nevertheless the classical, or "idealist," impetus was not extinguished by the romantics, but continued in opposition, though rarely in outright hostility, to the romantic throughout the nineteenth century. The tension between these two poles was to give German acting its peculiar mark and particular richness.

NOTES

1. Rudolph Genée, *Lehr- und Wanderjahre des deutschen Schauspiels* (Berlin: Hofmann, 1882), 361. All translations in this book are my own.

2. Eduard Devrient, *Geschichte der deutschen Schauspielkunst,* new ed. (Berlin: Elsner, 1905), I, 436.

3. Friedrich von Reden-Esbeck, *Caroline Neuber und ihre Zeitgenossen* (Leipzig: Barth, 1881), 37.

4. Johann Christoph Gottsched, *Ausführliche Redekunst,* vol. 7 of *Ausgewählte Werke,* ed. P. M. Mitchell (Berlin & New York: De Gruyter, 1975), 438.

5. See Justus Moser, *Harlekin,* ed. Henning Boetius, Ars poetica 4 (Bad Homburg, Berlin & Zurich: Gehlen, 1968).

6. Johann Elias Schlegel, *Ausgewählte Werke*, ed. Werner Schubert, Textausgaben zur deutschen Klassik (Weimar: Arion, 1963), 566-67.

7. Gotthold Ephraim Lessing, *Hamburgische Dramaturgie,* ed. Friedrich Schröter and Richard Thiele (Halle: Verlag der Buchhandlung der Waisenhauses, 1877), 13.

8. J. H. F. Müller, *Abschied von der k. k. Hof- und National-Schaubühne* (Vienna: Wallishausser, 1802), 180.

9. Lillo's *George Barnwell; or, The London Merchant* was first performed by the Schönemann troupe in Hamburg in 1754, Lessing's *Miss Sara Sampson* and Moore's *The Gambler* in 1756. See Hans Devrient, *Johann Friedrich Schönemann und seine Schauspielergesellschaft*, Theatergeschichtliche Forschungen 11 (Hamburg & Leipzig: Voss, 1895), 367-68. Series henceforward abbreviated to TF.

10. Heinz Kindermann, *Conrad Ekhofs Schauspieler Akademie*, Österreichische Akademie der Wissenschaften, Philosophisch-historisch Klasse, 230, 2 (Vienna: Rohrer, 1956), 12. Kindermann includes all documents relating to the dealings of the academy.

11. Letter from Ekhof to Nicolai in *Schauspielerbriefe aus zwei Jahrhunderten*, ed. Manfred Barthel (Munich: Funck, 1947), 53.

12. Johann Friedrich Schink, *Dramaturgische Fragmente*, extracted in *Conrad Ekhof: Ein Schauspieler des achtzehnten Jahrhunderts*, ed. Hugo Fetting (Berlin: Henschel, 1954), 195.

13. Quoted in Ed. Devrient, *Geschichte*, I, 404.

14. Friedrich Ludwig Schmidt, *Denkwürdigkeiten des Schauspielers, Schauspieldichters und Schauspieldirektors (1772-1841)*, ed. Hermann Uhde (Hamburg: Mauke, 1875), I, 228.

15. Quoted in Hermann Uhde, "Konrad Ekhof," *Das neue Plutarch* (Leipzig: Brockhaus, 1876), IV, 184.

16. Adolf Winds, *Der Schauspieler in seiner Entwicklung vom Mysterien zum Kammerspiel* (Berlin: Schuster & Loeffler, 1919), 71.

Chapter 2

THE IDEALIST ACTOR, 1777–1828

The *Hamburg Dramaturgy* ends on a note of despair. Lessing laments the fickle Hamburg public that goes to the theatre only to be titillated and the pallid dramatic fare they are accordingly offered. He also suggests that, despite Ekhof's example, progress made toward extricating the German actor from dependence on the French-dominated Leipzig school has been in vain. This is due partly to the enslavement of public taste to all things French, partly too to a seeming failure to discover the principles of acting. "We have actors but no art of acting" (Lessing, 596) is his famous complaint. He continues by calling for "special rules, understood by everyone, drawn up with clarity and precision, by which, in a specific case, praise or blame can be accorded to the actor." Whether such rules are desireable can be questioned, but in the decades following the Hamburg enterprise, the specific language of the body, through which emotions, thoughts, prejudices, attitudes, and motives are expressed or betrayed received much attention.

Several attempts to describe this "language of the body" were published during the second half of the eighteenth century, of which the most popular and accessible was J. J. Engel's *Ideen zu einer Mimik* (*Ideas about Imitation*), published in 1785, running through several editions in the next sixty to seventy years. Engel's ambition, which arose directly from Lessing's challenge to discover the rules for acting, was to provide a catalogue of the various gestures, facial expressions, and postures by which human beings express unspoken meaning. This was given quasi-scientific legitimacy as he based his work partly on Lavater's *Physiognomy* (1775-1778), though it has been pointed out that in effect he did little more than collect ideas current in English, French, and German acting manuals.[1] Nevertheless, Engel's work is

2. From J. J. Engel's *Ideen zu einer Mimik.*

painstakingly detailed, and so provided the actor with models to be used in order to give acting exactitude. For example, in describing how different people drink, Engel writes of "the man who drinks for pleasure."

He stands bent backward, his feet placed slightly apart, his free hand gently drawn into the body without any muscular tension and placed just beneath the other hand, which holds the beaker or glass. His eyes are half-closed, but without the intense expression of the thorough connoisseur. Sometimes they are almost completely closed, tightly shut. His head is upright. The whole man seems to be concentrated on the one experience.[2] [See Figure 2.]

And so on, for four hundred pages! Although few actors could be expected to master or, in the course of performance, even to remember each of Engel's postures, his book, one of the first extensive chironomia in the German language, provided a standard of reference by which the actor's performance could be judged. Engel's writing is based on the assumption of uniformity in human behavior and social discourse, an assumption that, as will be seen in the next chapter, could be challenged. For the actor who worked to any extent from "intuition," from re-creating the feelings of the character, the obligation to follow an externally established set of gestures could appear to be as formal a requirement as the old Leipzig style had been, however more "realistic" those gestures were claimed to be. But for most actors, the clear lines of guidance offered by Engel were welcome. The way in which this new "realism" in acting became formalized into a gestural and vocal code is epitomized in the career of the most lionized actor of the late eighteenth and early nineteenth centuries—August Wilhelm Iffland.

AUGUST WILHELM IFFLAND

Iffland was unusual to his time, as he gave up the comforts of a well-established bourgeois home for a life on stage. He was born in Hannover on 19 April 1759, the son of a government registrar. His family intended him for the church, but from the age of five, when he saw the Ackermann troupe, his heart was set on the theatre. Amateur theatricals at school only inflamed his enthusiasm and, to avoid a confrontation with his father, he ran away from home when he was seventeen to find a troupe willing to hire him. He was lucky enough to be engaged by Ekhof for the Court Theatre in Gotha. Here Iffland received the best training then available to the actor, as Ekhof was scrupulous in ensuring that his actors performed with total concentration and attention to the most minute of details. The Gotha company was disbanded in 1779, mainly as a result of Ekhof's death, but Iffland, whose good fortune it was never to struggle for a living, was at once contracted to the newly constituted Mannheim Court and National theatre. With his two friends Heinrich Beck (1760-1803) and Johann Beil (1754-1794), he soon be-came a mainstay of the Mannheim theatre, which in its organization and repertoire was an exemplar for other German theatres in the late eighteenth century.

Much of the credit for the high quality of the Mannheim theatre must go to the intendant Baron Heribert von Dalberg (1749-1806), who fos-tered a repertoire ranging from popular comedies through to the classics of Shakespeare and encouraged new plays; Schiller's *Die Räuber* (*The Robbers*—1781) received its first performance in Mannheim in 1783. Furthermore, as Dalberg expected of his actors a high degree of expertise on stage, combined with an ability to think and write about their acting, he formally asked them questions to answer in writing. In their replies, they examined acting in a more systematic and far-reaching fashion than had been the case with the Schönemann Academy some twenty-five years before. Iffland was central to the growth of this theatre, first as actor, then as playwright and dramaturg. By the time he left Mannheim in 1796, he had become the most celebrated man of the theatre in Germany. His guest appearances in numerous cities, starting in 1784, had created for him a huge following, while his plays—*Rührstücke*, mild domestic melodramas that ingratiatingly embody an unchallenging, bourgeois morality—were immensely popular and of a quality that ensured their survival in the repertoire for almost a hundred years.

Iffland left Mannheim because of differences between him and Dalberg and because of the heavy damage done to the theatre and city during the early stages of the Napoleonic wars. After impressive guest appearances at Weimar and Hamburg, he was appointed director of the Berlin National Theatre, which had been founded by Döbbelin in 1786. From 1796 until his death in 1814, under Iffland's direction, the Berlin Royal Theatre, as it came to be called, grew to be the richest and most prestigious theatre in Germany. These were years of ceaseless activity for Iffland. He staged Shakespeare and other classic European dramatists and the new plays of Schiller and Goethe, in lavish productions with spectacular scenery and vast crowd scenes. He also continued to appear as a guest throughout Germany, maintaining his reputation as the foremost actor of his day. In doing so, he commanded a salary and luxury of accommodation previously unheard of in the German theatre. Iffland was the "new man" of his profession, his career bringing a heightened public esteem to the theatre and inspiring many younger people to take up the stage for a living.

As a young man, Iffland's views on the function of theatre were, not surprisingly given his training, an extension of those of Ekhof and Lessing. This is readily apparent in the essays he wrote in response to Dalberg during his early Mannheim years. For Iffland, the purpose of art was to reflect nature as completely as possible. Replying to the question, "What is nature and what are its true limits in theatre?" Iffland wrote, "In the whole of nature there is nowhere uniformity, nowhere incongruity. Nothing is inappropriate. One thing requires the other. Each small part has a specific relationship to the whole. Beauty lies in the perception of the whole."[3] He saw the actor as one who led the audience to this perception of unity in multiversity. In doing so, he argued, the actor must ensure that in performances "there is nothing too much, nothing too little—nothing missing. Nature and completeness are thus synonymous" (Koffka, 431). But to our eyes that "completeness" seems strangely exclusive, for Iffland made clear that it does not include all phases of human emotion. In particular, any feeling that requires rawness in tone or gesture to be expressed accurately should be avoided. For Iffland, as for Lessing, the sensitivities of the audience must never be offended. Indeed, in his memoirs Iffland deplored any seemingly uncontrolled outbursts by the actor. "How often," he complained, "has screaming been used for strong expression, coarseness for power, rawness for nature"[4] A mild temperance, even when representing extremes of experience, must govern all. Iffland equated this modified sense of completeness in nature with moral goodness. Hence, if the actor possesses this sense, it should just be relied upon in the representation of character and, involuntarily, the audience will be guided toward a morally uplifting view of mankind: "If naturalness in representing humankind does not violate the most delicate feelings for the morally beautiful, then the morally beautiful is also the limit [of nature] itself" (Koffka, 431-32).

The sensitivity required by the actor led Dalberg to ask what constitutes true decorum on stage and what qualifications an actor needs to guarantee it. To this Iffland responded that the actor called upon to represent people of noble feelings must also be noble. As personality is the means by which nobility is revealed, then the actor's personality must be sensitive, educated, and morally spotless: "The most certain means of appearing to be a noble man would ... be to try to be one" (Koffka, 461). Nobility should not, however, be identified with high social rank or, in actorial terms, with the Leipzig style, and here distinctly nationalist sentiments began to color Iffland's thinking. When he first went to Mannheim, Iffland, along with Beck and Beil, was afraid that the city's proximity to France would mean that on stage they would have to be "graceful" rather than "true." They were delighted, however, when the public enjoyed the "undecorated" truth of the acting they had learned from Ekhof (Iffland, *Leben,* 44). Hence, in Iffland's Mannheim essays, the virtues of honesty, sensitivity, warmth, and directness came to be seen as distinctly German. The true German actor, he argued, reveals inner feelings and impulses, eschews the display of skills in declamation, gesture, and movement, in contrast to the French actor who tends to use such display to hide character. Any actor who adopts the French style of acting, Iffland claimed, will eventually debase that inner nobility of character that is the hallmark of the German. "The French give presentations," he wrote, "the Germans representations. Their paintings of the passions are splendid, ours true. Decoration is varnish that covers ugliness, making corrupt passions into beautiful blemishes" (Koffka, 473). With such thinking, Iffland established an identity between the educative and nationalistic missions of the theatre, which he pursued with ever greater energy as his career progressed. To be natural was to be noble, which in its turn was to be German.

The "Mannheim school," cultivated by Iffland, Beck, and Beil, represents initially an extension of the Ekhof-Lessing view of acting as a means of bringing the audience to recognize the harmony of nature. If this is done simply and directly, it will inevitably be to the audience's moral betterment. But whether the Mannheim school and Iffland in particular sustained this simplicity is a question fraught with difficulty. Iffland's innumerable guest appearances in the various theatres that were being founded in German cities engendered a copious literature that is far from unanimous on the quality of his acting. All who saw him acknowledged his polish, his flawless technique, the richness and variety of his nuances, his ability to pictorialize on stage, and the certainty of his acting in which each attitude adopted was as clearly defined in meaning as Engel could have wished. But opinions as to how effective he was in representing character differed.

Karl Costenoble often acted with Iffland during his many guest appearances in Hamburg, and no one could have been more generous in his praise. For him, Iffland was everything that was perfect in acting. His subtle transitions, the dexterous play of his eyes, his gestures that seemed infinite in their variety were all, Costenoble claimed, impossible to imitate. They also cast an air of magic over the stage. Despite his slight build, his premature pot-belly, and his inferior vocal powers, Iffland had presence. Warmth flowed from him, he was the center of the performance. "The master possessed a wonderful suppleness that accommodated itself to all the moods and ideas in his surroundings."[5] Similar sentiments from colleagues and audiences can be found in the dozens of pamphlets and hundreds of reviews published on him. He was praised for "the originality of his perceptions, humor, and behavior, the upright unpretentiousness of his mind, the unforced polish of his bearing, his good-natured frankness."[6] When he visited Weimar in

1796, Karl Böttiger wrote a detailed description of the fourteen roles he played and claimed Iffland demonstrated he was master of all the positions prescribed by Engel in his *Ideas*.[7] Nothing was vague, nothing left to chance. Among his most enthusiastic devotees was Goethe.

He has the advantage of being able to give meaning and variety through the slightest nuances, and everything that appears arises from this deep source. His body is most adroit, and he is master of all his vocal organs, the deficiency of which he knows how to hide, even to exploit. The great capacity of his mind to fasten upon human peculiarities and to represent them with their individual features arouses as much astonishment as does the range of his performance and the speed of his representation. But first and last, what most arouses my admiration is his great understanding, through which he grasps single elements of character and gathers them together so that they make a whole different from all others.[8]

But although Goethe may have been expressing the opinion of the majority, he was not speaking for all. Some found the very wholeness Goethe admired crucially lacking. At times Iffland seemed so concerned with finding precisely the right nuance from moment to moment that he could lose the overall grasp of the character. To many he was a "mosaic artist," whose representation was a series of striking but discrete moments with little spontaneity. Early in his career, Dalberg criticized him for being at times too calculating in the use of his voice and straining after character (Koffka, 360). Charges of mannerism, overextension, and playing for effect in order to win the applause of his audience were to follow him all his life. So persistent were they that one of his most vigorous apologists based a whole book on refuting them, at times one feels with too great a protestation.[9] Calculation was probably the most consistent complaint about Iffland's acting. He had "an evident knowledge of his physical and representational powers. . . . He knows precisely what has an effect and where one must apply it to have an effect."[10] This meant some felt him lacking in feeling. Schiller, who had been impressed by his Franz Moor at the premiere of *The Robbers,* later deprecated him, claiming "never in his life has Iffland been able either to feel or to represent enthusiasm or any sort of exulted feeling"[11]—while Ludwig Tieck, an adamant foe, felt that although Iffland had the ability to play high comedy, "his imagination was not creative, his humor not poetic,"[12] so that his characters were totally lacking in magnitude and depth. At best his detractors would grant him a facility in comedy, but in serious roles he did little more than, in the words of Schröder, "reduce a serious character to a comic caricature."[13]

Today it is even less possible to come to a final decision about Iffland's acting. But some useful pictorial material is still available in a series of sketches of his major roles, rendered by the Henschel brothers during rehearsals and performances.[14] In some ways these sketches confirm the more negative judgments. Iffland's Lear, for example, often seems to be verging on parody (see Figure 3). His dumpy figure does not suit the role, and, to make matters worse, the sizeable beard he wears puts his head out of proportion. The curse on Goneril is realized in rhetorical gestures reminiscent, if it were not for the folds of drapery over his arms, of the Leipzig school. In the storm scene, his chin-clutching makes him seem more puzzled than desperate, while in the mad scenes he is elegiac, like a sea-god from an Italian mannerist painting. The impression given by these sketches seems to confirm the description of Iffland as a "mosaic artist," as little unity can be seen among them. But critical accounts do not always tally. When Friedrich Schmidt saw Iffland as Lear in Berlin, he was powerfully moved. "My whole soul was broken up, my emotion was quite unmanly" (Schmidt, 147-48), while others found psychological accuracy in his performance. In particular, some found he registered the onset of madness well, through "long, dull stretches of daydreaming, through jumps in diction, through uncertain hand movements."[15] Costenoble recalled that his representation of madness was as unnerving as that of Ludwig Devrient in the role,[16] which indicates a surprising parallel to romantic acting. But perhaps the key to the popularity of Iffland's Lear was best identified by a Viennese critic who found it acceptable because "he softened the harshness of Shakespeare's design, gave Lear dignity where the poet shows him as a foolish child, placed tragic greatness into the originally farcical character of the old king."[17] What Iffland had done with Lear was to harmonize a disharmonious text, re-forming the character to complement orthodox images of venerable old age. In any event, one senses there was little in his performance to offend the ear or eye, and that the appeal to his audience was to their pity rather than their fear.

Despite the comment of the Viennese critic, Iffland's strongest supporters generally admitted he lacked heroic stature, that he was unable to fill tragic roles with protean fullness, but humanized them, often reducing them to the scale of a bourgeois father. It is doubtful whether the humanization brought the experience of the play closer to the au-

3. Henschel brothers' sketches of August Iffland as King Lear. Reproduced by permission of Gesellschaft für Theatergeschichte.

dience. In fact it could belittle the role. The Henschel sketches show a schoolmasterly Wallenstein, with gestures more appropriate to the lecture hall than the battlefield in which a hero sets himself against the power of the Habsburg Empire. Even Costenoble conceded that in this role he lacked the necessarily heroic size, that he was convincing only as a human being, not as a warrior or statesman (Costenoble, *Tagebücher* II, 11), while August Klingemann found him monotonous, treating Schiller's verse as if it were the most commonplace prose.[18] His Philip II in Schiller's *Don Carlos* appears in the sketches as little more than a serious, introspective courtier. It has none of the ponderous gravity that can be given the part, so that audiences would both fear the man, as Carlos does, and feel for him, as Posa does. He was kingly perhaps, but not a despot.

Throughout his career, Iffland never really departed from the fundamental principle that the purpose of acting was to portray the essential harmony of the human condition. Whatever the character he played, he projected from it a strong illusion of inner worth and nobility. Such idealized representations of humanity clearly offended those few who wished for a more energetic theatre, one that was closer to life as normally experienced, but it appealed strongly to an ever-increasing audience that looked to theatre primarily as a source of pleasure and as an escape from normal life. One of Iffland's admirers prefaced his pamphlet on the actor's appearances at Hamburg with a definition of this theatre. ''For us the true end of acting is pleasure, an elevating, refined pleasure, to the extent that this is achieved through moral means. Through art and artists we wish . . . to be transported from odious and boring reality that chains us by day to the bench, the money-market, the desk, or the workshop . . . into another new, ideally beautiful world.''[19] And Iffland responded to this need. What is more, he reinterpreted ''odious and boring reality,'' feeding back ''idealized . . . ennobled'' images of everyday life that might reconcile his audiences to it. Hence, the immense popularity of those roles that figured more prominently in Iffland's repertoire than tragic ones, the mild benefactor, the slightly errant but eventually warm-hearted father, and the miserly but ultimately compassionate merchant, all of which were central figures in Iffland's own *Rührstücke*. He appeared most frequently not in the classics but as characters in plays now forgotten, as Forester Warberger in *Die Jäger* (*The Huntsmen*—1785), as Councillor Reinhold in *Die Hagestolzen* (*The Old Bachelors*—1791, or as Bittermann in Kotzebue's

Menschenhass und Reue (*Misanthropy and Repentance*—1789), characters who are all fine examples of that inner German "nobility" Iffland prized so highly.

The quality of such performances can still, perhaps, be partially captured today by his portrayal of Harpagon in Molière's *Miser*, which was, according to his biographer Funck, his greatest role (Funck, 93). He played it not in a direct translation of Molière's text, but in an updated version by Heinrich Zschokke in which Harpagon, renamed Fegersack (Empty Purse), is a courtier of the late eighteenth century. The Henschel sketches show Iffland's Fegersack to be a relatively good-humored gentleman with chubby features and well-rounded gestures; there is also a distinct touch of kindness in his attitudes. Moments of high passion have an air of parody about them, as if Harpagon/Fegersack were himself a performer. It is difficult to see how his miserliness was in any way represented as evil or as more than just a passing quirk of character. As Funck remarked, throughout the performance one felt with him, not against him. Everything was decent, nothing included that might disturb the audience or break the bond of sympathy between them and the actor.

With Iffland's career, the acting profession acquired a new status in the eyes of the German public and the stage a heightened prestige. In perfecting what Ekhof had begun, the art of "*schöne Rundung*" (beautiful rounding-out), Iffland established for the actor a double function. The first was the actor as paragon for his audience. In 1753, Ekhof had had trouble in persuading his colleagues even to adapt to the manners of bourgeois life; fifty years later, Iffland was busy making the actor into the model of aristocratic manners. Due to the importance of the Berlin Royal Theatre, actors were ever more frequently seen in fashionable salons, where they would display their vocal and physical talents to best advantage. Iffland especially was prominent in the social life of the city, cultivating its manners so assiduously that the "inner" nobility he valued so highly seemed to be extended into a concern for a more conventional "outer" nobility. As August Haake recalled,

In life Iffland appeared to be modern, elegant, paying homage to the fashion of the day, keeping step with the times. Dignified, aristocratic, he spent much time with princely personages and other highly placed people. In him Racine's demand that the actor be raised in the lap of queens was fulfilled. Whoever did not know him must have considered him to be an elegant diplomat rather than an actor. The dignity with which he appeared, especially in higher social circles, even drew upon him accusations of presumption.[20]

Haake felt, however, that such aspersions were unjust, particularly as even in his palmiest days Iffland sustained an overriding interest in acting and the theatre.

The truth of this was borne out not only by Iffland's indefatigable administration of the Royal Theatre and his continuous appearances on stage, but also by his voluminous writings. These appeared in a series of publications issued almost yearly between 1807 and 1812, the *Berliner Almanachen* (*Berlin Almanacs*). In them he defined the second important function of the actor, the artistic. Although he was never as comprehensive nor as specific as Engel in the *Ideas,* he called for far greater exactness than was usual in acting, expounded basic principles concerning the relaxed composure necessary for success on stage, listed the various physical attributes and attitudes required to represent different character-types—"The unhappy lover walks with rigid step, lowered head, sunken chest, with glances that wish to attract everyone and hold them fast"[21]—and categorized ways in which particular emotions are expressed—"protruding or stretched lips blaze out anger—the corner of the mouth and the trembling chin betray resentment" (Iffland, *Almanac*, 86). Other essays describe how villainy should be represented on stage. In a detailed analysis of his own approach to Franz Moor, one of the few out-and-out villains Iffland played, he argued that the humanity of the character and the causes of his malice should be emphasized in performance, softening his harsher features, bringing his experience within the understanding of the audience. He also wrote at length on the need for education as a prerequisite for the performing artist and on the virtues of good deportment both on stage and in society at large. The essays are comprehensive and detailed, establishing with clarity both an ethic and methodology for the actor.

The clarity that Iffland brought to acting, as well as the enhanced eminence he achieved for the theatre, makes him a crucial figure in the history of the German theatre. Although his technical virtuosity was rarely equalled, Iffland, who copied superlatively the manners of the *beau monde,* himself became a model to imitate, a shining example of social success, and an artist who had mastered and tempered all phases of human experience. With Iffland a new decorum was established for the actor, who was to create a harmonious image of humankind through "elegant manners achieved by the union of nonchalance with refined deliberation" (Haake, 157). Once this Olympian condition was achieved, the actor, with a broad and particular knowledge of all means of human expression, could interpret to the audience the multifareous, though harmonious experience of the human race. With Iffland, the actor became master of the audience.

Although Iffland and the "Mannheim school" undoubtedly had "idealist" tendencies in the constant purpose of presenting an image of the human being as a creature of harmony, most historians of German theatre have placed him in the middle of the polarity that evolved with the growth of the theatre. Such placement is just, as Iffland never abandoned the realistic mode for a grander style of acting. Furthermore, despite the clarity of his axioms for the actor, he never designed a composite system of acting, retaining throughout his life an awareness that the best actors must find their own way to excellence. However, a school of acting that did provide the actor with an aura of grandiosity and seemingly unequivocal directives as to how this was to be created was founded at the Weimar Court Theatre during the years of Goethe's direction, between 1791 and 1817. Although, as Haake observes, Goethe's and Iffland's ambitions for the actor were aligned, the actorial style cultivated at Weimar reached toward a level of abstraction that Iffland would never have encouraged (Haake, 152).

GOETHE AND THE WEIMAR SCHOOL

When he was appointed to the directorship of the Weimar Court Theatre, Goethe's feelings about his new post were ambivalent. His early plays, written in the 1770s, had been widely performed in German theatres, but his later dramatic work, classical in form and written in highly concentrated blank verse, seemed unsuitable for the stage. Soon after his arrival in Weimar, he had acted in the amateur court theatre, appearing with Ekhof in Cumberland's *Jew* in 1778, but his interest in theatre had since waned. Even worse, his opinions of actors were not of the highest. *Wilhelm Meister's Apprenticeship*, despite the vigor and color of its descriptions of theatrical life, betrays a familiar distrust of the actor as one whose egoism and lack of moral fibre and artistic integrity are seen to stand in the way of creating a serious art form out of the theatre.

Goethe therefore had reservations about assuming the leadership of the theatre, especially as the company he formed out of the troupe of Joseph Bellomo, the previous director, and other actors brought in from elsewhere, possessed few skilled artists. None of them seemed able to fulfil his particular ambition, which was to create an ensemble in which no individual would stand out, in which harmony was perceived primarily through the whole rather than within each actor. It was unambiguously proclaimed in the prologue he wrote for the theatre's opening production of Iffland's *Huntsmen*.

Allein bedenken wir, dass Harmonie
Des ganzen Spiels allein verdienen kann,
Von euch gelobt zu werden, dass ein jeder
Mit jedem stimmen, alle miteinander
Ein schönes Ganze vor euch stellen sollen....[22]

>   [Our sole concern is that only harmony in the whole performance
>   deserves to be applauded by you; that each agree with each, that
>   all of us together should set before you a beautiful whole....]

But there were problems. For a start, the older actors still preferred the stilted bearing and bombastic tone of former days, while the younger ones, misguidedly under the influence of the realism that had arisen from Ekhof's acting, were content mainly to play themselves. In addition, while the company was more cohesive than it had been in Bellomo's time, it was unambitious and unwilling to rise to Goethe's challenge to rid the theatre of "the abominable slovenliness in which the majority of German actors comfortably drone on" (Goethe, *Briefe* II, 137).

Goethe achieved little until Iffland's guest appearances at the theatre in 1796 and 1798. Iffland's influence both on the director and the company was invigorating, as at last they had a model. Soon many Weimar actors showed a potential for sharper characterization and greater resourcefulness as well as economy in their expression. Even though Schiller, by now co-director of the theatre with Goethe, cast doubts on Iffland's powers, Goethe never lost faith in him. This influence was, however, only transitional. Goethe's interest could not be held indefinitely by the drama for which Iffland's acting was most suited, *Rührstücke* and the popular comedies and melodramas of August von Kotzebue. Improvements in the company's attitudes encouraged him to find a less quotidian style of acting that might suit his hitherto unperformed classical dramas, the verse dramas of Schiller, and the accomplished verse translations of Shakespeare by A. W. Schlegel and his collaborators, which were beginning to supplant the rough-and-ready prose versions commonly in use. Such drama seemed to posit a theatre beyond the humane mission of arousing compassion for others. It also searched for the ideal, creating in the audience an awareness not only of what humans are, but of what they can be. Although Goethe never abandoned the idea of the theatre as a school for morals, he projected this function onto a higher plain, seeking through the performance of tragic drama to "elucidate and deepen human nature, to raise belief in the godlike spark in man and in his ability to master life."[23] This desire to dignify the human race, extolling its strengths and achievements, was analogous to Iffland's mission in the theatre, though with more heroic dimensions and an extra-human frame of reference.

Not surprisingly, few actors were immediately capable of responding to this high call, as none could radiate the almost superhuman presence it required on stage. Goethe had therefore to look for models. He turned first to the French theatre. In 1799, Wilhelm von Humboldt visited Paris, where he saw François Joseph Talma, whose performances of classical French roles were rejuvenating the turgid acting of the Comédie Française. On stage Talma was not spontaneous, simple, and realistic, as he preserved the poised artistry characteristic of the best French classical acting. But he did infuse it with a vitality and continuity missing in the acting of his contemporaries. Humboldt wrote Goethe a letter describing Talma.

Every situation he thinks of is present in his imagination as a pictorial figure. . . . Each of his movements in the theatre is beautiful and harmonious, his bearing [is] noble and gracious throughout. He may sit, stand, kneel, and the painter will always find the study of these positions valuable. Among other actors, one probably finds single beautiful pictures here and there . . . [but Talma's] acting exhibits an unbroken succession of them, a harmonious rhythm in all movements.[24]

Humboldt's description suggests an abstract quality in Talma's acting. Psychological details are not mentioned, neither is there any concern for human warmth or Germanic "nobleness." Instead his interest has been taken by the combination of the statuesque with the fluid, as if the principles of sculpture have been fused with constant motion, so that Talma creates an aura of naturalness while giving the character a

dignified stature. Lessing had described acting as an art "halfway between the plastic arts and poetry" (Lessing, 25), in which the actor
must guard against the tendency to sustain a single posture until it
becomes offensive to the audience. In Talma such a fine balance between
stasis and fluidity had been achieved. When Goethe saw Talma in 1808
at Erfurt during the Napoleonic occupation, he felt he did not live up
to his reputation, but Humboldt's description still provided a basis from
which he could work.

The creation of the Weimar style of acting occurred principally through
the production of Schiller's mature tragedies, of adaptations of foreign
tragedies, notably *Macbeth* in 1800, Voltaire's *Mahomet* in 1800 and
Tancred in 1801, and of pseudo-Greek imitations by the Schlegel brothers. Its basic principles are preserved in Goethe's famous *"Regeln für
Schauspieler"* ("Rules for Actors"), written down in 1803, though not
collected until 1824, and only published after his death. Throughout
the "Rules," Goethe enjoins the actor to observe a scrupulous respect
for outward beauty, always carrying the body with elegance. The actor's
aim must be to portray constantly an ideal, humanity as it could be,
purged of the commonplace and gross gestures of everyday life. This
enjoinder gives the "Rules" a stuffy tone, reminiscent of some of
Ekhof's charges to the Schönemann Academy, though it must be admitted that if, as Goethe claimed, actors did hawk, spit, and blow their
noses on stage, his dictates against such habits are all to the good.[25] So
too are his observations on vocal delivery. In most theatres of the time,
even Iffland's in Berlin, verse was delivered as if it were prose and was
written out as such. Goethe, however, wished to emphasize the verse.
To do this, clarity of utterance is the salient issue. In order to achieve
"the clean and perfect pronunciation of each word" (Goethe, *Schriften*
XV, 204), the actor must avoid a conversational tone, be deliberate and
exact in pronouncing each syllable, and pause at the end of each line,
even at punctuation marks. In practice Goethe encouraged speaking that
was more akin to music than normal discourse, and even beat out the
rhythm in rehearsals. According to the "Rules," other artificialities are
to be observed. Proper names, for example, are to be given special
emphasis, so that the audience is never confused over who is speaking
to whom. Goethe also draws a distinction between "recitation" and
"declamation." When reciting, the actor "does not disown his nature,
his individuality" (Goethe, *Schriften* XV, 208), but suggests emotions
rather than portrays them. Declamation, however, requires the actor to

"leave [his] innate character, disavow [his] nature and place [him]self wholly in the attitude and mood of the one whose role [he] declaims" (Goethe, *Schriften* XV, 208). But this does not require total self-abandonment, as the actor must always keep carefully under control, playing upon the voice as if on a musical instrument, in a manner that is both beautiful and complete.

On physical deportment Goethe is less original. Willi Flemming has pointed out that many of his requirements, including the famous one that the actor stand with face three quarters turned toward the audience and only a quarter toward the character addressed, were common in the theatre before the advent of realistic acting. Such rules had already been applied by the old Leipzig school and had been codified in the writings of Franciscus Lang, a teacher in the Munich Jesuit school eighty years before (Flemming, 161). Nevertheless, the revival of such distinctly stylized acting had its freshness. The actors of the old baroque theatre had worn costumes that determined the form each gesture took, but Goethe, who took classical sculpture for a model, dressed his actors more sparsely—in historical plays in an approximation to the costume of the period, in plays with classical settings in tunics and togas. This tended to reveal rather than hide the limbs and gave greater freedom to the Weimar actor. However formal they were, gestures did not appear to be determined by outer necessity, but seemed to be a natural expression of the body, which accordingly appeared more dignified than it did in the older theatre.

Goethe included the almost obligatory rules that an actor must strive to be a model of good deportment on- and off-stage, but in some notes he wrote to his actors in the course of rehearsals, not included in the "Rules," he suggests they go further than merely looking noble. They should project a presence that has a superhuman quality. He instructs them always to maintain the impression of unusual bouyancy and grace. In order to expedite this, all props and furniture should be made of especially light material "so that it never becomes labour to move them, but always remains play" (Goethe, *Schriften* XV, 229). If the physical world must offer little in the way of hindrance to actors, they must also show mastery of the more intangible world of the emotions. The successful actor, wrote Goethe, must demonstrate a perfect understanding of emotions to explain them to a less enlightened audience. "The different emotions have such inner correspondence and similarity, one so easily appearing in the place of another, that the average person scarcely understands them. Whatever it is in the great actor that strives to determine their species is called genius, in the clever and capable actor it is judgment" (Goethe, *Schriften* XV, 230-31). Few if any of the Weimar actors displayed "genius," but the idea of the omniscient actor, whose work was a logical extension of Lessing's conception of "genius" as the ability to clarify the mainsprings of human action and to show their purpose, was to be an attractive ideal for actors in the coming century.

The limitations of the Weimar company were substantial, due partly to Goethe himself. Close to the end of the "Rules" he places a *caveat* that should have prefaced the collection. "One must make one's own sense of all these technical-grammatical rules and constantly practice them so that they become habit. Stiffness must disappear, and the rule become only the hidden outline of the living action" (Goethe, *Schriften* XV, 225). In other words, they should provide a framework within which the "free mood" of the actor can operate to create a character from the imagination. In practice few managed this. Some of Goethe's directives even belie the possibility. For example, if the actor must always remain aware of both the audience and of being positioned within the stage picture (Goethe, *Schriften* XV, 224-25), it is very difficult to be ruled by the character's needs. Then Goethe suggests that the "Rules" are a "grammar," as if they give the actor access to creating meaning on stage. In fact they are not. The writings of Engel and Iffland have a greater claim to be called "grammars," and these, it should be noted, were of little interest to Goethe and inimical to Schiller. In fact the "Rules" establish principles of conduct, defining the decorum of the theatrical event, creating a framework to guarantee dignity of proceedings. They do not suggest how an actor can gain access to or realize his role.

At the heart of Goethe's theatre, there is a contradiction. While he encouraged the actor to adopt a dignified, even superhuman posture, he also demanded submittance to a whole larger than the self, the play and the production that realized it. This requirement was dictated no doubt by his interest in the harmonious whole of the stage, as well as by his distrust of the actors, which was reflected in the strict discipline he enforced upon them. In the casting of plays he insisted that actors forego the pleasure of standing out from their colleagues and refused to allow anyone to decline a role, however small. Even though he had some problems with the duke's mistress Karoline Jagermann, whose beauty, vanity, and Mannheim training prompted her to seek only leads, generally the ensemble ethic prevailed. Ironically, to contemporaries who were accustomed to seeing single actors prevail over the whole, each member of the company appeared mediocre. Even if one or two had possessed the magnetism of an Ekhof or Iffland, it would have been difficult for that actor to be felt in the company. Moreover, as the salaries paid in the theatre were modest in the extreme, it was impossible to attract a leading actor who could have perfected the manner of performance outlined in the "Rules," and then encourage the other actors' emulation. Instead they were trained by Goethe, whose bent for the theatre was theoretical rather than practical. He could tell his actors what to do, rarely how to do it. None of them, unfortunately, was a Talma.

The reception of the Weimar company was, understandably, mixed. Within the city, there were some like Kotzebue who disliked the theatre because of Goethe's aloof personality. Others, like Karl August Böttiger, preferred the more realistic acting of Iffland; Böttiger even travelled to Hamburg in his final years to see the ultra-realistic Schröder in order to create antagonism between the Weimar theatre and an important actor whose work was antithetical. Even Iffland, when he made his final guest appearance in 1812, felt less at home in the theatre, complaining that the acting was wooden with little life. But others welcomed the discipline of the company. Eduard Genast quotes an article from the influential Leipzig newspaper *Zeitung für die elegante Welt* in which the company is praised for its aspirations after the ideal and their avoidance of the "everyday [talk] of normal life."[26] In Weimar, the reviewer commented, the old and new were combined in a perfect example of theatre, an institution that, under the wise supervision of a prince and a poet who was his close associate, educated and refined the taste of its audience while never encouraging them to question the foundations of the society on which it was built. The reviewer also praised the company's excellence not only in verse tragedy, but in the higher species of comedy. In fact a survey of the theatre's repertoire shows that although the higher drama of Weimar Classicism had an honorable position, even at the end of Goethe's tenancy, opera, operetta, and the plays of Kotzebue and Iffland were seen more frequently than most of Schiller's and Goethe's works.[27] While the "Rules" applied primarily to the performance of tragedy, the discipline they created clearly influenced the actors beneficially, so that they became adept at the quieter realism required by the average drama.

Toward the end of his life Goethe, in conversation with Eckermann, claimed that only one actor had really mastered the "Rules," and could therefore be regarded as his follower. "I know very well that our older, local actors have learnt much from me," he said, "but in a real sense I can only call Wolff my pupil."[28] Pius Alexander Wolff (1782-1828) arrived in Weimar in 1803. After a few months of instruction, during which Goethe wrote the "Rules," he rose to become a leading member of the company, developing into a most impressive tragic actor. His best roles were the lead in Goethe's *Torquato Tasso* at the play's first performance in 1807, Hamlet in 1809, and the Prince in Calderon's *Constant Prince* in 1811. In 1816, he left Weimar for the Royal Theatre in Berlin where he became the leading tragic actor and was responsible for introducing the Weimar style to a wider audience.

Acting did not come easily to Wolff. "He lacked fresh humor," wrote Genast, "and, if he forced it, he always became morbid. He was not one of the intuitive actors, but his considerable talent was supported by methodical training and inexhaustible diligence" (Genast, 174). Almost all who wrote about him found a stiffness in his gestures and movement, and few were able to sense much spontaneity in him. Even in his greatest roles he "seem[ed] to supply that which nature had denied him."[29] That Wolff conceived of acting as the exercise of mind over matter is clear from some interesting essays he wrote on vocal delivery during his Berlin years. "Every voice, even the most beautiful, needs art in order to be used to advantage on stage; but even the worst can please when one knows how to give it value. In the hands of a blockhead, a violin from Cremona lacerates our ears, while a master knows how to entice pleasant sounds from the most miserable of instruments."[30] Although Wolff's natural "instruments" were not of the best, he attracted audiences by creating the illusion of an inborn nobility that gave gravity to his stage presence and serenity to almost all the roles he played. When he appeared, a "grand artistic stillness"[31] settled over the stage, remaining throughout his slow and steady performance in which nothing was allowed to disturb the harmony of his voice and movements, in which everything was deliberate, clear-cut, and unfailingly unambiguous. "How he acted!" recalled Goethe, "how reliable he was! how secure! It was impossible for me to detect even the slightest offence against the rules I had implanted in him" (Goethe, *Gespräche* IV, 37).

Not surprisingly, Wolff's Hamlet was a model of clarity. He did not show a prince uncomprehendingly angry at the world, nor a man crippled by fear, self-pity, or indecision. Rather he played him as a pleasant, intelligent young man who, on returning home to find all order overthrown, unquestioningly accepts that he is the person to set it right. While this rather straightforward interpretation gave the part a unity and momentum, it did not prevent him from exploring extreme states of mind, the experience of which served mainly to make Hamlet's goal clearer. Notable above all were his scenes with the Ghost, which, after he reached Berlin, he acted against the Weimar rules with his back to the audience, as he felt it impossible to convey with his face the terror Hamlet feels at the vision. But, by the time he turned slowly back to the audience after the Ghost had disappeared, he had prepared the most desolate of expressions. "Youth, life, belief, and hope seemed to have been extinguished for ever from this deathly pale, disturbed face. He stood there, blanched, his lips twisted painfully—broken—crushed. Only with difficulty were his words wrested from his broken heart."[32] From henceforth the suffering Hamlet underwent was used to underline the nobility of the prince, which would go to waste at the end of the play. Moments of liveliness occurred during his scene with the Players; he also maintained the most courteous demeanor toward Ophelia. Throughout he invested the role with a "deep melancholy and a most sublime, noble pathos" (Bauer, II:268), adopting poses that provided "a worthy lesson for pictorial art and sculpture."[33] As he died, instead of lowering his voice in defeat, he spoke loudly and clearly, passing from the world every inch a prince. The gravity he gave the role was to provide a model for several actors over the next hundred years.[34]

By 1828, the year of Wolff's death, the "idealist" approach to acting had been firmly established. While the harmonious and yet various image of humanity, conveyed through surface realism and an infinitude of nuances, was the ideal that many actors strove for, the idealism of the Weimar school became the predominant style for most actors until the end of the nineteenth century. Few achieved the high dignity Goethe had envisaged. All the same the "Rules" were widely followed, as they provided actors with a model that, in the absence of any systematic training, they could follow with some confidence. Furthermore, Goethe's "Rules" posited a status for the actor that was distinctly superior to

the actual low social status still endured by the majority of the profession, despite the celebrity enjoyed by Iffland and Wolff. But, in the
hands of the untalented actor, the Weimar style tended to appear as a
parody of itself and, despite Goethe's claim that he wished the actor to
be the servant of the playwright, it frequently came between the audience
and the play. Although Ludwig Tieck admired Wolff, he could never
bring himself to appreciate the imitators of the Weimar school who
sprang up in his wake. As he observed in 1831,

The tone that wishes to elevate itself to dignity and nobility will, in order to
avoid being prosaic, unnoticeably rise too strongly, become bombastic and
sobbing, or by-and-by change into a sort of singing. Once the ground was laid,
actor and listener became accustomed to this mode, so that abnormality became
even stronger, recitation often became false song from a coarse voice and when
it was strained it broke into howling. Thereupon this too found its admirers
and passed for great tragic tone, for the wonderful and the superhuman. Recently, associated with these monstrosities has been a sudden crying jerk and
exaggerated emphasis, which stresses excessively at least one word in each
verse, through which it is impossible to follow the sense of the author. (Tieck,
Kritische Schriften II, 341)

Hence, with those actors whose voices were untrained and movement
was inelegant, idealism in acting could easily become a travesty of
itself.

NOTES

1. Hans Oberländer, *Die geistige Entwicklung der deutschen Schauspielkunst im 18. Jahrhundert*, TF 15 (Hamburg & Leipzig: Voss, 1898), 173.
2. J. J. Engel, *Ideen zu einer Mimik,* vol. 7 of *Schriften* (Berlin: Mylius,
1844), 113.
3. Wilhelm Koffka, *Iffland und Dalberg* (Leipzig: Weber, 1865), 430. In
addition to his history of the Mannheim theatre, Koffka provides an extensive
selection of documents.
4. August Wilhelm Iffland, *Meine theatralische Leben* (Stuttgart: Reclam,
1976), 41.
5. Carl Ludwig Costenoble, *Tagebücher von seiner Jugend bis zur Übersiedlung nach Wien (1818),* ed. Alexander von Weilen, Schriften der Gesellschaft für Theatergeschichte 19 (Berlin: Selbstverlag der Gesellschaft für
Theatergeschichte, 1912), II, 63. Series hereafter abbreviated to SGT, publisher
hereafter abbreviated to VGT.

6. Johann Lochner, *Etwas über Herrn Ifflands Kunstaustellungen auf der Nationalschaubühne zur Nürnberg* (Nuremberg: 1802), 7.

7. Karl August Böttiger, *Entwickelung des Ifflandischen Spiels in vierzehn Darstellungen auf dem Weimarischen Hoftheater im Aprillmonath 1796* (Leipzig: Goschen, 1796).

8. Letter from J. W. Goethe to J. H. Meyer, 18 April 1796, in Johann Wolfgang Goethe, *Briefe*, ed. K. R. Mandelkow (Hamburg: Wagner, 1962-1967), II, 219-20.

9. Z. Funck, *Aus dem Leben zweier Schauspieler: August Wilhelm Ifflands und Ludwig Devrients* (Leipzig: Brockhaus, 1838).

10. *Iffland auf Hamburgs Bühne* (Hamburg & Altona: Vollmer, 1805), 23.

11. Letter from Schiller to Goethe, 24 April 1798, *Der Briefwechsel zwischen Schiller und Goethe*, ed. Emil Staiger (Frankfurt: Insel, 1966), 610.

12. Ludwig Tieck, "Die geschichtliche Entwickelung der neueren Bühne," vol. 2 of *Kritische Schriften* (Leipzig: Brockhaus, 1848), II, 345.

13. Friedrich Ludwig Schmidt, *Denkwürdigkeiten des Schauspielers, Schauspieldichters und Schauspieldirektors, 1772-1841*, ed. Hermann Uhde (Hamburg: Mauke, 1875), I, 169.

14. In Heinrich Härle, *Ifflands Schauspielkunst*, SGT 34 (Berlin: VGT, 1925).

15. Heinrich von Collin in Monty Jacobs, ed. *Deutsche Schauspielkunst*, rev. ed. Eva Stahl (Berlin: Henschel, 1954), 322.

16. Karl Costenoble, *Aus dem Burgtheater, 1818-1837* (Vienna: Konegen, 1889), II, 334.

17. F. L. "Herr Iffland in Wien" (Vienna: 1808), 382-83.

18. Quoted in Schmidt, *Denkwürdigkeiten*, I:179.

19. Johann Friedrich Schütze, *Dramaturgisches Tagebuch über Ifflands Gastpiele in Hamburg* (Hamburg: Nestler, 1805), 8-9.

20. August Haake, *Theater-Memoiren* (Mainz: Kunze, 1866), 155.

21. A. W. Iffland, *Almanach fürs Theater* (Berlin: Salfeld, 1808), 78.

22. Goethe, "Prolog," 7 May 1791, *Poetische Werke, Vollständige Ausgabe* (Stuttgart: Cotta, n.d.), III, 1227.

23. Willy Flemming, *Goethe und das Theater seiner Zeit* (Stuttgart: Kohlhammer, 1968), 119.

24. Letter from Wilhelm von Humboldt to Goethe, 18 August 1799, *Gesammelte Werke* (Berlin: Reimer, 1843), III, 144.

25. Goethe, "Regeln für Schauspieler," in *Schriften*, vol. 15 of *Gesamtausgabe* (Stuttgart: Cotta, n.d.). The complete "Rules" are available in English translation by Marvin Carlson in *Goethe and the Weimar Theatre* (Ithaca & London: Cornell University Press, 1979). Strangely enough, it has been claimed in Toby Cole and Helen Krich Chinoy, *Actors of Acting*, new ed. (New York: Crown, 1970) that the rule against spitting was in reaction to Ekhof's habit of spitting on stage (274).

26. Eduard Genast, *Aus dem Tagebuche eines alten Schauspielers* (Leipzig: Voigt & Gunther, 1862), I, 165.

27. Between 1791 and 1817, 87 plays by Kotzebue and 31 by Iffland were produced. In contrast only 19 by Goethe, including light occasional pieces, 18 by Schiller, including translations, 8 by Shakespeare, and 4 by Lessing were given. The most frequently performed pieces were *The Magic Flute* (82), *Don Giovanni* (68), *The Abduction from the Seraglio* (49), *Don Carlos* (47), Iffland's *Bachelors* (40), Beck's *Chess Machine* (36), and Iffland's *Huntsmen* (35). Altogether 601 plays were produced of which 17 were farces, 31 *Singspielen* (plays with singing), 77 tragedies, 104 operas, 123 contemporary dramas, and 249 comedies. From C. A. H. Burckhardt, *Das Repertoire des Weimarischen Theaters*, TF 1 (Hamburg & Leipzig: Voss, 1891), xxxvi-xxxvii.

28. *Goethes Gespräche*, Gesamtausgabe, ed. Flodoard Frh. von Biedermann, 2d ed. (Leipzig: Biedermann, 1909-1910), IV, 36-37.

29. Letter from Zelter to Goethe, 20 April 1816, in *Briefwechsel zwischen Goethe und Zelter*, ed. Friedrich Riemer (Berlin: Duncker & Humblot, 1834), II, 248.

30. Pius Alexander Wolff, "Bemerkungen über die Stimme und ihre Ausbildung zum Vortrag auf der Bühne," in Max Martersteig, *Pius Alexander Wolff* (Leipzig: Fernau, 1879), 299.

31. Karl von Holtei quoted in Martersteig, *Wolff*, 82.

32. Karoline Bauer, *Aus meinen Bühnenleben*, ed. Arnold Wellmar (Berlin: Decker, 1877), II:268.

33. Adolf Mullner quoted in Wilhelm Widmann, *Hamlets Bühnenlaufbahn (1601-1877)*, ed. Joseph Schick & Werner Deetjen (Leipzig: Tauschnitz, 1931), 198.

34. Alexander von Weilen, *Hamlet auf der deutschen Bühne* (Berlin: Reimer, 1908), 161.

Chapter **3**

THE ROMANTIC ACTOR, 1771–1832

In the early nineteenth century, the schools of Mannheim and Weimar provided the most widely admired and imitated styles of acting. But for those associated with the romantic movement in art, music, and literature, the "idealist" actor these schools produced was a phenomenon viewed with suspicion. True artistic experience, the romantics considered, resided in a meeting between the actively enquiring imaginations of artist and audience. Such a dynamic was not, however, possible in a theatre where each movement, gesture, and change in vocal inflection was carefully predetermined by the actor. Furthermore, the actor's concern to project an image of "worth," be it moral, social, or artistic, tended to stand between the audience and the character.

The impact of the romantic movement on the development of the German theatre is difficult to identify. The first phase of romanticism, the *Sturm-und-Drang* (Storm and Stress) movement of the 1770s, had declared itself primarily through theatre, in plays that challenged the Enlightenment view of humans as harmonious beings. With plots articulated in a series of loosely connected episodes, they dramatized the predicament of the social misfit, of those confused by a contradiction between their inner promptings and the necessity to adapt to patterns of conduct that were externally imposed. But the movement was short-lived. Over the turn of the century, when romanticism was giving German culture a new identity and a European stature, the theatre, for all the nationalist ambitions that had earlier been expressed for it, remained almost untouched. This was not for want of trying. Almost all romantic writers had ambitions to write great drama, as, in common with their eighteenth-century forebears, they saw in the theatre a means of uniting people from varying walks of life in a common experience.

August Wilhelm Schlegel eulogized the way in which emotions are strengthened by the presence of an audience, encouraging friendship among men. "We feel ourselves strong among so many companions and all souls flow together in a great irresistible stream."[1] Although his ideas on the humanizing influence of theatre are akin to those of the eighteenth-century theorists, they have a more populist and irrational ring to them. His ambitions for the theatre were also more universal in nature. Like his fellow romantics, Schlegel looked to the past, to Periclean Athens, Elizabethan London, and Golden Age Spain for models of a theatre where audiences comprised the whole citizenry and whose plays had timeless themes beyond the interests of any one class. Perhaps it was the romantics' preoccupation with the past that brought about their failure in the theatre. Refreshingly they protested against the limited worlds of Kotzebue and Iffland, against a dramatic action that did little but point out some rather unremarkable moral, but they failed to find an adequate alternative. Their use of historical forms and their interest in the arcane, the supernatural, the extraordinary, and the grotesque rarely found popular recognition. Only Zacharias Werner, who perfected the *Schicksaltragödie* (the fate tragedy) and wrote effective historical dramas, was widely performed. But his work had little staying power beyond his time. Sadly the most salient features of the romantics' lyrical and prose writings, their mysticism, their interest in the composition of the psyche and its identity with the natural world, did not inform their dramatic output. In the words of Joseph von Eichendorff, himself a disappointed dramatist, "The romantics failed entirely to establish a common basis with the people. As a result all the ground of reality disappeared slowly beneath their feet and most of their plays went beyond or above the real stage. With willful obstinacy and pride they ignored the stage instead of developing it."[2] Later in the century playwrights such as Franz Grillparzer and Ferdinand Raimund and operatic composers such as Carl Maria Weber, Heinrich Marschner, and Richard Wagner ensured the theatre was not entirely lost to the romantics, but in its heyday romanticism was only tangentially involved with the theatre.

The involvement of the actor in the romantic movement was, not surprisingly, minimal, especially as the growth of idealist acting did nothing to help toward the successful staging of romantic drama. But Ludwig Tieck, a leading romantic writer and an indefatigable critic and historian of the theatre, provided in his essays a commentary on acting that amplified perceptions of the actor's potential outside the realm of idealist performance. While Tieck acknowledged the accuracy of Iffland's powers of observation and his technical versatility, he always dismissed him as a man without imagination, deficient in the stature needed to play great tragic or comic roles. The great actor, Tieck argued, must radiate a presence so compelling that his audience is taken far beyond the limits set by the imagination of the playwright. He is not just to complete what is incomplete in the text, as Lessing had posited, but he must dominate the stage. "The true actor must not only understand his writer, in several places he must be able to surpass him. . . . In the greatest of poetic works there are several places where the poet must stand back and the mastery of the stage begins, where the genius of the actor has to reign alone."[3] Tieck does not here define that peculiar "genius," but clearly it is not the superlatively rational explicator of the playwright's text as Lessing had described. Rather it is closer to "genius" as described by J. G. Herder, an intuitive, entirely spontaneous impulse that can powerfully reveal to humanity its relation to the natural world and its place within a universe that cannot be grasped by the intellect alone. As, given the prosaic nature of most contemporary drama, the actor's "genius" was rarely, to Tieck's thinking, stimulated, he felt him entitled to go beyond the limits set by the playwright. "It would be a sad restraint for the pure actor with his lucid knowledge or poetic instinct, if he were never to conceive more freely and bravely the so frequently meagre and silly characters offered him, and, in his own domain, be allowed to create a work of art for us. Often, if he were merely faithful to the so-called writer, it would be impossible for him to create such a work" (Tieck, *Kritische Schriften* III, 64-65).

Tieck, as we have seen, disliked the average actor who practiced "sing-song declamation and elevated false pathos." Instead he recommended naturalness in speech and gesture, not in the interests of plain realism, but as a way to make credible a theatre that transported the audience from everyday life into the realm of the marvellous. This should not be done through mesmerizing them—they should always remain aware of the illusion—but as a deliberate strategy. Instead of revealing aspects of character until all is clear, the actor should always give the impression that something more remains hidden, while the audience, sensing this hidden entity, should never fully understand what it is. They should remain fascinated by the actor's portrayal of character, because their imagination is led to fill out this empty space. If the actor reveals all, the audience's attention is lost. "The most agitated feeling, the deepest, most violent emotion must still leave in the imagination a presentiment of something yet more terrible, which does not appear but always hovers near in the mind. Once this unseen quantity really appears, the imagination grows lame and the illusion and enjoyment is destroyed'' (Tieck, *Kritische Schriften* IV, 86). Thus the crucial meeting of the actor's imagination with that of the audience could be achieved.

FRIEDRICH LUDWIG SCHRÖDER

Tieck's writings were not based entirely on theory. One actor especially he admired as having "creative imagination in the highest sense of the word"[4]—Friedrich Ludwig Schröder. Schröder was born in Schwerin in November 1744, the son of the actress Sophie Schröder and either her estranged husband or Konrad Ackermann. His childhood, spent with the Ackermann troupe, was unhappy, due to serious tensions between himself and his (step)father. These resulted in his being abandoned by his parents at the age of twelve in Königsberg, when the town was about to be occupied by Russian forces during the Seven Years War. But, after two years of penury, he rejoined his family, and for the next several years was an active member of the troupe, despite the continuation of his feud with Ackermann, which at times erupted into violence. His *Fach* was the First French Servant, and he specialized in dancing, acrobatics, and improvised comedy. When the troupe came to form the Hamburg National Theatre company, he refused to be part of it, preferring to spend several months with the Viennese improvisational actor, Felix Kurz-Bernadon (1717-1783), then touring in the Frankfurt and Mainz area. He rejoined Ackermann after the demise of the Hamburg project. The next few years were marked by his constant harassment of Ekhof, whose "mistakes" Schröder insisted on pointing out, until the exasperated older man left the Ackermann troupe to join Abel Seyler.

Ackermann died in 1771, leaving the artistic leadership of the troupe to his volatile son. At this juncture, Schröder changed entirely, and over the next nine years, during which he established the troupe in its own permanent theatre in Hamburg, achieved much of the work that makes him such an important figure in the history of German theatre. With a company that included for a time the urbane, courtly actor Johann Brockmann (1745-1812), the "intuitive," heroic actor Johann Reinecke (1747-1787), and Schröder's two celebrated, beautiful sisters Dorothea

(1752-1821) and Charlotte Ackermann (1757-1774), he prepared for "the most splendid period of Hamburg theatre history, earning world renown for this theatre and the Hamburg audiences, whose tastes it improved."[5] This improvement was achieved partly through Schröder's expansion of the repertoire, as he introduced drama of greater scope, with more breadth of action, more vigorous plots, and more complex characters than were generally available in the plays of the time. Shakespeare was the cornerstone of this new repertoire. Between 1776 and 1779, Schröder staged *Hamlet, Othello, The Merchant of Venice, Measure for Measure, King Lear, Richard II, Henry IV, Macbeth* and *Much Ado About Nothing*. Not all productions met with equal success. *Othello*, for example, was too strong for the audience's delicate feelings, and had to be taken off even after a happy ending had been tacked on. Also, not all the plays were new to the German stage. But Schröder's Shakespeare cycle and the wide interest it aroused prepared for the universal adoption of Shakespeare as a "national" dramatist in the German theatre. Of equal importance was Schröder's staging of many *Sturm-und-Drang* plays, especially of Lenz's unorthodox comedies *Die Soldaten* (*The Soldiers*—1776) and *Der Hofmeister* (*The Tutor*—1778). No other theatre practitioner was so closely associated with this early romantic dramatic movement as Schröder. When he left Hamburg in 1781, he had earned acceptance for the new drama, and had augmented the repertoire in a way that was to have lasting impact.

Schröder's departure from Hamburg was due partly to old actors of the Ackermann troupe leaving the company and partly to his ambition to achieve wider recognition. Spurred on by the success of Brockmann, who had toured as a solo actor when he left Hamburg in 1778, in 1780 Schröder gave guest performances in Berlin, Vienna, Munich, and Mannheim, all of which were received enthusiastically. This led to an invitation to join the Vienna Burgtheater, which he did in 1781. His four years here were not the happiest, despite the interest taken in him by Josef II. He was constantly frustrated by intrigue and by favoritism in the casting of plays. He therefore returned to Hamburg in 1785 to take up the management of his theatre again. The next thirteen years saw a significant improvement in production standards and a vast increase in the theatre's stock—apparently it had 120 different sets[6]—but Schröder's energies were flagging. He maintained his old repertoire, adding to it his own plays, bourgeois genre-pieces and adaptations from the English theatre, and those of the young Schiller, but the spark of the old days was gone. He retired in 1798, worn out by fighting with an undisciplined company and by a futile struggle against the public demand for opera. On his departure the theatre went into decline, so much so that for eleven months in 1811 and 1812 he took over the management once more. This failed due to the crippling censorship of the occupying French troops and to his own lack of contact with the contemporary theatre, so he retreated back to his home in the village of Rellingen. He died in September 1816 at the age of seventy-five.

Schröder, like Ekhof and Iffland, was physically unremarkable. He had a tall, slender figure but lacked elegance. His eyes were "small, lustreless, and inexpressive, his voice a hollow tenor."[7] Pictures suggest nothing grand in his appearance. Given his limited resources, during his early years with Ackermann, Schröder specialized in training his body, mastering the most torturous of acrobatic stunts and using his wonderfully fertile imagination in prolonged bouts of improvisation. Speed in transitions, physical flexibility and grotesque characterization were the hallmarks of his early work. "Schröder was . . . unique in the comic dryness or uncontrollable wantonness of his Truffaldino and similar servants, in exaggerating comic figures as is required of caricature roles, in grotesque caricature, in the accentuated expression of speech, in the always-changing, never-failing play of his hands, feet, and facial muscles" (Schütze, *Hamburg,* 406-7). Only after taking over the Ackermann troupe did Schröder shift to serious, literary roles. He did this both because of his new responsibilities as actor-manager and the accelerating disappearance of the improvised drama from the repertoire. But sharpness of characterization, constant movement, and the ability to project an impression of boundless energy remained with him to give his roles in the bourgeois drama and the classics an acuity and vigor unique among his contemporaries.

During his first Hamburg period, Schröder perfected his realistic approach to acting. In some ways, it appears to differ little from either Ekhof's or Iffland's, as Schröder claimed merely to be fulfilling the playwright's demands and remaining true to nature. "I have consulted no other mirror than the truth. . . . I do not think about shining and being conspicuous, but about filling out and being. I wish to give to each role whatever belongs to it, no more and no less. In this way each [role] must be what no other [role] can be."[8] But in contrast to his contemporaries, Schröder exhibited a range of expression that magnified his characters. He also invested them with a special tension. His major criticism of Ekhof had been that his representation of character was too deliberate, "blunt and stiff, premeditated and without temperament."[9] In addition to personal antipathies, such judgment may have been due to Ekhof's rounding out of the character and resolution of conflicting traits. Schröder did not round out or resolve; instead his characters' contradictions were allowed to abide. No doubt this attracted Schröder to *Sturm-und-Drang*. In these plays characters are torn by irreconcileable needs, while their attitudes toward others, especially family members or sexual partners, can be strongly ambivalent. Conflicts are expressed in a language that is often ecstatic, exaggerated, or convulsive, and they impel an action that can be abrupt and violent. Schröder's achievement was not to smooth out these conflicts, but to embody them credibly, allowing them to be seen as possible. In so doing, he brought rougher aspects of human nature to light, ones that could not always be harnessed and were often outside the restraints of social conditioning. Notable among his *Sturm-und-Drang* roles were the Major in Lenz's *Tutor*, a man torn between overwhelming love for his daughter and his impulse to play the tyrant over her, Grimaldi in Klinger's *Zwillinge (The Twins—* 1775), and Constantin in Leisewitz's *Julius von Tarent* (1776).

The quality of Schröder's acting, the sharpness of his characterizations, and the way in which he embodied conflicting traits of character can be gathered from his interpretation of Harpagon in a revival of *The Miser* in 1775. Harpagon had been one of Ackermann's most popular roles, which he played with high good humor, as if miserliness were just an unfortunate shortcoming. Later, Iffland was to play it mildly. Schröder, however, showed miserliness as a deeply engrained obsession, determining Harpagon's whole personality. But he also allowed that personality to be seen from two different sides. When Harpagon first appeared he was a grotesque figure, familiar from the improvisational theatre.

Lean, scrawny, with sparse white hair on his half-bald crown, a famished, mortified face, an emaciated, sharply pointed chin; his neck thin and bony, protected by a short, white bandage. The upper part of his body a skeleton covered in skin.... Long fingers like the feet of a spider projected from his almost fleshless hands.... His whole form was wretched, decayed, his whole physiognomy the picture of niggardliness, of self-martyrdom, of the fear of being robbed.[10]

Naturally Schröder concentrated on Harpagon's paranoia. Every noise and movement startled him, as did the slightest suggestion that his money was in danger. But the moment he was left alone with his treasures, he was a different being, for he loved them as others would a wife. "His eyes glittered with happiness, he clung to his idols with loving, yearning looks, a sweet smile swam across his mouth, his voice cooed accents of love. He was possessed by a truly dithyrambic rapture when he apostrophized his gold, calling it 'the comfort of mankind, the solace of the wretched, the magnet of the heart' " (Schink, 69). This Harpagon was therefore, at one and the same time, niggard and bounteous lover. When it came to the theft of the strong box, audiences were uncertain how to respond to him, for he had been seen both as a figure of fun and as a human being who attracted sympathy. Clarity of response to character, the dominant appeal of the idealist schools, was denied the audience for a less certain experience. Harpagon's needs were as legitimate as those of the lovers. This did not trivialize evil, but made it more real and understandable.

Whatever his claims, Schröder did not see the actor as just the obedient servant of the text. Foreshadowing Tieck's later writings, he stressed the actor's primacy in performance. "The actor must overcome the very playwright; the greater [the playwright], the harder the battle, the more glorious the victory.... Woe to the actor when the spectator, instead of leaving the theatre silently with tears in his eyes or a smile on his lips, says loudly, 'The play is beautifully written.' Then it is a literary society he has just left."[11] Given this opinion, Schröder felt himself entirely justified in excluding or rewriting any passages that he found not true to nature, and would radically alter those texts that failed to stretch his imagination. But although he upheld the centrality of the actor, and was concerned as much as any of his contemporaries about the social status of the profession, he did not expect the actor to be a paragon on stage. The character, rather than the actor's skills, should draw the audience's attention. To do this, the actor must be able to achieve a transformation of self so as not to be recognized. But while the audience might be deluded by this transformation, the actor should never be. Despite his reputation as an "intuitive" actor, Schröder was able to assume or drop his role at will. "The actor," he claimed, "in order to be forgotten must never forget himself."[12] Successful transformation required imagination and originality in both the conception and execution of the role, which meant that Schröder adamantly refused to be influenced by anything external to him. "The art of acting," he commented, "is very debased when it is associated only with the imitation of various models. . . . An actor should be no antiquary who receives his forms through tradition and repeats them!" (Schmidt I, 206-7). Each performance should be original, vitalized by new insights. This is only possible if, while representing character on stage, the actor also allows imagination free play around the representation. In this way the performance will have a genuine spontaneity as well as that "unseen quality" that Tieck felt definitive of the greatest acting.

Schröder's enthusiasm for Shakespeare was due mainly to the challenge offered by his roles. He echoed Ekhof's opinions on the English playwright, though in a far more positive sense, when he claimed that Shakespeare caused him little trouble, for "he makes everything easy for me and puts me so much in his debt" (Meyer I, 338). But if, as Schröder also asserted, the stage can be a battlefield between actor and playwright, the meeting of his energetic imagination with Shakespeare's major characters must have created theatre of great intensity.

When *Hamlet* was first produced in Hamburg in 1776, Brockmann acted the lead elegiacally, as a melancholic who played with people, at times even verging on the comic as he highlighted the prince's pleasure at fooling the court. Although Schröder had supervised the staging of the production, when he took over the title role after Brockmann's departure, he did not treat it as lightly. In fact he rather impatiently dismissed Brockmann's Hamlet as "very often affected."[13] From the very start, Schröder's Hamlet was a man as angry with himself as with the world around him. His first soliloquy—"Oh that this too too solid flesh would melt"—gave him opportunity to show the conflicting forces of sorrow and anger that divide and confuse Hamlet. His encounter with the Ghost introduced a powerful element of fear, effected through Schröder's pliable body. "Full of astonishment he staggered back; in doing so his hat fell off. Gasping and trembling in every limb, he bent his body further backwards. He remained some moments in that position, then slowly bent forward again, looking very closely at the Ghost, and then for the first time found words, though his tongue was only half able to articulate them."[14] But he lost all fear as he heard of the murder, becoming filled with "pity, revenge, and the bitterest of pain" (Schink/Litzmann, 256), all of which were swamped in a wave of fury as he delivered the soliloquy "Oh all you host of heaven!" The end of the scene was effectively touched with a moment of compassion for his father.

The immensity of his anger gave the remainder of the play its momentum; Brockmann, one senses, never dominated the action so completely. Schröder was quite prepared to drop the mask of madness when he needed to expose the injuries suffered by Hamlet. Also his prince was not entirely devoid of feelings for others. The scene with Ophelia was played with deep pity, both for her and himself, as if he were thinking back to a time of lost happiness. The high point of his performance was the bedroom scene with Gertrude. This he acted with the exactitude that, despite his constantly sustained energy, never left him. He passed "from pain to bitterness, to the highest anger, and after this to reawakening childish affection" (Schink/Litzmann, 258). The appearance of the Ghost was an especially telling moment. "Schröder dashed down the portrait of his uncle so violently that it shattered. 'His eyes followed the pieces rolling on the floor and, as he was on the point of raising them again, he caught sight of the Ghost'" (Schink/Litzmann, 259). The Ghost seemed to arise as an image of his mind, called up by the broken physical image, a phenomenon that might have no objective existence.

Schröder, obedient to contemporary taste, did not give Shakespeare in the original version. In fact his *Hamlet* ended lamely, with Hamlet and Laertes, neither dead, joining hands and swearing to rule Denmark with honor and justice. Schröder's version of *King Lear* also differed from Shakespeare's, notably in the omission of the opening scene, not given at that time, as it was believed physical representation would strain the audience's credibility too far. This, of course, altered appreciably the audience's initial perception of Lear, for he entered not as a monarch about to expose himself and his land to ruin, but as a vigorous huntsman whose strength was still unbroken. His abdication seemed therefore to have been motivated by nothing more than a desire to spend his old age in comfort. So the first time Goneril crossed him, far from calling on the audience's pity for Lear, Schröder had him fly into a titanic rage, which Schink's mixed metaphors capture well. "He stood before the insolent Goneril, a volcano of whirling flames, hurling out fireballs, and the curse, a sea of furious waves, roared over her" (Schink, *Charakteristik*, 47). It was such a breathtaking moment that whenever

4. Friedrich Ludwig Schröder as King Lear. Reproduced by permission of Theatermuseum der Universität zu Köln.

he played the role outside Hamburg, supporting actors were so taken aback they hardly dared speak to him.

After such a mighty start, Schröder's Lear could rise to few higher peaks of fury. Instead, as the king declined into madness and extreme old age, Schröder mixed, in his characteristic fashion, the irrascible, the majestic, and the pathetic aspects of the character (see Figure 4). The most famous detail of his performance first occurred when he played the role for his debut at the Burgtheater. Brockmann, already a favorite with the Viennese, always played the scene with the blind Gloucester on a tree stump, like a hedge-preacher. Schröder was about to do the same, but, at the moment he was to climb up, he had Lear's strength give out, and he fell to the ground. This was a nuance that earned him ovations. The climax of his performance came where it would with all future actors, at the awakening with Cordelia. Schröder's capacity to register accurately changing emotions meant that this was not a scene of hollow pathos. He seemed to recapture the entire experience of the play. When he was first seen, he was sitting as if dead. Then "lighter breathing indicated he was waking up. He raised his opened eyes weakly and, with sight half-dimmed, turned them on the bystanders" (Schink, *Charakteristik*, 49). His reaction on hearing Cordelia speak was not instant joy, in fact there was a touch of anger in it, as if he were trying to recall her offense against him. This passed, he gathered himself together, and then her image became clearer to him. This led to a memory of their earlier love and a rapturous reunion. Schröder's acting in the death scene—in his version Lear dies while Cordelia, through some deft stage management, survives—was strong and graphic. His emotions over Cordelia's "corpse" built to a climax of anger as immense as the one that started the play. This, however, proved too much for Lear's strength and, as if he were possessed by forces too strong for him, he died of a heart attack.

With Schröder, the realistic Hamburg school of acting, conventionally regarded as antithetical to the Weimar school, was founded. No doubt Schröder, given his antipathy to the imitation of models, would have disowned the very notion of a "school," but his seemingly unconstrained, often harsh realism was an unequivocal alternative to acting that required the performer to be a paragon of uprightness and "natural nobleness." Even though Schröder was the most self-aware of actors, he, more successfully than any of those contemporaries whose acting was similar to his, such as Reinecke and the volatile, intuitive actor David Borchers (1744-1807), represented on stage emotions and impulses that had the appearance of being uncontrollable and even incomprehensible to rational faculties. Coexistence of opposites, rather than their mingling and resolution, was the principle of his performances. Schröder prepared the way for the handful of actors who can be regarded as part of the romantic movement.

FERDINAND FLECK

While Tieck had deep respect for Schröder, his affections were drawn most strongly to Johann Friedrich Ferdinand Fleck (1757-1801), "the idol of the romantics."[15] Tieck saw Fleck when he was a schoolboy in Berlin, when Fleck, as a rival to Iffland, was the leading actor of the Berlin Royal Theatre. No greater contrast between actors could be imagined than between Fleck and Iffland. While the dumpy actor with a reedy voice made the best of his limitations, Fleck had an over-abundance of natural talent, physical beauty, and vocal resource. For his most ardent admirers he was nothing less than a *"Gottmensch"*[16] (a divine being) who represented everything that created the peculiar magic of the theatre. He was slender in frame, with an Apollonian profile, and he possessed a magnificent voice that could express "tenderness, supplication and devotion [in] truly flutelike whispers," while it "could roll like thunder in restrained fury and roar like a lion in unleashed passion" (Tieck, *Schriften* V, 467). Like Schröder, with whom Fleck acted briefly before going to Berlin in 1783, he had great powers of transformation, though he was lacking entirely in any method. More than any other contemporary actor, Fleck embodied that instinctive "genius" prized by the romantics. This meant that he never had to work at a role, but acted it from his initial impressions. Fortunately his imaginative grasp of character was thorough enough to comprise all facets, though his acting rarely had the particularity of Schröder's. This could work to his advantage. Tieck, for example, found his Lear more impressive than Schröder's because "he did not work so obviously at the origin and development of madness [but just] let it be shown in its fullest grandeur" (Tieck, *Schriften* V, 468). His intuitive approach also allowed him to yield more easily to the role, so that the humor in tragic heroes such as Shakespeare's surfaced freely, an unusual circumstance at that time.

The chief reason for the idolization of Fleck was the almost visionary quality of his stage presence. Unlike Schröder, Fleck made little effort to control the fire of his imagination when he was ignited by the vital feelings of his characters. While this lack of discipline threatened to reveal the "hidden quantity" Tieck felt definitive of great acting, the spontaneous arousal of his imagination gave Fleck unexpected stature, as if he were in touch with a level of consciousness outside the experience of the audience. His seeming possession by external forces was described as "demonic" acting, "as if a higher genius spoke out of him and gave itself being" (Tieck, *Schriften* V, 469). He was no longer a mere actor, but one who saw things few others could ever see. Fleck, irradiated by elements of the unearthly, was a medium for a supernatural world. "In those plays compatible with Fleck's disposition, the whole stream of brightest and noblest poetry flowed toward him, embracing him and drawing him into the land of marvels. Everything came to him as a vision and this poetry and inspiration, moving him deeply, created through him such great and sublime things that we will with difficulty see them again" (Tieck, *Schriften* V, 466).

Fleck, always best in the classic repertoire, was a disquieting Macbeth and an aristocratic Shylock, who degenerated as his revenge possessed him, ending the play "horrible and ghostlike, but never common, always noble" (Tieck, *Schriften* V, 468). His Karl Moor was a magnificent figure, torn between maudlin self-pity and towering wrath, while Wallenstein, his most famous role, provided a standard for actors throughout the nineteenth century. Fleck's Wallenstein was a reflective man whose belief in astrology was so persuasive that his downfall appeared as a reversal of order as established by fate. Naturally, the climax of his performance was the dream speech. "For a second time he actually saw the vision with his inward eye, and was so powerfully affected by it that his face was drained of all expression as he told of it."[17] At the end of the final play of the trilogy, he stood transformed, and elevated "the spectator above all levels of ordinary life on earth,"[18] a condition that might, arguably, be seen as correlative to Schiller's conception of the Sublime.

Such acting has its dangers. Fleck was, as Tieck observed, great only in those parts suiting his temperament. Generally he was unremarkable in contemporary, realistic drama, and he was always subject to his moods. He could lose concentration entirely in the course of a performance and often had to fall back on the mannerisms of the average late eighteenth-century actor. Indeed, one of the few pictures that have survived of him in performance, of the dream speech in *Wallenstein,* suggests that even at his best he was not above resorting to affected poses. The idolization he enjoyed also bred arrogance. Once, when playing Karl Moor, he was so offended by the initial unwillingness of the audience to applaud that he lost all interest in the part. His slovenly acting, which included trying to balance his sword on the tip of his finger, naturally gave rise to groans, hisses, and catcalls from the audience. These stung him painfully, so he stalked down to the footlights, raked the auditorium with a formidable scowl, and then returned upstage to "play the rest of the role with so much passion and truth that the audience forgot everything and thanked him with jubilant applause."[19] One wishes that for their own and Fleck's sake, they had not been so easily carried away.

Fleck's moodiness and inconsistency mean that he cannot be counted among the most formative actors of the German stage. In fact his influence was possibly more negative than positive as through him developed the cult of the actor not as a social model, but as an extraordinary being to be unquestioningly admired. Nevertheless, his memory was to be relatively short-lived, as it was soon overshadowed by the most legendary figure in the history of the German theatre, Ludwig Devrient.

LUDWIG DEVRIENT

Few actors more thoroughly suited contemporary, popular preconceptions of the actor than Ludwig Devrient. Born in Berlin in 1784 into a family that was prospering in the haberdashery trade, as he grew up, he found it impossible to settle into the regular habits of commercial life. After an unhappy upbringing, which caused him to make several attempts to run away, he spent some years in the family business. However, an unfortunate incident in which, during a journey to Russia, he gambled away funds entrusted to him, led the family to give up on him. At this point he saw the heroic actor Ferdinand Ochsenheimer (1767-1822) playing in Leipzig, and was so stirred by him that he determined at once to make his living in the theatre.

He was hired in May 1804 by J. W. Lange, whose troupe toured small towns in the Thuringia Wald. These beginnings were inauspicious, as stage-fright rendered Devrient's voice all but inaudible and his movements unbelievably awkward. Nevertheless, the stage director had confidence in him, and advised him to specialize in intrigue and character *Fächer*. In these Devrient was a success, so much so that the following year he was hired by the Dessau Court Theatre, which performed for six months in Dessau, six months in Leipzig. As opera was more popular than the spoken drama, Devrient, whose singing voice was negligible, had to waste much time playing small supporting roles rather than developing his powers as an actor. He did, however, make his mark as a highly skilled comedian, especially in plays, very popular at the time, that required him to act out several different roles in the same performance. His greatest success was in a comedy, *Die Drillinge* (*The Triplets*), in which he played three brothers, all with distinctly contrasting personalities and appearances. So convincing was he in creating the illusion that each was a separate character that the play stayed in his repertoire for the rest of his life.

In 1809, he joined the City Theatre in Breslau (now Wroclaw, Po-land), then one of the leading companies in Germany. The five years he spent here are normally considered to represent the zenith of his career, as it was in Breslau that he perfected the comparatively few tragic roles with which he made his name. Above all he was noted for his intense and disquieting Franz Moor, Lear, and Shylock, and for pathetic roles such as Schewa in Cumberland's *Jew*. He also continued to play a broad range of character-types with great inventiveness and comic vigor. By 1811, when Iffland gave some guest performances at Breslau, Devrient was beginning to acquire a national reputation, so Berlin seemed the next logical step for him.

In 1815, Devrient was hired by the Berlin Royal Theatre on Iffland's recommendation, though not until several months after the director's death. By this time Devrient's own health was in serious decline, brought about mainly by his incessant consumption of alcohol. He had already passed out in the middle of a performance of *King Lear,* having to be carried from the theatre "like a dead man from battle."[20] By the time he arrived in Berlin, his alcoholism was chronic. His first year in Berlin, during which he played all his greatest roles, was a triumph, gaining him a reputation that eclipsed even that of the deceased Iffland. But, in 1816, the new intendant Count Karl von Brühl, a disciple of the Weimar school, hired Wolff. After Wolff's immense success in *Hamlet,* the unwritten law was that Wolff played tragedy while Devrient stuck to comedy. After his last great comic role as Falstaff in the two parts of *Henry IV,* Devrient's powers were visibly in decline. He played in fewer and fewer premieres, even though the plays of Grillparzer, which would have offered him some superb vehicles, were just being intro-duced into the repertoire. His neglect by the Berlin management and his need to pay off his huge drinking debts made him take increasingly to touring. Although this sapped his energy even further, there were brief periods of renewal. In 1828, he appeared as a guest at the Vienna Burgtheater, where his reception was tremendous. He played to packed houses and was greeted by the press with positive rapture. Two years later, by now a dying man, he appeared at Weimar, and visited the aging Goethe. On his return to Berlin, Zelter, one of Goethe's corre-spondents, reported him as "a corpse putrefying in alcohol."[21] Not long after, on 30 December 1832, he died, forty-eight years old.

Devrient was a man about whom myths were made. From his child-hood, when, sitting on a tree stump, he used to imitate weirdly the vocal patterns of a French pastor he had heard preach, through his adulthood, when he engaged in intense bouts of midnight drinking with E. T. A. Hoffmann, to the moment of his death, which occurred while his wife was playing on the piano the last scene of *Don Giovanni*, to after his death, when a prominent actor, Friedrich Lemm, received a note signed by Devrient saying that he would be the next to die, a prophecy that proved true, Devrient's life was marked by the extraordinary. No doubt many stories about him are apocryphal, many were invented by himself, but they show clearly his contemporaries perceived him as an unusual man. Devrient has become part of the legend of romantic Germany, a wild genius, driven by his appetites to an early death, a prodigy whose interests in the weird and grotesque have suffused his reputation in a nimbus of diabolic light.

In fact the man was not as mysterious as his reputation would have it. He had a most engaging personality. Although with Hoffmann he indulged in vehement, often morbid flights of the imagination, most people were struck by his childlike naiveté and helplessness. Inept in the practical things of life, he could never keep his money; he was forever giving it away. He was dearly loved by his colleagues. "When the wine glowed within him," wrote Costenoble, "he embraced the whole world with heartfelt love, and, as a friend, recognized each of his comrades' talents, and rejoiced with kindred souls."[22] His inner warmth was complemented by his attractive appearance. Pictures show a man slight in build with finely chiselled features, an unusually long nose, which is bent in the middle, and, above his jutting chin, an expressive, flexible mouth. Most striking of all are the eyes, either staring as if transfixed in horror, or twinkling in ingratiatingly good humor. All is crowned by luxuriant, black hair. "That picturesque head," wrote his close friend Heinrich Anschütz, "with the soft, glossy, black hair, with the sharply cut and yet so noble profile, with those glowing and yet so clear and tender eyes."[23] All in all, Devrient's ductile and winning personality seemed to contradict the myth that surrounds him. How, therefore, can the man and his notorious reputation be reconciled?

No doubt much of the popular fantasy about Devrient arose from the uncanny influence he exercised on his audience from the stage. All who saw him paid unstinting tribute to his powers of transformation, which filled each character he played with a life unique to itself. Even in 1828 he had lost none of this ability, as Eduard von Bauernfeld observed.

He played individually each time. He was never schematic or mechanical in the conventional fashion of the theatre. He knew how to contain everything within beautiful proportion, but he also appeared with sharp and individual features, without ever overacting. He developed to the highest degree the art of choosing a distinct appearance and of maintaining the assumed character in bearing and voice. Occasionally the deception became so great that [when he played two roles in one night] we really had to believe that we had before us a man different from the one who had left us a short time before.[24]

So different and yet inwardly consistent were each of his characters, so seemingly accurate each of his representations, that one of his contemporaries observed, "It is scarcely possible to say anything else about him but that [he always chooses] the right person."[25]

The intense individuality of each of Devrient's characters led him to place utmost value on originality. While at Dessau, tempted by an offer of reconciliation with his father if he gave up his disreputable career, he staked his whole future on whether he was original or not. "You have no idea," he complained at the time, "of how I thought of the scene in my imagination, of how it appeared quite different from what I had intended—it comes from that damned copying."[26] He therefore determined that he would give up the stage if he could not act the role of Chancellor Flessel in Iffland's *Mündel* (*The Ward*) so individually as to convince himself and his colleagues that it was created solely from his imagination. Fortunately he managed to do this.

As his national standing grew, his acting came to be regarded as the antithesis of the Weimar school. He refused to allow himself any posture or vocal mannerism that came from anywhere but his own perception of what the role needed. Even though as a young man he had admired Iffland for his resourcefulness, his approach to a role was entirely his own. As Rachel Levin commented, he worked "*not* like Iffland, but from the inside out, formed on his own model and not that of the parterre" (Altman, 146). The inner origins of the character were communicated to the audience with a notable directness that created another distinction between Devrient and Weimar. His imagination could grasp an uncommonly broad range of emotions, while his physical flexibility and lightness, coupled with his tractible if not altogether attractive voice, meant that he could render emotions with subtlety. Furthermore, as his skills allowed him to pass from the expression of one state of mind to another with great speed, the audience could never grasp the precise, present mental condition of the character, even though they sensed its rightness. In this way Devrient communicated viscerally the disturbing experience of change within the character's psyche and the emotional fluctuations to which it was subject. The Weimar actor was self-possessed; Devrient, it appeared, was entirely subject to the labile flow of emotion.

By temperament Devrient was given to representing neither the ideal humanity of the Weimar school, nor a "naturally noble" but average human being as Iffland had done. He was fascinated by the extremes of experience. "All purely rhetorical roles were unsuited to him," wrote his nephew Eduard Devrient, who had acted with him. "It was not within Ludwig Devrient's temperament to represent ideal humanity in pure harmony. He did not have beauty of form. With a sort of demonic air, his spirit hunted to the borders of humanity after its extreme manifestations ... the extraordinary, the terrible, the horrid, the bizarre, and the laughable" (Ed. Devrient, *Geschichte* II, 138). His power as an actor lay in his ability to terrify audiences by convincing them of the immanence of exceptional passions within his characters. The effect he had was not ennobling nor always aesthetically pleasing. Rather, it could be disintegrative, as he could unsettle his audience by realizing the baneful powers within the character in such a way as to make them feel themselves infected by them. Revealing is the reaction of Rachel Levin, who refused to go to the theatre after Fleck's death, but returned to see Devrient. "I was utterly delighted *once again* to be touched by imagination and art! *Merely being touched* made my eyes weep and my completely disordered nerves vibrate as if in convulsions.... I applauded so much that I instantly contracted a migraine" (Altman, 147).

Tieck often found Devrient too unnerving, so for a link between Devrient and the romantic movement we must look to his relationship with E. T. A. Hoffmann. Hoffmann, who had done much work as a dramaturg and opera composer, visualized a theatre with action more violent, appearances more abnormal, and experiences more uncommon and intense than was then customary in most theatre. How the actor could realize such a theatre is one theme of Hoffmann's essay in dialogue form, *Seltsame Leiden eines Theaterdirektors (Strange Sorrows of a Theatre Director*—1817). The conversation between "Grey" (possibly Count Brühl) and "Brown" (possibly Hoffmann himself)[27] provides withering analyses of many aspects of theatrical life, but the most constant complaint is the egotism and exhibitionism of performers. Only

Devrient, referred to throughout as "little Garrick," is able to fulfil "the first requirement of the performing art . . . the complete denial or forgetting of one's own self" (Hoffmann, 391). This does not, however, require a blind surrender of the self to the role. Rather, entering into a state of intense concentration, Devrient imagined "the face of [a] spectator benumbed in fear, terror, and horror" (Hoffmann, 387). A corresponding horror took hold of himself, with peculiar effect, for "in this terror a higher intelligence awakens within him, formed like the person of his role, and this intelligence, not *he* continues to act, although it is constantly observed and checked by his own self, whose consciousness never abandons him" (Hoffmann, 387). Hoffmann's description may be a shade fanciful, but it establishes a key point. Devrient experienced the role as both part of himself and as outside himself, as though he were the medium for an experience not entirely his own. Slightly later, Hoffmann compares dramatic characters to figures from the actor's dreams. Hence, when he is realizing such figures on stage, the actor cannot give them lineaments that reflect the external world; instead they arise from the imaginative logic of the dreamed form. Hoffmann continues by describing the total stillness Devrient required around him, as the slightest disturbance could throw him off and therefore dispel the presence of the imaginary figure that both controlled and was controlled by his consciousness.

Although Hoffmann provides no detailed description of Devrient's roles, he was deeply moved by his Franz Moor. In this role more than in any other we can grasp the fascination Devrient exercised over his audience and can identify the particular nature of his "demonic" acting. Most actors in this part, following Schiller's stage directions about humps and other conventional paraphernalia for villains, presented Franz Moor as a hackneyed, melodramatic figure, overlaying their features with lurid makeup and adopting the conventional, red, "malcontent's wig." However Devrient played him with little makeup, no wig, and an undeformed body. In the harsh glare of the footlights, his face appeared ghastly white in contrast to his jet-black hair. He also chose his costume to delineate the character, not on historical grounds, as was increasingly becoming the convention. He wore plain, sombre clothes, shot through with threads of gold, covered by a dark red Spanish cloak with a white collar, from which stuck his neck, "long and scraggy like a bird of prey's."[28] Later, a few changes in detail, such as the appropriation of an ermine coat on which the count's star was pinned, was all Devrient used to establish Franz's ambitions.

Although Devrient as Franz dominated any performance of *The Robbers* he played in, at the start he was so quiet that many, when they first saw him in the role, were disappointed at how ordinary he was. Initially Devrient focussed on those traits that motivated Franz, especially his spite and cowardice. He was no confident villain but uncertain both of those around him and of himself. His first monologue was an act of self-questioning rather than a declaration of villainy, while his anathema of his ugliness, coming as it did from an outwardly not unattractive figure, could only be taken as descriptive of inward deformity. August Klingemann referred to "inner moral ugliness creeping from spiteful, warped eyes," finding this more repulsive than any physical blemish as "one can come to love pockmarks and external ugliness, but inner ugliness pushes love away as an opposite pole is pushed by the magnet."[29] Nevertheless this inward ugliness, masked in public by a "nun's veil of holiness" (Rellstab, 315), allowed Devrient to show Franz as "a rebel out of inner necessity, an exponent of a truly tragic experience" (Altman, 209).

It was only in the violent confrontations with his father and Amalia in Acts 2 and 3 that Devrient allowed Franz to utter raw defiance. But these moments were comparatively rare, vulnerability remained the essence of the character, especially in Act 4 when he first experienced spasms of conscience. These came as he stood before the picture of Karl, and realized that his brother had just entered the house in the guise of "Count Brand." His realization was soon followed by a violent altercation with Hermann, ending with the brandishing of pistols. Here Franz's nerve broke. As he slunk away from the departing Hermann, still determined to murder his brother, the bell struck. The sound hit him like a stroke of conscience. What followed was Devrient's greatest moment, described here by Ludwig Rellstab.

Never have I seen a more splendid, physically sensitive performance than Devrient's. Each step, each twitch of his hand, each turn of his head had meaning. He hastily threw back his black coat, for he was still in mourning for his father, as if his involuntary contact with it had terrified him. He looked around timidly, as if wanting to see whether the spectre in his breast were actually following him. At last he dared to turn around completely, and stood

5. Ludwig Devrient as Franz Moor. Reproduced by permission of Theaterhistorische Sammlung-Walter Unruh, Freie Universität, West Berlin.

once again with his face to the audience. But he was no longer the same person whom a few moments before we had seen leaving, full of resolute malice. His features were pallid, his muscles quivered as if trembling with fever, his teeth rattled together, his hollow eyes rolled uncertainly here and there, his hair was standing on end in terror. (Rellstab, 321)[see Figure 5.]

His fear extinguished any resolution to murder. Uttering half-articulated sounds, he began to steal off-stage when, unintentionally, he let drop the dagger in his hand. It fell "with a clattering noise. This unexpected sound, at which everyone involuntarily jumped, pierced the criminal's desolate horror of death with such powerful fear that it overcame him and he sank down unconscious" (Rellstab, 322). The stunned audience allowed the curtain to descend in silence.

The breakdown in Act 4 was preparation for the final collapse. Here, at last, Franz's inner tensions broke out with eruptive force. The Day of Judgment speech allowed Devrient to portray a soul in the agonies of despair, expressed in a seemingly reflex way, for words poured from his mouth as if the character had lost control of himself. Klingemann observed, "Thoughts ran short of words, but he carried on mechanically as his fear of death rose, so that sounds flowed away unconnectedly from his lips"; after his performance "all other [actors] appeared artificial in comparison, and even Iffland's performance evaporated like a shadow in the memory" (Klingemann, III, 345).

Devrient's demonic acting clearly did not consist, as his nephew Eduard might be interpreted as implying, of outwardly grotesque poses or aggressive villainy. To draw a parallel with Hoffmann's fictional figures, Devrient did not create a René Cardillac, a Dr Coppelius, or a Councillor Krespel, knowingly malign characters. Rather his creations were closer to figures such as Nathaniel in "Der Sandmann," passive beings whose psyches are the battleground for forces that seem to have their genesis beyond normal consciousness, that cannot be controlled by the will. His characters were "demonic" in the sense of being possessed, not of taking possession. In contemporary critical language, such experience was described in quasi-religious terminology; from our own more secular viewpoint, we can see that Devrient, in direct opposition to the idealist schools of acting, brought the unconscious of his characters to the fore.

Like his Franz Moor, Devrient's Lear was remarkable for the strangely few moments of fully unleashed passion. He has been credited as the first German actor to perform the opening scene,[30] so, in contrast to Schröder, he started from a standpoint of weakness. This was a dying Lear "upon whose face lay all the traces of great passion that may in his youth have ruled his breast entirely and that still had not left him completely" (Rellstab, 332). The division of the kingdom was, therefore, conducted as an act of reconciliation, in utter trust of his daughters. So great was his love for them that his anger was muted at their first betrayal, his love continuing to shine through even at moments of deepest suffering. Only when it came to the curse on Regan, where Devrient often broke down, did the king finally give way fully to his grief.

In the mad scenes, Devrient's acting was quiet, with few unnatural or peculiar moments. The onset of madness was heralded lightly by the words "I would not be mad" accompanied by a brush of his hand across his forehead. His fear was contained solely in his eyes, which seemed to gaze on madness like a "threatening ghost" ready to seize him. When he succumbed, he played as if the pain were over, but with no less uncanny an effect. Costenoble recalled how he "would not always utter the words of pain with the tones of pain. It sounds all the more terrifying when the monstrous speaks as if it were a deformed joy" (Costenoble, *Burg* II, 334). By the end of his career, Devrient relied solely on his eyes to create the impression of inner turmoil, aided where necessary by movements of the hands and fingers. Few details are available of the scene of reconciliation with Cordelia, though many considered it his finest moment, as in it Lear returned to his natural state of dependence. The young Richard Wagner was deeply moved by the influence he had on the audience. After the performance they stayed for a long time in their seats, "scarcely whispering, silent, nearly motionless, as if they were bound by a magic force no one had the power to resist."[31]

Devrient's Shylock was famous. The role had been open to various approaches; Schröder had played it sympathetically with Jewish mannerisms, Fleck had maintained Shylock's nobility, while Iffland had trivialized it—"At the end of the trial scene he collapsed like a ridiculous scarecrow."[32] Devrient, however, emphasized the character's harsher, uglier aspects. Hoffmann found that when Shylock was played by Devrient, his fate was more painful than that of accepted tragic figures as, still alive, he faced the annihilation of his whole existence. While Iffland had tottered around with tiny steps, Devrient moved in long strides that lent a majesty to his bearing. While Iffland had made of Shylock a Europeanized Jew, Devrient played the Oriental, the peer of his Venetian enemies. His exotic foreignness was displayed most strikingly in the trial scene as, sitting cross-legged on the floor, he whetted his scimitar on the soles of his feet. So moved, afraid, and confused were the audience by the strange beauty of Shylock in defeat that Zelter, Goethe's correspondent, felt that they were divided between their own beliefs and those of the character (Goethe/Zelter, *Briefwechsel* II, 175). When he left the stage, he had conferred "a certain sinister greatness" (Rellstab, 336) on the role, seeming to speak not only for himself but for the whole persecuted race of Jews. As a result they did not know how to respond; an alien belief, rigorously upheld, seemed to have greater legitimacy than their own.

Devrient played other Shakespearean roles, Mercutio, Parolles, and a splendid Falstaff, who displayed the "natural, primitive humor of a depraved genius" (Parthey, II, 94). But his greatest role would have been Richard III, a part that fascinated him throughout his career. He was always ambitious to play it, but even though it was promised him soon after he had arrived in Berlin, Wolff's engagement stopped any production of the play. Only in 1828, after Wolff's death, did he have the opportunity to act it. By then his powers had declined, and he was unable to bring to his performance the insights he had accumulated over so many years. These included a perception that only the "holy truth" of his mother's curse and prophecy check Richard's ruthlessness, and an approach to costuming that, like his Franz Moor, would soften the normally grotesque appearance of the character so that the inner life had more freedom to develop. In performance, Devrient's voice was weak and his lapses of memory meant he had to shorten the part considerably. Nonetheless there were splendid moments. The Lady Anne scene was most convincing, due to the strange mixture of elegance and humor Devrient brought to it, while his indifference as he ordered Hastings's execution was unpleasantly powerful. But, by the time he reached the Bosworth field sequence, his strength was so sapped he could do little more than struggle to keep on stage until the end of the play. As a result, the completeness he was normally able to bring to his roles was lacking. His Richard remained a series of striking episodes, little more.

In his lifetime, Devrient created over 500 roles, a formidable number even by the standards of the time, though it must be stressed that several of these were in one-act plays. For the regular Breslau and Berlin audiences, seeing him in the great tragic roles was the exception rather than the rule, as he appeared most often in light comedy. This was a source of distress to Hoffmann, who, in the guise of Brown, upbraids Grey-Brühl for making him play trivial roles. Devrient's accommodating mentality, argues Brown, makes it difficult for him to refuse whatever is offered him, and this means his talents are being eroded by roles that do not challenge his imagination sufficiently, allowing that imagination to range freely without being tempered by the discipline required by great dramatic characters. There is a danger, according to Brown, that if Devrient's imagination feeds only on itself, he will soon be unable to perform the great roles. Moreover, the exploitation of Devrient in trivial drama can debase public taste, as an audience "very soon comes to the point where it considers the diamond that has been shown it in a false light to be a common pebble" (Hoffmann, 403). Although

Devrient's decline was no doubt caused by drink, the predominantly light repertoire of the day, as well as Wolff's presence in Berlin, severely limited his range. In Berlin he played Schewa in *The Jew* fifty-five times, Shylock forty-four times, Franz Moor twenty-five times, and Lear a mere seventeen times, but he was seen far more frequently in plays such as *The Triplets,* in light comedy, and Kotzebuean melodrama.[33] On tour, however, he kept more to classic parts, from which his reputation had sprung. Hence, on a national level he was known as much for his serious as his comic roles. These created for him the legend of the "demonically" possessed actor that has ever since been sustained in the German theatre.

It is a contradiction in terms to speak of a "romantic school" in acting. Others created finely individual characterizations, filled with warmth, passion, spontaneity, and, at times, a grandiosity that owed little to the formality of the idealist schools. Notable in this respect were Sophie Schröder (1781-1868), a powerfully emotional actress who spent several years at the Burgtheater, and Ferdinand Esslair (1772-1840), a widely celebrated actor, whom Tieck admired for his ability to realize heroic roles fully and naturally. But no "school" was established. The essence of the romantic actor was the denial of tradition and the insistence on total originality in rendering the role. Although Friedrich Schröder and Devrient did not play themselves on stage and could tackle roles entirely different from their own personalities, their acting was solely a product of themselves and of their insights into the necessity of the characters. Comparisons with other famous actors are fruitless. Devrient has repeatedly been compared with his great contemporaries Edmund Kean and Frédérick Lemaître but, beyond a similarity in their ways of life, the comparisons do justice to no one. Kean was by strategy irregular, assaulting his audiences with sudden, breathtaking outbursts of passion, while Lemaître started from a basis of outrageous parody to develop an acting that was unequalled in its flamboyance. Devrient, however, was quieter, more inward, more regular, allowing his role to seep into the sensitivities of the audience, until they too felt themselves influenced by the impulses swaying his characters. Like Schröder and Fleck, though to a degree more intense, he led audiences to feel extraordinary emotions, visceral in their intensity. In both character and audience, though, if we are to believe Hoffmann, not entirely in the actor, these feelings appeared to be beyond the power of the will to control, hence the label "demonic" and the strange reputation of Devrient. His acting, as we have seen, realized the powers of the unconscious. Later actors who could penetrate their audiences as effectively came to be known as *Nervenschauspieler*—actors who touch the nerves. Devrient was the first of this kind. In taking his audiences beneath the comforting surface, he opened to them an experience beyond the immediate grasp of the rational mind, yet it was still recognizable to them. While the idealist actor reassured by presenting an image of human beings as harmonious and rational, the romantic actor gave a vision of human vulnerability. Such perceptions could, at one and the same time, exhilarate and yet disturb profoundly.

NOTES

1. August Wilhelm Schlegel, *Dramaturgische Vorlesungen*, vol. 5 of *Sämmtliche Werke,* ed. Eduard Bocking (Leipzig: Weidmann, 1846), 34.

2. Joseph von Eichendorff, *Zur Geschichte des Dramas,* vol. 3 of *Werke*, ed. Marlies Korfsmeyer (Munich: Winkler, n.d. [1970]), 505.

3. Ludwig Tieck, *Dramaturgische Blätter,* vol. 3 of *Kritische Schriften* (Leipzig: Brockhaus, 1852), 62-63.

4. Ludwig Tieck, *Phantasus* II, vol. 5 of *Schriften* (Berlin: Reimer, 1828), 464.

5. J. F. Schütze, *Hamburgische Theatergeschichte* (Hamburg: Treder, 1794), 385.

6. Karl August Böttiger, *Friedrich Ludewig Schröder in Hamburg im Sommer 1795* (n.p., n.d.), 290.

7. Eduard Devrient, *Geschichte der deutschen Schauspielkunst,* new ed. (Berlin: Elsner, 1905), I, 455.

8. F. L. W. Meyer, *Friedrich Ludwig Schröder*, new ed. (Hamburg: Campe, 1823), I, 338.

9. Heinz Kindermann, *Theatergeschichte der Goethezeit* (Vienna: Bauer, 1948), 147.

10. Johann Friedrich Schink, *Friedrich Ludwig Schröders Charakteristik als Bühnenfuhrer, mimischer Künstler, dramatischer Dichter und Mensch* (n.p., n.d.), 68.

11. Friedrich Ludwig Schmidt, *Denkwürdigkeiten des Schauspielers, Schauspieldichters und Schauspieldirektors,* ed. Hermann Uhde (Hamburg: Mauke, 1875), II, 136.

12. Quoted in Paul J. Hoffman, *Friedrich Ludwig Schröder als Dramaturg und Regisseur,* SGT 52 (Berlin: VGT, 1939), 279.

13. Alexander von Weilen, *Hamlet auf der deutschen Bühne* (Berlin: Reimer, 1908), 52.

14. From a review attributed to J. F. Schink, quoted by Berthold Litzmann in *Friedrich Ludwig Schröder* (Hamburg & Leipzig: Voss, 1894), II, 256.

15. Wolfgang Drews, *Die grossen Zauberer*, 3d ed. (Munich: Donau, 1953), 64.

16. Karl Costenoble, *Tagebücher von seiner Jugend bis zur Übersiedlung nach Wien (1818)*, SGT 18 (Berlin: VGT, 1912), I, 13.

17. J. G. Rhode in Monty Jacobs, ed., *Deutsche Schauspielkunst*, rev. ed., Eva Stahl (Berlin: Henschel, 1954), 217.

18. Z. Funck, *Aus dem Leben zweier Schauspieler: August Wilhelm Ifflands und Ludwig Devrients* (Leipzig: Brockhaus, 1838), 137.

19. Edgar Gross, *Johann Friedrich Ferdinand Fleck,* SGT 22 (Berlin: VGT, 1914), 121.

20. Karl von Holtei, *Vierzig Jahre*, ed. Max Grube, 4th ed. (Schweidnitz: Heege, n.d.), I, 74.

21. Letter from Zelter to Goethe, in vol. 6 of *Briefwechsel zwischen Goethe und Zelter,* ed. Friedrich Riemer (Berlin: Duncker & Humblot, 1834), 98.

22. Karl Costenoble, *Aus dem Burgtheater (1818-1837)* (Vienna: Konegen, 1889), II, 317.

23. Heinrich Anschütz, *Erinnerungen aus dessen Leben und Wirken* (Stuttgart: Reklam, n.d. [1900]), 61.

24. Eduard von Bauernfeld, *Aus Alt- und Neu Wien,* vol. 12 of *Gesammelte Schriften* (Vienna: Braumüller, 1873), 171.

25. Gustav Parthey, *Jugenderinnerungen* (Berlin: n.p., n.d. [1871]), II, 93.

26. Georg Altman, *Ludwig Devrient: Leben und Werke eines Schauspielers,* Deutsche Lebensbilder (Berlin: Ullstein, 1926), 37.

27. Suggested originals for Brown and Grey have included, among others, Franz von Holbein, a prominent theatre director, and Devrient himself. As the editor to vol. 3 of Hoffmann's *Gesammelte Schriften* (Berlin & Weimar: Aufbau, 1977) observes, they are really "artistic characters in a poetic dialogue" (529). Nevertheless the two figures most closely resemble Brühl and Hoffmann, though Grey-Brühl shows more appreciation for Devrient than possibly he did in real life. Brown articulates many of Hoffmann's beliefs about the theatre and is the dominant partner in the dialogue. All references to the *Seltsame Leiden* are taken from the above edition.

28. Ludwig Rellstab, "Ludwig Devrient," in vol. 9 of *Gesammelte Schriften* (Leipzig: Brockhaus, 1860), 314.

29. August Klingemann, *Kunst und Natur: Blätter aus meinem Reisetagebuche* (Brunswick: Meyer, 1819-1828), III, 344.

30. Altman, *Devrient,* 87. Wolfgang Drews in *König Lear auf der deutschen Bühne,* Germanische Studien 114 (Berlin: n.p., 1932) claims that Iffland had played the opening scene in Mannheim as early as 1784 (82-83).

31. Richard Wagner, "Über Schauspieler und Sänger," in vol. 9 of *Säm-

tliche Schriften und Dichtungen, 5th ed. (Leipzig: Breitkopf & Härtel, n.d.), 160.

32. August Haake, *Theater-Memoiren* (Mainz: Kunze, 1866), 171.

33. Altman (149-50) quotes some interesting box-ofice figures from Devrient's first season in Berlin. *Unser Verkehr* (*Our Business*), a popular comedy about Jews, was given eleven times for an average Box-office intake of 816 talers. *The Triplets* was given five times for an average intake of 585 talers. The following plays were all staged once only, not always with Devrient cast, for the following intake: *Intrigue and Love*, 382; *The Merchant of Venice* (with Devrient as Shylock), 352; *King Lear* (with Devrient in the lead), 335; *Don Carlos*, 330; *Emilia Galotti*, 211; *Wallenstein's Death*, 194; *Hamlet*, 194; *Nathan the Wise*, 187; *The Bride of Messina*, 187; *Minna von Barnhelm*, 172.

Chapter **4**

MID-CENTURY VIRTUOSI, 1815–1868

Eduard Devrient (1801-1877), the second of Ludwig's actor-nephews, later stage director and historian of German acting, considered that the 1830s saw the start of a severe decline in the quality of German theatre. Logically, the middle decades of the nineteenth century should have seen the theatre in its prime, fired by the still youthful spirits of its years of growth. But Devrient felt its homogeneity had gone.[1] Actors no longer led their own troupes; in their place, bureaucrats, responsible for the administration of grants from royal governments, dictated artistic policy with little concern for the quality of the repertoire or the well-being of the actor. In this impersonal atmosphere, all potential for a harmonious ensemble vanished, and the isolated individual was able to display him or herself on stage to the disregard of his fellow actors. Such vanity was encouraged by a press, which, instead of attempting to help create good theatre, fed upon scandals and the clash of person-alities. Standards of production were, according to Devrient, also in-appropriate. As spectacular opera increasingly came to dominate public taste, in the richer theatres plays were given against grandiose sets and performed in a broad, rhetorical fashion, a degenerate form of the Weimar style with the gestures of grand opera, that prevented audiences from establishing intimate rapport with the action. To make matters worse, triviality seemed to characterize the repertoire to an even greater degree than earlier in the century.

For one who, despite his antipathy to the formal dictates of Goethe's "Rules," had inherited the ideals of Weimar, Eduard Devrient's sense of alienation from the theatre of his day is understandable. But the middle decades of the nineteenth century should not automatically be dismissed as representing a decline in theatrical standards. Rather, the growth of German theatre changed direction as it began to respond to a changing world. The court theatres were, as Devrient rightly observed, becoming overladen with bureaucracy, were rife with favoritism in the conduct of artistic affairs, and were concerned primarily with providing an imposing show. But they were also facing growing competition from other theatres, often under private management. In 1824, the Königs-tädtische Theater opened in Alexanderplatz, Berlin, under a royal patent that cancelled the monopoly of the Royal Theatre. Three years later in Hamburg, the Thaliatheater set up in competition with Schröder's old foundation, the City Theatre. By the middle of the century, with the liberalization of censorship laws after the 1848 revolutions, in Berlin five theatres were competing with the Royal Theatre and, in other German cities, court theatres were being challenged by private entre-preneurs. All this prepared the way for the lifting of all restrictions on theatre, with the exception of censorship, when Germany was finally united in 1870.

The growth of a more diverse theatre was a mixed blessing for the actor. Opportunities for employment were multiplied, but in a profession where, despite financial instability, supply has always outstripped de-mand, even now the majority of actors were not assured of regular employment. This was partly because most directors, in both court and private theatres, hired actors by the method of *Bühnenproben* (stage trials), by which several aspirants were hired for a month at the begin-ning of the season, but only those most popular with the public or the management were given extended contracts. The rejected actors found themselves out of work and destitute for the remainder of the season. With the growth of the theatre and improved transportation between cities, professional organizations came to be founded. The first of these was a cartel of the most prestigious theatres, the *Deutsches Bühnenverein* (Alliance of German Stages), which was founded in 1851 to safeguard managerial interests and to ensure that those actors who were employed held rigidly to their contracts. A potentially adversary group, the *Gen-ossenschaft Deutscher Bühnenangehöriger* (Society of Associates of the German Stage) was set up by Ludwig Barnay and other actors in 1871 to protect the interests of actors and, above all, to provide them with a pension scheme, but the financial position of the average actor was not substantially improved until the end of the century. The theatre, while being socially more acceptable, was still a highly uncertain oc-cupation to choose. Furthermore, despite constant demands by prominent figures for the regular training of actors, no training schools were set up. Most actors still picked up what they learned on stage.

Eduard Devrient's complaints about the repertoire have some justice. As the classics could only be performed by the court theatres, the repertoires of the newer theatres tended to be lighter in vein. Comedies, farces, and, by the late 1850s, French operetta were highly popular and, as happened with the London patent theatres at the start of the nineteenth century, the court theatres responded by offering equally undemanding plays. At their best these were not too bad. The well-made play, which had been created almost single-handedly by the French dramatist Eugène Scribe, provided playwrights with a model upon which to order their plots neatly and effectively. This model proved adaptable enough to suit serious playwrights who wished to question covertly the values of the *status quo,* such as Karl Gutzkow and Heinrich Laube. It was also ideal for those playwrights whose work was less problematic, such as the comic writer Roderich Benedix and the universally popular Charlotte Birch-Pfeiffer. These two playwrights' studies of contemporary German life might be regarded as the mid-century equivalents to the plays of Iffland and Kotzebue in the early decades. It was, however, difficult to find a stage for drama of a higher calibre by serious writers such as Franz Grillparzer, Christian Dietrich Grabbe, and Friedrich Hebbel. This was not a theatre that encouraged its audiences to ask questions of an existential nature. There were also dreadful attempts to perpetuate a tradition of high drama, most notoriously in the work of Ernst von Raupach, the "Shakespeare of triviality,"[2] who produced a seemingly endless stream of historical tragedies in both prose and verse—he was paid more for verse. These provided actors with "clamorous tirades, during which they can spread wide their legs, fling out their arms, run hither and yon, and make their exits to hurrahs."[3] Raupach, rather than Schiller or Shakespeare, had the lion's share of the repertoire.

It was in this recognizably more modern environment that the virtuoso actor, the soloist who attracted audiences mainly through a demonstration of technique or through compelling personality, rose to preeminence. This was not an entirely new phenomenon; Iffland had undoubtedly anticipated it. But, in the middle of the nineteenth century, with a general dearth of challenging drama, lack of coherent ensembles, and, most importantly, with fortunes to be made from newer and larger audiences, the time was ripe for the virtuoso.

KARL SEYDELMANN

The first of the great virtuosi has been both the most admired and the most execrated actor in the history of the German theatre. Karl Seydelmann, the son of a shopkeeper, was born in Glatz, Silesia (now Gliwice, Poland) on 24 April 1793. After some unpleasant years as a recruit in the Prussian artillery, during which he deserted only to be reinstated some months later through his father's intercession with the military authorities, Seydelmann joined the Breslau theatre in 1815. His unexceptional physique and awkward speech made him unsuitable for the *Fach* of the young lover, so he specialized in low comedy roles, in "fools, chevaliers, fops, and bon-vivants."[4] After four years in Breslau, a time of wandering began. He played in Graz for the 1819-1820 season, impressing his audience in character *Fächer*, but had to move on when the theatre went bankrupt. After failing to find employment in Vienna and Pressburg, he was engaged for some months at a run-down theatre above a cattle-shed in Olmütz. Desperation drove him to apply for an underpaid position with the Prague theatre, then under the direction of Franz von Holbein. Here, given leisure to work at his craft, he began to develop a clinical style of realistic acting.

He left Prague in 1822 for the Court Theatre in Cassel, where for six years he continued to work at his technique and, through guest appearances, especially in Hamburg in 1826, began to build a national reputation. He left Cassel in 1828, as he could no longer tolerate the intrigue-ridden atmosphere of the theatre and was unable to secure a raise in salary in order to pay off debts accumulated through the treatment of his chronic ill health. His next engagement at Darmstadt was little short of disastrous, as his success with audiences led to a public demand for more drama, while the duke preferred opera. Once again, intrigue drove him out, this time to the Württemburg Court Theatre in Stuttgart. Here he remained for nine years. In roles from the classic and contemporary repertoire he perfected interpretations that, through the accuracy and variety of his nuances, caused many to compare him with Iffland. In Stuttgart, he became acquainted with some of the leading writers of the *Junges Deutschland* (Young Germany) movement, especially Karl Gutzkow and August Lewald. He was by far the most prominent actor in the company and, as *Regisseur* (an actor with responsibility for staging productions) he attempted to impose some discipline on his recalcitrant colleagues, insisting on a lengthier rehearsal schedule than was then customary. But his aloofness, caused no doubt by his earlier struggles with poverty and his persistent ill health, militated against the ensemble spirit he was attempting to create, and his strictures on the company earned him enemies among both the actors and the administration. Yet again, intrigue was rife, leading to a crisis in December 1837, when Seydelmann was threatened with arrest and banned from ever again appearing on the stage of the Stuttgart theatre.

Fortunately this crisis was not as calamitous as it could have been. Appearances at Weimar in 1830, the Vienna Burgtheater in 1831, and with Immermann's company in Düsseldorf in 1833 had consolidated Seydelmann's national standing, while his immensely popular, though critically controversial appearances in Berlin in 1835 had made him the most discussed actor in the German theatre. His second series of Berlin guest performances in 1837 had won him uniform acclaim so, following the Stuttgart debacle, he left for the Berlin Royal Theatre, where he was popularly regarded as the successor to Ludwig Devrient. Here, despite fundamental differences between his and Devrient's acting, he won easy acceptance, acquired an unusually wide circle of friends, and was besieged by playwrights, including Gutzkow and Laube, who urged him to appear in their plays. For a brief period his health seemed to improve, but in 1840 he suffered a physical and nervous breakdown, which sent him into deep depression. His health continued to decline, and he became obsessed by thoughts of death. His last stage appearance was in January 1843; two months later, on March 17, he died painfully, of heart disease complicated by cancer.

For Seydelmann, life was a constant struggle. A graphic idea of this can be gathered from his letters, classics in the literature of acting, written with a biting directness, an exuberance, and a healthy anger that seem to have eluded him in his more public dealings. He wrote at length on the mediocrity of contemporary theatre, on the shortcomings of uneducated actors, on the paucity of good new plays, on inefficient and corrupt managements, on the vanity, ignorance, venality, and moral turpitude of actors, managers, and *Regisseurs* that everywhere bedevilled the theatre. Like Iffland, though with far greater urgency, he regarded artistic achievement and moral worth as identical. "You want to become an *artist*! Then first and foremost be an *honorable, able human being*! This is very difficult, *very* difficult, and yet *so essential* in order to satisfy higher demands. Every time you feel the *actor* is incomplete, the *human being* appears to be worm-eaten."[5] Constant attention to self-education and unceasing work was, he claimed, essential for actors, as very few had the apparently easy intuition of a Ludwig Devrient. Despite his being a Catholic, Seydelmann is the voice of the Protestant work ethic in the German theatre.

If, after quiet examination of your whole being, you should fear that you do not possess as much talent for your chosen career as seems necessary to be *successful,* then stick all the more *persistently* to hard work. Strength grows wonderfully with hard work.... In order to grow strong, one does physical exercises, lifts weights, and makes one's limbs supple.... So with a not especially remarkable talent, one can achieve most enviable results, as practical, persevering hard work strengthens and elevates weak, natural gifts. (Seydelmann, 98)

In this advice to his son Seydelmann was drawing upon years of his own experience.

Like many serious men with perception, intelligence, and uncompromising standards, Seydelmann was withdrawn, a quality of character that made him ill suited for the stage. Naturally he aroused keenly conflicting reactions among his friends and associates. Eduard Devrient, who was an actor at the Berlin Royal Theatre with him, abominated him. His diaries are riddled with comments on Seydelmann's haughtiness, egoism, and untrustworthiness. Even after his death Devrient could only describe him as "furtive, suspicious, a sham, caustic and sarcastic."[6] Others, however, were deeply attached to him, as, for example, the playwright Karl von Holtei, whose obituary notice, written with an extravagance characteristic of the time, raises him to the level of a hero. "In him has died a model of strong, serious, unshakeable will, an example of how spiritual power and endurance can finally achieve every victory in every earthly battle. With him a fine character, an exceptional human being has died, a rare human being."[7]

The critical controversy aroused by Seydelmann's acting was caused only partially by differing reactions to his personality. It has, in fact, more consequential, historic causes. When he appeared in Berlin in 1835, Seydelmann was naturally compared to Ludwig Devrient who, in the eyes of conservatives, possessed far greater warmth on stage. This led, of course, to an extended debate over the perennial issue of whether an actor should think about or only feel his role. Seydelmann was regarded as the epitome of the "thinking" actor. But the debate was complicated by his refusal to present idealized characters, which, in the tradition established by Iffland, were commonly regarded as the legitimate domain of the thinking actor. There is no doubt that Seydelmann's characters were most carefully formed, all aspects "were clearly united in subordination each to the other"[8] and they unfolded logically as "at the beginning everything to come [was] apparent in him, as he progress[ed] he recall[ed] everything he [had] done." But instead of being harmonious, his characters struck his audiences as being askew and not whole. "He does not discover everything, not the beautiful, not the poetry of the character. He takes only the lower half, the worse side, and enlarges this side with all his virtuosity. This virtuosity, however, assures him high standing as an artist."[9] In Seydelmann, the thinking actor, the master of technique, was using his skills to an end previously considered unfitting for them. This unfamiliar nexus of technique and final result caused great critical discussion in which, importantly, the polarities that had evolved since Ekhof's day between idealist and romantic acting were first fully brought to public consciousness.[10] While Seydelmann's career anticipated those of future virtuosi, his approach to acting also allowed the German theatre to become aware of its past.

Actors do not, however, draw audiences solely by their historic significance; they must also exercise a more instant appeal. In Seydelmann's case, the appeal can first be identified through the analogy often drawn between his acting and the literature of the *Junges Deutschland* writers. Their novels, plays, and polemical essays not only criticized the complacency of public life but, with their greater objectivity, cynicism of outlook, and unembellished style, they represented a reaction against the primarily subjective and lyrical writings of romanticism. An equivalent clarity and hardness was characteristic of Seydelmann's acting, so that through him the theatre seemed to acquire a new authenticity that was distinct from both the idealism and romanticism of the past. The words he spoke were, according to Heinrich Laube, "a sword, a protestant sword, against our romanticism, which was formed from mist."[11] But when Seydelmann arrived in Berlin early in 1838, the *Junges Deutschland* movement had been effectively suppressed by the arrest and brief imprisonment of its leading members. Seydelmann was then taken up by the young Hegelian movement, prominent in which was the writer Theodore Rötscher, whose biography of the actor is still a major source. Rötscher welcomed Seydelmann as an antidote to those actors who, following the dangerous example of Ludwig Devrient, felt that all they need do on stage was to be inspired from moment to moment. Rötscher argued that Seydelmann was not only a thinking actor, but intuitive too. He imaginitively expanded his initial insights and then realized them in a wholly conscious, deliberately constructed manner. While this caused a certain lack of spontaneity, his characters clearly benefitted as they received both strongly individual coloring and an abstraction that related them to types. Moreover, Seydelmann's simple and extraordinarily intelligible speech led the audience to follow with ease his demonstration of how character was constructed. His acting consisted in "disclosing the human heart to humankind, making accessible to them the mysterious abysses of human passion, demonstrating the threads that have been spun from the visible actions of the individual, by which the character arises before us with compelling necessity" (Rötscher, 185).

Although everyone who saw him realized he lacked the emotional lability of Ludwig Devrient, his forceful personality endowed the roles he played with a palpability that seemed argumentative in its confidence. This led to charges that he was rarely concerned with the playwright's intention, but wished solely to demonstrate the brilliance of his talents and intellect. Seydelmann, of course, denied such accusations, claiming he subordinated himself entirely to his perception of the playwright's intention, with little concern for his own predilections. But even his most sympathetic critics could not acquit him. "It is his peculiarity," wrote Gustav Kühne, "to catch hold of a single trait and assemble a complete figure around it" (Kühne, 333). Seydelmann as actor often appeared to be less a purely mimetic artist who just realized the character, than one who commented upon character as if he wished overtly to guide his audience's perceptions of it. This resulted in a breaking of the illusion that, at that time, was unquestionably assumed as the basis of all theatre. From our present-day viewpoint, Seydelmann would seem to have anticipated certain principles of "alienated" acting. The correspondent for the *Hallische Jahrbücher* described this well. Seydelmann, he wrote,

always stands next to his performance as the interpreter. We do not merely feel, he also tells us why he plays this way, on what principles and to what purposes. While we become aware . . . of his reflective consciousness, we have more work than pleasure, or rather we have pleasure, but one not suited to [the theatre], pleasure in understanding, in coming to a comparative judgment. We must solve a mass of riddles where in fact everything should immediately be clear for us. We see reasons where we wish only to see effects. The artist shows us more the why than the what and the how. We see him make models when we are hungry for the completed figure. Finally, of course, we understand from the standpoint on which the artist himself has set us, that "everything beautiful is difficult."[12]

Few of Seydelmann's contemporaries described his acting with such discrimination, probably because the very conception of an actor standing both outside and inside his role was unthinkable. This meant that many failed to detect the logic with which he constructed his roles and led to widely differing opinions on the nature and the quality of his acting. Heinrich Anschütz, a Burgtheater actor bred on the Weimar style, considered him merely a "mosaic artist, [an] industrious collector of colored stones."[13] Eduard Devrient, who was scathing in his comments on Seydelmann, recognized that he and his enemy were men of entirely different breed. Whereas Seydelmann appealed to those who preferred "strength, energy, and sensationalism," Devrient wrote in his diary, "I [consider] that true power demonstrates itself only in harmonious development and suppresses all grasping after sensationalism" (Ed. Devrient, *Tagebücher* I, 62-63). Although Devrient was capable of granting Seydelmann isolated moments of genuine theatrical strength, in general he found him scrappy, often platitudinous, usually raw and discordant, and the man himself eager only for applause, unmotivated by a true love of art. Eduard Devrient, as an actor very different from his uncle, was in spirit an idealist of the older schools. Nevertheless, in his history of acting, even he had to concede, albeit unwillingly, Seydelmann's importance, devoting twenty-nine full pages to him in contrast to the mere fifteen given to his uncle, whom, despite differences in style, he revered. The new phase Seydelmann represented in acting was most sympathetically described by Laube, who saw in his work neither the formality of idealism nor the passion of romanticism. He considered it to be a new, calmer, and, in contrast to other judgments, complete realism that seemed to fuse the two extremes of German acting.

[Ludwig] Devrient was the hero of all passions, of genius, of the extraordinary, of the superhuman, of whatever reaches into our world from another. All that, he seized instantly, with titanic strength, terrifying in our midst. He was a thunderstorm at night with all its dazzling beauty. Seydelmann possesses none of these extraordinary intuitive powers. He is a serene, quiet day whose appearances do not catch our interest by surprise, but through their bright reality and truth, defined on every side. Whatever he lacks in lustre, he replaces with artistic moderation [and] the artistic completeness of his forms. If one wishes to make an exaggerated comparison, he stands to Devrient as Goethe does to Shakespeare. (Laube, *Charakteristiken* I, 337-38)

In his choice of roles Seydelmann stayed away from heroic, declamatory parts and romantic leads, due to his physical unsuitability and his difficulty, caused by his extremely long tongue, in articulating fluently and rapidly. His strengths and inclinations lay either in the contemporary drama of Gutzkow and Laube or in classic roles that involved tortured or strangely artificial personalities. His favorite role was Iago, played only in Stuttgart, though Eduard Devrient heard him read it in Berlin and observed, not without irony, "Iago will be Seydelmann's most splendid role; he is him completely" (Ed. Devrient, *Tagebücher* I, 165). Seydelmann's initial view of Iago was surprising. "He seems to me," he wrote, "to be the most adaptable, companionable, faithful and obedient being . . . all these admirable qualities embellished by cheerfulness and wit" (Seydelmann, 109). As he observed, everyone trusts him and throughout the play should continue to feel that trust residually, regarding him not as some emanation of hell but as a man with potentially noble qualities that have never been called into use. Iago is a hero in reverse. With thinking partially reminiscent of the late eighteenth-century mentality, Seydelmann continued to write on how the villain should always be represented as a human being, not a monster. In this way, audiences will become aware of the normal conditions under which evil can grow, of the relative rather than the absolute nature of good and evil. The stage will then be able to educate audiences by making them aware that "our indulgence for a so-called small, innocent mistake can become the source of the most terrifying transgressions" (Seydelmann, 109-10). Seydelmann's approach to representing evil on stage can be gauged by examining three roles for which he was celebrated: Carlos in Goethe's *Clavigo,* Mephistopheles, and the ubiquitous Franz Moor.

Reconstruction of Seydelmann's roles is helped by the survival of some of his personal prompt-books. So that he did not have to learn his roles from the illegible copies normally provided actors, he wrote out his parts for himself in immaculate handwriting. While so doing, he recorded, often in the most meticulous detail, his interpretation of the role. Words to be stressed are underlined, sometimes even with the degree of stress marked, pauses are indicated, as are his movements on stage and appropriate gestures, while margins contain a liberal number of comments on the motivation of the character. Frequently he included exhaustive descriptions of costume and of dates and places at which he performed the part, occasionally with notes as to how his performance had changed from his initial representation of the role. These are invaluable documents, unique to the theatre of the time.

Carlos, one of the roles recorded in his prompt-books, was widely regarded as his finest achievement. Given the sympathy aroused in *Clavigo* for Marie and her brother Beaumarchais, it is not surprising that Carlos was normally represented as a cold-blooded villain. Seydelmann, however, neutralized melodramatic potential not only by presenting the demands of political expediency as if they were as legitimate as those of the heart, but by having Carlos, a high-ranking civil servant, deeply concerned about the future of his young friend Clavigo. In this way he fulfilled Goethe's intention. "In Carlos I wished to have pure understanding of the world work with true friendship against passion, inclination, and external affliction, so as to motivate a tragedy."[14] From the start Seydelmann's Carlos exhibited "decorous manners, lightness of speech [and] a refined, quietly cold bearing. . . . He thinks only of his friend whom inwardly he loves, however withdrawn he is, however much he despises mankind. . . . He is prosaic, even hard in contrast to the pliable Clavigo. He goes to work with him in a thoroughly honest manner . . . demanding only that he behave decisively. He should know what he really wants."[15] In order to make credible Carlos's attachment to the vacillating Clavigo, Seydelmann tried to convey a sense of blood relationship between the two; hence, Carlos's desire to make something of the young man's potential and his resolve to deter him from a marriage he considers disastrous appeared humane in intent.

Act 4 is the climax for Carlos. Seydelmann's notes disclose he played the scene with a gradual strengthening of the voice and ever sharper gestures, in order to work more effectively on Clavigo's wavering resolve and to denigrate the image of Marie in his mind. As a result, he took care not to arouse laughter; Marie had to be seen by the audience as a genuine threat to Clavigo's well-being, not as a bagatelle to be thrown aside without thought. The notes show above all how exact Seydelmann was in establishing the degree of insinuation needed to work Clavigo round. He did not assault him with reproaches, rather his anger was like an "inner fire . . . burning beneath a cover of snow, out of which swirl from time to time single pillars of smoke, which suggest the progression of a volcanic flame" (Geiger, 140). Then his voice was not harsh, rather his words "evaporate in Clavigo all bitterness over his disappointed ambition, without being improperly furtive. . . . There is a smearing tone of voice that, used properly, spreads the poison in floods, even though it sounds like the rustle of a fine drizzle" (Geiger, 140).

Critical accounts indicate a correlation between Seydelmann's notes and his performance on stage. He did not try to make Carlos likeable; though his ambitions were praiseworthy, the means used still seemed unpalatable, so the interpretation aroused ambiguous responses toward the character. Laube, who saw Seydelmann first play the role in Breslau in 1829, was so overwhelmed by the clarity of Carlos's stratagems and the force with which they were communicated that at once, he claimed, he became aware of a range of expression in the theatre previously unknown to him. Others, predictably, were less ecstatic. Eduard Devrient disliked Seydelmann's Carlos as he ensnared rather than confronted Clavigo, while Anschütz, who always looked for beautiful harmony in stage characters, felt it was too sensational. But Seydelmann was widely acclaimed in the role, so much so that he became identified with it, as if in the character he had found a true double.

Seydelmann's Mephistopheles, not included in the prompt-books, though famous, was more controversial, as in the opinion of many, even he failed to comprehend "the creature of popular superstition with all his physical coarseness . . . instilled [with] transcendental substance, the principle of evil, completely certain in his knowledge of himself" (Rötscher, 208-9). Given his choice only to play the more noisome aspects of the character, he was the perfect devil. August Lewald, who found he raised both laughter and fear in his audiences, described him well.

His costume is of bright red, glittering material, with yellow ornaments. His little cloak of silk is grass green. A small, black sword-belt girds his extremely long trunk. His body is as thin as a wasp's, his fingers twisted like claws. As he walks, his cloven hoof is dragged after him with eminent gravity. Bristly black hair covers his skull, his eyes are asquint and sharp, his mouth, drawn back to the furthest limits, exposes his teeth. This expresses the most horrible mockery. His nose, monstrously misshapen, sinks to his chin.[16] [see Figure 6.]

Lewald described how, as the performance progressed, the malice within Seydelmann's Mephistopheles magnified until "the whole of hell" sounded in his voice. Notable was his parody of academics in the student scene, when his voice uttered "strange tones, hollow, doleful, like the cooing of the turtle dove mixed with the sound of evil howling" (Lewald, 163). He created such a malign atmosphere that Gretchen's complaint about the oppressive air seemed literally to be true. Gutzkow, who saw him in the role in Stuttgart, found his Mephisto "the most forcible as well as the most scholarly"[17] interpretation he had seen, though he felt the role had become too contrived by the time Seydelmann arrived in Berlin. Eduard Devrient, strangely enough, first enjoyed him as Mephistopheles, but later retracted his rash judgment, considering him "offensive . . . grotesque . . . even farcical" (Ed. Devrient, *Geschichte* II, 445), while Immermann, who directed him in the part in Düsseldorf, complained that he almost drove the audience out with his infernal "croaking, puffing, and bungling."[18]

Despite Laube's claim that Seydelmann was a "serene, quiet day" in the German theatre, he was undoubtedly capable of a coarseness that disconcerted some of his audience. At times this stood him in good stead, as when playing the Russian serf Ossip in Raupach's tragedy *Isidor und Olga,* or the Moor in Schiller's *Fiesko,* a well-nigh bestial interpretation with "the whimpering, teeth-baring and gesturing of the ape, the leap of the tiger, the flexibility and look of the snake" (Lewald, 60). His Franz Moor was also a hideous creature, somewhat far from the rather humane villain that Seydelmann's writings on Iago would have led one to expect. Only the prompt-book of the first act is available. This indicates he oscillated between gushing sentiment for his father and seemingly spasmodic outbursts of hatred that were directed as asides to the audience, as if they were being taken into his confidence. The monologue following his father's departure was carefully built to run over a whole scale of moods from sarcasm to malicious humor, from self-pity to deep bitterness, to end in an explosion of wild humor as Franz determines to break all family bonds. Such fluctuations in mood and attitude were, apparently, standard for the complete part, and they were met by the usual flurry of critical controversy. Most interesting among the various accounts is that of Gustav Kühne, who felt that

6. Karl Seydelmann as Mephistopheles. Reproduced by permission of Deutsches Theatermuseum, Munich.

Seydelmann communicated perfectly "the unalloyed dark side [of the character], the gloom of the soul, the hell of destiny" (Kühne, 334), though he concludes that while Ludwig Devrient ultimately gave the audience pleasure through the role, Seydelmann caused pain, as if the audience were victims of Franz's malice instead of collaborators, as his asides seemed to suggest.

Whether Seydelmann fully succeeded in making human the causes of evil and in fully explaining the complexities of a tortured psyche is now impossible to establish. The detailed prompt-books of his Philip II and Shylock suggest that he worked hard to demonstrate how people could be driven by the harshest and most vindictive of motives and yet still retain a warm humanity; indeed his Philip finally emerged the tyrant only because he realized how totally he had been betrayed in his private dealings. Once again criticisms of these roles vary widely in their perceptions.

This disagreement, ironically over an actor who strove for absolute clarity on stage, was caused partly by his personality, partly by his unorthodox interpretations, and partly by the detachment he sometimes displayed from his characters. If such detachment was similar to more modern conceptions of "alienated" acting, then it would undoubtedly have caused puzzlement, as both practically and theoretically the theatre was still a century away from incorporating it. In any event, more than any previous actor, Seydelmann became someone to argue over. This might also be regarded as symptomatic of the ego-oriented theatre Eduard Devrient deplored, and it certainly served to elevate the actor to the dominant position of virtuoso he enjoyed in the middle decades of the nineteenth century. But Seydelmann was also decisive in bringing the theatre to an awareness of the polarities that had evolved since the late eighteenth century. He was deeply antipathetic to the idealist schools and, even though he was unstinting in his praise of Ludwig Devrient's powers, he realized these were unique to the man who possessed them, so that his acting could be imitated by others only to the grave disadvantage of the theatre. Seydelmann, like most great actors who did not create models, is impossible to classify.

Few nineteenth-century virtuosi evinced as serious and original an approach to acting as Seydelmann. His style had its imitators, notably Theodore Döring (1803-1878), whose warmer personality recommended him more easily to audiences, though he lost none of the sharpness of his original mentor. But most virtuosi were content either to master the rules and techniques of the idealist schools or, throwing themselves with abandon into their roles, to produce what were little better than travesties of Ludwig Devrient's acting. Among the former was Friedrich Haase (1827-1911), in Martersteig's opinion the doyen of the virtuosi, whose imitation of the manners of high society was so polished that he "outaristocrated the aristocrats."[19] His finished technique, enclosed characterizations, and tendency always to place himself in the middle of the stage meant that, despite some well-meaning efforts, he was unable to settle with a permanent company of actors. Until near the end of the century he continued to tour, in Germany and America, repeating a handful of roles, earning for himself a respectable, if not a splendid reputation.

EMIL DEVRIENT

Perhaps the most distinguished perpetuator of the Weimar school was the third of Ludwig Devrient's actor-nephews, Emil.[20] He was born in Berlin in 1803. His most impressionable years as a young actor were spent not under the influence of his uncle but with August Klingemann, the director of the Brunswick theatre, who was a follower of Goethe. This training, coupled with his admiration for Pius Alexander Wolff, ensured that Emil would master the harmonious style of idealist acting. He was engaged for varying lengths of time at Bremen, Leipzig, Magdeburg, and Hamburg, but it was only in 1831, when he was hired by August von Lüttichau, the Weimar-inspired intendant of the Dresden Court Theatre, that he found a company congenial to his talents and temperament, and here he stayed until his retirement from the stage in 1868. He did not, however, remain known only locally. The extraordinarily advantageous terms of his contract with Dresden meant that he could spend several months each year on tour. By the early 1850s, he had acquired a national following, so that in 1852 and 1853 he was chosen to head the first company of German actors to play Shakespeare and German classics in England, at the St James Theatre in London. This mainly successful venture increased his prestige at home, and after it he continued to pack houses with enthusiastic audiences until his retirement. When he died, four years later, he was, despite the emergence of a reformulated realism, still for most people the image of the ideal actor.

This image was created in part by his exceptionally good looks and

7. Emil Devrient. Reproduced by permission of Gesellschaft für Theatergeschichte.

superior voice. "He was of slender, noble build, his voice was a sonorous, rich bass-baritone, his eyes a dark, softly radiant blue. With these personal attributes he was certain above all of his triumph with women."[21] Portraits show he had finely shaped, well-balanced features, which, with his wavy brown hair (a wig), suggest both self-possession and youthful innocence. Even late in life, the burden of years did not hang heavily on the eternally young Emil (see Figure 7). His physique and voice were ideally suited to realizing the beauty and harmony sought by Goethe in his "Rules," so, early in his career, he learned them, and stuck to them with tenacity for the rest of his life.

As a beginning actor, Emil Devrient's range was remarkably broad. He sung in opera—Sarastro in *Die Zauberflöte* and Kaspar in *Der Freischütz* were two of his roles—and he acted in legitimate drama. His voice, however, lacked the strength necessary for opera, so soon he concentrated solely on spoken theatre, in the first ten years of his career mastering almost three hundred different roles. But his distinctive technique soon led him to limit the type of role he specialized in, and he made his name as the Young Lover and Hero, playing such parts as Posa, Egmont, Hamlet, and Tasso, all of which allowed for the expression of noble sentiments and ennobling affections. He also played maturer parts such as Bolingbroke in Scribe's *Glass of Water*. The darker side of human experience and psychologically complex characters he could not realize on stage, so Shylock, Lear, and Franz Moor were never in his repertoire. Strangely, in view of Seydelmann's identification with the *Junges Deutschland* movement, he was an ideal interpreter of many of Gutzkow's and Laube's leading characters. He "had the nobility of appearance, proportion in acting, the warmth and sensibility of feeling to present these *Junges Deutschland* heroes in winning fashion."[22] In particular he could make palatable these passive heroes' disdain through "fastidiously guarded Byronic gestures, noble, often cynical, often sentimental, always contemptuous of the world."[23]

Emil Devrient was the virtuoso supreme. His unmistakeable figure and bearing ensured that audience interest was focussed upon him as actor, not on the characters he played. In fact he had little respect for the actor who worked through transformation. "Every day he takes another wig, every day he puts on new makeup, rolls his eyes this way today, another way tomorrow, and the great character-actor is ready. But look at people like us, every day the same appearance, the same exterior, and yet each time we are another. That is art."[24] That art was essentially a demonstration of physical and vocal restraint and of the actor's sensitivity. Gustav Freytag defined it as "a fixed tempo in speech and acting, gradual and established transitions from one mood to the other, an aversion to all violence and subtle affectation, a striving always to be as gracious in bearing, gesture and speech, performing as beautifully and as nobly as the role possibly allows, developing most carefully the voice and powers of mimetic expression."[25] Naturally such acting implied vanity, and Emil Devrient was not without his critics, among whom was his brother Eduard, whose diaries describe a running battle between the two, and contain several anguished comments on Emil's desire perpetually to be the center of the audience's attention. Such vanity even led Gutzkow, for several years dramaturg in Dresden, to adapt plays such as *Coriolanus* and *King John* so radically that Emil's role was the sole element of interest remaining.

In fact, he was not a great actor of the classics, preferring mainly contemporary works set in the gracious world of the drawing-room. But his most celebrated role was Hamlet. Obviously he did not act the part as Schröder had done, as the rebarbative prince angry at himself and the world, neither did he play the philosopher searching for answers to metaphysical problems. Also he could not represent Hamlet's madness or establish a tension between the prince's apparent distraction and the possibility of some inner resolve. Such complexities were no part of his style. As he grew older, he worked consistently toward a polished interpretation in which prime emphasis was placed on Hamlet's melancholy and his feelings for his mother. He was "the weak, affectionate son of his mother, the sweet, beautiful speaker, the elegiac youth of moonlight."[26] Consequently he was best in his scenes with Gertrude. But this cannot carry Hamlet through the whole play, so all too often Devrient had to resort to mannerism, isolating key moments, playing them for pathos rather than as crucial phases in the development of Hamlet's character. "He lays the soliloquy 'To Be or Not to Be' before the audience as if it were a sweetmeat upon a plate" (Kurnik, 209). This was a Hamlet "weak-hearted, dreamy, rich in words and poor in deeds."[27] There were, however, some finer aspects. When he played the role in London, he impressed English audiences with his "noble expression and poetic magic."[28] Henry Morley, a leading London critic, found "most acceptable" his expression of horror at Hamlet's hearing of his father's murder, and authentic the reading that Hamlet's reaction to his mother's crime destroys his entire faith in womankind.[29] Nevertheless the Prussian ambassador's daughter was probably enthused by nationalist pride or plain infatuation when she reported that Lord Ellesmere had told her that Emil Devrient was a greater actor than John Philip Kemble, Edmund Kean, and Talma.

After his death, with the rise of a more widely adopted realistic style of acting, it became easy to laugh at Emil Devrient. He was, no doubt, a child of his time, the perfect actor for what "the German audiences wanted and needed in the middle of the nineteenth century. Surrender to a beautiful form whose threatening relation to something real should never be felt'' (Bab, *Devrients,* 199). Such a demand led actors, be they virtuosi or company people, to indulge in empty, flowery rhetoric and extravagant gesture. Emil Devrient, while catering to public tastes, provided some discipline in comportment and vocal delivery, which, though it lacked dramatic excitement, provided audiences with an example of how restraint and deliberation gave idealist acting its attraction.

BOGUMIL DAWISON

Restraint was apparently the one thing lacking in Emil Devrient's most determined and consistent foe, the truculent Polish-German virtuoso, Bogumil Dawison. Dawison was born in Warsaw on 15 May 1818 into a genteel Jewish family. From the age of twelve, poverty forced him to earn his living working for a Warsaw newspaper, but in 1838 he gave up a promising career in journalism to join the theatre. He began by playing in Polish companies in Warsaw, Vilna in Lithuania, and Lemberg (now Lvov, Soviet Union). He remained in Lemberg for six years, building up a substantial repertoire in both Polish and German. His spontaneity on stage distinguished him from his affected, stiff colleagues, so much so as to make him a local celebrity. A brief visit to Vienna in 1841 kindled his ambition to become part of a larger theatre system, so, after mastering the German language, in 1846 he left Lemberg to try his fortune.

After several rebuffs, he was engaged in 1847 by the Thaliatheater in Hamburg, where from his very first appearance he was acclaimed for his fieriness and natural speech. This naturalness was in part an acquired trait as Dawison, not a native speaker of German, took great pains to learn each role syllable by syllable, writing it out in full from memory. Nevertheless he learned quickly, so that when he left Hamburg in 1849, he was master of over 130 roles, all delivered with an almost perfect native accent. He left for the Vienna Burgtheater, but his arrival there concided with the appointment of Heinrich Laube to the theatre's directorship. This was not an auspicious sign for Dawison, as his developing tendencies toward virtuosity would undoubtedly clash with Laube's ambitions to perfect the ensemble style for which the theatre was known. Dawison's four years in Vienna were marked by increasing tensions between him and Laube, which came to a head in December

1853 when the two had such a row in the wings during a performance that Dawison was unable to go on playing. He was reported to the police, suspended from the company, and, in February, told to leave Vienna and never return.

Fortunately for him, he had already attracted national attention through guest appearances, and was especially prized in Dresden, where his appearances at the Court Theatre in 1852 and 1853 had been welcomed as an alternative to the "slow, agreeable, prudent pathos" (Freytag I, 8, 313) that, under the influence of Emil Devrient, characterized the theatre's acting style. The ten years Dawison spent in Dresden were the best in his career. His engagement with the Court Theatre had initially been with the intent of bringing about a historic union of the two extremes of German acting through cooperation between him and Devrient. Unfortunately, neither was the most modest of men, and, though they appeared on stage together twenty-eight times in all, no reconciliation of the antipodes took place. Instead personal bickering over who upstaged whom resulted. On the whole, the two men avoided each other, which was easy as both were also busy touring. Dawison, while appearing regularly in Dresden, travelled widely, appearing several times in Berlin and in Vienna, where the ban against him applied only to the Burgtheater. He appeared at Nestroy's Carltheater and in the Theater an der Wien. Throughout Germany and Austria, he was fêted for his performances of the classics and for his highly developed technique and originality, which was vitalized by his remarkable aggression and energy.

But, by 1864, this energy had started to flag. For some years Dawison had suffered the occasional lapse of memory, and increasingly he seemed to be straining for effect rather than achieving it with ease. He left Dresden to devote himself entirely to touring, appearing both in Germany and Austria, and abroad, in Amsterdam, Warsaw, Paris, and finally the United States, where he played in New York, Philadelphia, Baltimore, and Boston. At times he would even appear with an English-speaking cast, most notably when he acted Othello in German to Edwin Booth's Iago, an arrangement that did not strike contemporaries as particularly odd. The American tour was a financial success, but it exhausted Dawison. After a final appearance as Lear in New York, he returned to Germany where he suffered a total breakdown. During his last years he was insane, his time being spent in various spas where he declined into "a childish old man with a fixed stare and a babbling tongue" (Kurnik, 257). He died on 1 February 1872, fifty-four years old.

While Emil Devrient radiated charm and elegance, Dawison was a fount of rawness. He was not a large man but

impressive, of medium build, [with a] powerful body and an expressive face, well suited to a variety of roles, with eyes full of vivacious and changing life, and eyebrows slanting sharply to his nose, making him ideal for crafty and gloomy characters. His emotions were active and sharp, his intellect acute and receptive, and his bearing one of a man who may have experienced much in life, who, with brilliant success, attacks a predetermined goal with deliberation and energy. (Freytag I, 8, 313)

While Emil Devrient was passive, Dawison was active; while Devrient was the eternal youth, Dawison was the often embittered man of experience. He placed little value on beauty and harmony for their own sakes. "Beautiful speech and rhetoric," he wrote, "fine acting and the noble play of gesture do not make an actor. What makes an actor is the ability to disguise oneself, effective expression, and readiness of tongue. Truth is the highest law of art. Only that which is true is beautiful."[30] The "truth" of his acting did not, however, appear through prosaic realism. Like Ludwig Devrient, to whom he was constantly compared, he was drawn to portray extremes of experience. But the comparison can be misleading as Dawison's "demonic" impulses were assertive. He played his characters with distinctness and deliberation, so that each appeared to be "a sharply defined being, a mightily outspoken, thoroughly thought-out personality."[31] But, as with Ludwig Devrient, Shakespeare rather than the classical drama of Goethe and Schiller was his forte. He had difficulty in realizing characters that required clear, unambiguous outlines, but was a "colorist," who worked most happily with figures whose needs, emotions, and perceptions of the world were in conflict rather than unity with each other. Hence he rescued from oblivion many roles previously considered to be unplayable because of their difficult motivation. One of these was Leontes in *The Winter's Tale,* a character whose behavior is a mixture of intense jealousy and childish trust. Dawison's rendering of this role was most effective. "Those raw tirades of blind jealousy would repel the hearer were he not fascinated by the wandering, mysteriously fiery eyes, were his pity not drawn by the pallid, suffering face, by an expression portraying the whole despair of the heart and yet fervent love, while the tongue speaks of hatred, primitive revenge, and loathing."[32] Dawison did not lull audiences into gentle acquiescence, he alerted them to passions and emotional turmoil.

The immediacy and potency of Dawison's stage presence did not always meet with the approval of his critics. He was often accused, maybe with justice, of paying too little attention to the overall development of the character, concentrating instead on a moment-to-moment approach. This could all too easily lead to charges of self-indulgence, which carried weight as Dawison, being abrasive and rebellious by nature, was frequently involved in violent altercations with colleagues. But he also had an invigorating influence on a theatre that was always in danger of becoming too stuffy. One of his champions described him as the voice of the proletariat in an overrefined cultural institution, one who could "rage in pure anger, rejoice in real joy, struggle with genuine pain, [and] weep pure tears."[33] Although he did not identify correctly Dawison's origins, this advocate recognized, along with most of his contemporaries, that he reintroduced on stage the reality of human experience without idealist stylization or the careful framing of the role as had been practiced by Seydelmann.

Given the eminence of *Hamlet* in the German theatre, Dawison, not surprisingly, included the lead among his most frequently played roles. His prince was antithetical to Emil Devrient's "elegiac child of moonlight," though precisely how antithetical is difficult to establish. As with Seydelmann, different critics saw different things in Dawison. All agreed he was aggressive, there was nothing in him of the wilting lover, of the young man overcome by external compulsion and inner weakness. Rather, he was active and certain in his goals. Naturally, this led to problems. Laube pointed out that Dawison's Hamlet should have had no difficulty in despatching Claudius in Act 1, and that his failure to do this meant that later in the play he was just a comic figure. But the psychologist Jakob Moleschott found a more sustained conflict. "Dawison's Hamlet is not weak-hearted, timorous, lacking in will. On the contrary, he is passionate, irrascible, determined, but his conscience is yet more powerful than his passion and the battle between the two . . . is highly exciting, moving, and right for the stage."[34] The delay in the murder was the result both of this struggle and of Hamlet's need to know thoroughly all the consequences of the murder beforehand.

For some this interpretation was strangely intellectual, despite Dawison's emotional strength. Gutzkow felt one could only grasp the unity of his performance after much thought, not spontaneously, finding the Hamlet who revealed himself in conversation and the one who delivered the soliloquies to be entirely different people. Karl Frenzel, on the contrary, thought his Hamlet credible and consistent, while other critics welcomed the disparities Gutzkow had seen as, by establishing an irreconcileable cleft between intention as revealed in action and conscience as revealed in the soliloquies, Dawison had produced a distinctly modern Hamlet, a "pure son of the nineteenth century."[35] In concert with the empirical bias of contemporary thought, but in opposition to the tastes to which Emil Devrient appealed, he portrayed an actual condition rather than an idealized one. This actuality was undoubtedly a salient quality in his performance. Franz Liszt, who compared Dawison's virtuosity to his own on the piano, praised his anger toward Ophelia, as Hamlet was justifiably impatient at her refusal to grant him the "wine of love," offering instead "a drop of milk."[36] High points included the play scene, when he moved on his knees from Ophelia to Claudius, his hatred of the king growing by the moment, until it burst in a climax of hellish laughter. Dawison was without pathos. Even in Hamlet's scene with Gertrude, he made no attempt to draw the audience's sympathy. He seemed not to be upbraiding her for her lack of faith, rather to be searching for the principle by which she acted as she did. At the end he met his death in a nonchalant, defiant manner. "The pleasure with which Hamlet speaks, the rather blasé way in which he lets fall his baroque jokes against the courtiers is splendid. The negligent manner in which the king's son fences with Laertes elevates this otherwise weak scene" (Freytag I, 8, 318-19). Few, however, found Dawison wholly satisfying. He was often criticized for using overelaborate gesture, so that, for example, his scene with the Ghost was lacking in impact, there having been no earlier passages of simplicity. Also some found that his gestures tended to draw attention away from the inner state of the character toward his own virtuosity. He often overstated where understatement might have been more suitable. Such amplification was associated not with the idealist actor, who had become the soul of restraint, but still with the French. Indeed Dawison's affinity with the French—he knew the language and visited and acted in Paris several times—did not escape his critics' notice.

It is difficult to claim, as some of his devotees did, that he represented a "new realism," either by the past standards of Schröder and Ludwig

Devrient or by the future standards of naturalism. Dawison's acting combined, in no discernibly systematic manner or proportion, a realism of conception with a technique that often betrayed that conception. Problems in defining his style are also posed by critics' bias toward him personally, which often negatively colored their appraisals. He was also difficult to pin down as he sometimes changed radically his interpretation of roles, surprise being a major aspect of his appeal. Then he displayed a mixture of serious and comic on stage, which did not always seem to be intentional, and, despite Fleck's innovations earlier in the century, was still somewhat unpalatable to contemporary tastes. When he was at the Burgtheater, Laube complained about his unseemly antics as Mark Anthony over Caesar's corpse, insisting that his carelessness and exaggeration caused laughter. But others were more hospitably disposed toward his mixed effects; indeed, a Viennese colleague suggested that laughter at serious moments was one of Dawison's carefully planned strategies. For example, in *Richard III,* during the Lady Anne scene, "Dawison spoke the line: 'For I did kill King Henry' with the greatest vocal display and unnatural pathos. The following line: 'But 'twas thy beauty that provoked me' [was delivered] with folded hands and roguishly winking eyes in the most conversational of tones, as was the line 'Nay now despatch; 'twas I that stabbed your Edward—/But 'twas thy heavenly face that set me on.' "[37] Nevertheless the same author continues by describing how furious Dawison was in the final scene, when his ravings were accompanied by peals of laughter from the audience, caused not only by the wobbling backdrop against which he was performing, but by his exaggerated vocal patterns and his strange appearance in hacked armor. (See Figure 8.)

Richard III was one of Dawison's most frequently performed roles, and again contemporaries differed as to the humor or lack of humor he brought to it. Hebbel, for example, felt he tried to achieve far too high a level of pathos. But, on good nights, he emanated a baneful evil. During a guest appearance in Breslau, he thrilled his audience by portraying a king who was strong, confident, and completely lacking in self-pity. From the start he was a diabolic figure who would stop at nothing to destroy everyone in his way. Yet he was also fascinating. "The whole sequence of scenes in which the nemesis of history fulfils itself through this most magnificent of despots, was an unbroken chain of moments, performed with incomparable certainty, which conjured the spectator with truly demonic power into the circle of the guilt-laden

8. Bogumil Dawison as Richard III. Reproduced by permission of Theater-museum der Universität zu Köln.

tyrant'' (Kurnik, 151). But to balance this rather extravagant judgment, a Dresden critic, normally sympathetic to Dawison, failed precisely to see in him the massive, tragic figure fulfilling the "nemesis of history." In fact Dawison seems to have stayed too close to the reality of everyday life, his Richard being little more than an "elementary, insidious, and banally tyrannous sinner," following the logic that "the most warped of rogues seldom appear brutal, ugly, or outwardly gloomy, but . . . are masked with politeness, captivatingly painted with hypocrisy."[38]

Some development can be traced in Dawison's roles, which suggests that the hours he apparently spent in studying them did lead to progression. He was a popular Shylock, partly because he was the first Jew to play the role on the German stage. The press treated him roughly when he first gave the part in Dresden in 1852, claiming that he had neither the "demonic power" nor the "grand style"[39] necessary for the role. He was found to be trivial, losing himself in subtle psychological detail. By 1855, he was more satisfactory, if not outstanding, with an authentically Jewish appearance and a powerfully demanding attitude. But later he raised the character to heroic status, a benign, proud man, confident in his right. His hatred of the Christians was masked by his honorable bearing, undercut only by his vituperative behavior during the scene with Tubal. As he appeared in court, he was not sinister but a figure of simple dignity and splendor, wearing "a rich, oriental caftan worked over in gold."[40] His demand for vengeance seemed an authentic call for justice, and, when he left the stage in defeat, he went as a martyr to the absolute, to noble custom, and to the violated rights of humanity. The worrying ambivalence Ludwig Devrient had introduced into Shylock was absent. But, even in this role, some of the more negative aspects of Dawison were apparent. When he played it, he normally insisted that the whole of Act 5 be cut, so that *The Merchant of Venice* became a tragedy with Shylock as the central figure. Also he did not maintain his nobility. Eduard Devrient, who saw him play the part in the early 1860s, felt a serious decline had set in. He was annoyed at the artificial clarity of Dawison's speech, and felt that his failure to motivate the character sufficiently made him appear to be little more than a rich banker out to make a profit. The passages in which he defends himself in court were in no way passionate, but he was "like a juggler playing with a ball."[41]

As already mentioned, Dawison has customarily been labelled a "demonic" actor, as if he were standing in direct line of succession from

Ludwig Devrient. But this is plainly inadequate. Even though his acting tended more toward the realistic pole, which Devrient's acting was widely considered to represent, rarely was he able, or perhaps even concerned, to represent the character as being possessed by forces of the unconscious, never did he invest it with a dimension that made it part of a world beyond the immediate comprehension of the audience. Dawison was too brawnily human for such acting and almost certainly enjoyed applause too much to allow him to surrender as completely to a part as Devrient had done. In Devrient's most famous role, Franz Moor, he was totally different. Given his penchant for the overt expression of powerful emotions, Dawison was strangely muted as Franz. Constantly striving for originality, he did not play with Devrient's instability, or Seydelmann's oscillations, or as the red-headed monster of convention. Rather he made him a quiet, polite, aristocratic youth, not especially elegant, not hideously ugly, just somewhat unattractive. His conduct made it clear that his lack of attraction had caused his parents to center their affections on the more winning Karl; his misanthropy arose from resentment at their neglect when he was a child. Simplicity and repose remained with him throughout the early parts of the play, the attempted seduction of Amalia being done with unusual calmness. The cowardice and malevolence at the core of his personality could only be glimpsed at unguarded moments and during the soliloquies. When, finally, Franz began to give way to the promptings of his conscience, he did so not with the usual theatrical ravings but, as Rötscher observed, by tracing with minute accuracy the manner in which fear leads to powerlessness, then to insanity. Other villains Dawison portrayed successfully were Marinelli in *Emilia Galotti,* represented as a figure of boundless malice, and Mephistopheles, where his ability to combine the comic, even the farcical, with the serious stood him in good stead. Unlike Seydelmann, he was able to combine the contradictory traits of the character, especially as he emphasized Mephistopheles' constant intent to denigrate humankind. While he was the soul of life on stage, "a merry devil, always lively, fresh, entertaining, sparkling with wit and spirit" (Kurnik, 152), this energy and humor was directed specifically to the destruction in people of any sense of pride and nobility.

When Dawison died, the usual flurry of obituaries appeared in the German press, not all as complimentary as the occasion seemed to demand, but most acknowledging the man's unique contribution to the

German stage. A persistent theme in these writings was his failure to found a new "school" of realistic acting. "There was something meteoric in him," observed Karl Frenzel "that existed for itself alone, without predecessors or followers" (Frenzel II, 277). Critics and historians have searched for analogies to Dawison outside the realm of acting. In particular the grandiose, vividly colored paintings of Makart have been mentioned, as have the grand operas of Meyerbeer. The parallels are suggestive. Dawison, for all his rawness, was a florid actor, given to embellishment and following themes through to an extreme development, without always rooting them in a unified conception of character. His decorative approach, his tendency to surprise audiences by unusual, even arcane gestures and vocal patterns, and his unfailingly forceful personality were all antithetical to the appeal exercised by Emil Devrient, though no less popular for that. This was not, as partisans in the argument over the merits of the two might have argued, a conflict between "truth" and "beauty," but between acting that was abundant and infused with a heightened sense of life and a more measured, marmorial, Olympian conception of the actor. Both appealed widely, but they could not be reconciled. Despite the comparative modernity of the mid-nineteenth-century German theatre, the dichotomy established late in the eighteenth century remained, though in changed form.

NOTES

1. Devrient's complaints are listed in his *Geschichte der deutschen Schauspielkunst,* new ed. (Berlin: Elsner, 1905), II, Sect. 4, Chapters 4 & 5.

2. Karl Reinhold, "Erinnerung an Seydelmann," *Jahrbuch der Gegenwart* XII (1845), 986.

3. Heinrich Laube, *Moderne Charakteristiken* (Mannheim: Löwenthal, 1835), I, 302-3.

4. Theodore Rötscher, *Seydelmanns Leben und Wirken* (Berlin: Duncker, 1845), 8.

5. Karl Seydelmann, *Aus seinen Rollenheften und Briefen,* Studienmaterial für die künstlerischen Lehranstalten, 2 (Dresden: Ministerium für Kultur, 1955), 106.

6. Eduard Devrient, *Aus seinen Tagebüchern, 1836-1870,* ed. Rolf Kabel (Weimar: Bohlau, 1964), I, 172.

7. Karl von Holtei, "Karl Seydelmann," *Allgemeine Theaterzeitung,* 94, 20 April 1843.

8. A. Boden, *Seydelmann oder ein paar dramaturgische Versuche* (Mainz: Faber, 1841), 3.

9. Gustav Kühne, *Portraits und Silhouetten* (Hannover: Kius, 1843), II, 333.

10. An important and far-ranging discussion of Seydelmann in his relationship to actors of the past appeared in the *Hallische Jahrbücher*, 44-50, February 1838, soon after he had left Stuttgart (see note 12).

11. Heinrich Laube quoted in S. Troizkij, *Karl Seydelmann: Die Anfänge der realistischen Schauspielkunst* (Berlin: Henschel, 1949), 98.

12. "Seydelmann und die letzte Entwickelung der deutschen Schauspielkunst," *Hallische Jahrbücher*, 44, 22 February 1838, 362-63.

13. Heinrich Anschütz, *Erinnerungen aus dessen Leben und Wirken* (Stuttgart: Reklam, n.d. [1900]), 145.

14. Goethe quoted by Troizkij, *Seydelmann*, 138.

15. Quoted by Ludwig Geiger, "Seydelmann als Goethe Darsteller," *Goethe Jahrbuch*, 33 (1912), 138-39. Seydelmann's prompt-book for Carlos is only available, in edited form, in this article.

16. August Lewald, *Seydelmann und das deutsche Schauspiel* (Stuttgart: Liesching, 1835), 37-38.

17. Karl Gutzkow, *Aus der Zeit und dem Leben* (Leipzig: Brockhaus, 1844), 428.

18. Karl Immermann in Monty Jacobs, ed., *Deutsche Schauspielkunst*, new ed., rev. Eva Stahl (Berlin: Henschel, 1954), 20.

19. Max Martersteig, *Das deutsche Theater im 19. Jahrhundert* (Leipzig: Breitkopf & Härtel, 1904), 451.

20. The eldest, Karl (1797-1872), acted at Brunswick, Dresden, Karlsruhe, and Hannover. He did not achieve the prominence of his brothers and is perhaps best known as the one-time husband of the famous opera singer Wilhelmine Schröder-Devrient. In his later years he acquired a solid reputation as a tragic actor.

21. Max Kurnik, *Ein Menschenalter Theater-Erinnerungen (1845-1880)*, 2d ed. (Berlin: Janke, n.d.), 17.

22. Rudolf Gottschall, *Literarische Charakterköpfe* IV, vol, 6 of *Porträts und Studien* (Leipzig: Brockhaus, 1876), 313.

23. Julius Bab, *Die Devrients: Geschichte einer deutschen Theaterfamilie* (Berlin: Stilke, 1932), 202.

24. Quoted in Kurnik, *Erinnerungen*, 18.

25. Gustav Freytag, *Aufsätze zur Geschichte, Literatur und Kunst*, vol. 8 of 1st series of *Gesammelte Werke*, new ed. (Leipzig: Hirzel, n.d.), 309.

26. Quoted in Wilhelm Widmann, *Hamlets Bühnenlaufbahn* (Leipzig: Tauschnitz, 1931), 218.

27. H. H. Houben, *Emil Devrient: sein Leben, sein Wirken, sein Nachlass* (Frankfurt-am-Main: Rutten & Loening, 1903), 130.

28. Emil Kneschke, *Emil Devrient* (Dresden: Meinhold, 1868), 48.

29. Henry Morley, *The Journal of a London Playgoer* (London: Routledge, 1866), 49.

30. Quoted in H. H. Houben, *Emil Devrient*, 150.

31. Karl Frenzel, *Berliner Dramaturgie* (Erfurt: Bartholemäus, n.d.), 273.

32. Theodore Fasoldt, *Bogumil Dawison* (Dresden: Teubner, 1857), 21-22.

33. Adolf von Hirsch, *Bogumil Dawison* (Leipzig, n.p., 1866), 16.

34. Jakob Moleschott in Jacobs, *Schauspielkunst*, 282.

35. Gustav Liebert quoted in Peter Kollek, *Bogumil Dawison: Porträt und Deutung eines genialen Schauspielers*, Die Schaubühne, 70 (Kastellaun: Henn, 1978), 79.

36. Letter from Franz Liszt to "a friend," 18 January 1856, from *Franz Liszts Briefe an eine Freundin*, vol. 3 of *Franz Liszts Briefe*, ed. La Mara (Leipzig: Breitkopf & Härtel, 1894), 59.

37. Carl Sontag, *Vom Nachtwächter zum türkischen Kaiser!* (New York: Lauter, 1880), 60.

38. Otto Banck, *Aus der deutschen Bühnenwelt, Kritische Wanderungen in drei Kunstgebieten* (Leipzig: Durr, 1866), I, 282-83.

39. Julius Hammer quoted in Kollek, *Dawison*, 66.

40. Frenzel in Jacobs, *Schauspielkunst*, 364.

41. Letter from Eduard to Therese Devrient, 23 March 1861, *Briefwechsel zwischen Eduard und Therese Devrient*, ed. Hans Devrient (Stuttgart: Krabbe, 1910), 384.

Chapter 5

THE VIENNA BURGTHEATER, 1776–1909

Vienna is a special city in the history of German theatre, as, since the early eighteenth century, it had been especially hospitable to travelling troupes. By 1711, a permanent home for the *Haupt- und Staatsaktionen* had been found in the Kärntnerthortheater under the leadership of the improvisational actor Johann Stranitzky (1676-1726). From this beginning, for the next century and a half, there developed in Vienna a popular theatrical tradition that had no European rivals to match it in vigor, color, variety, and wit. Among this theatre's greatest works were Mozart and Schikaneder's opera *Die Zauberflöte* (*The Magic Flute—1791*) and the plays of Ferdinand Raimund and Johann Nestroy. But the Burgtheater also had equal importance in the life of the city and in the development of German theatre.

Since the middle of the seventeenth century, great state occasions had been marked at the Habsburg court by spectacular operatic performances, but it was not until 1741 that court theatricals were placed on a quasi-regular basis, when the Empress Maria Theresa had a ballroom in the Hofburg palace adapted for such purposes. Here, for several years, under various managements, Italian opera, high French tragedy, and popular comedy fought for elbow room. In 1776, Emperor Josef II, prompted in part by the writings of Josef von Sonnenfels, which reflected current Enlightenment thought on the nature and function of theatre, declared the company to be a national theatre, providing it both

Portions of this chapter appeared earlier in Simon Williams, "Shakespeare at the Burgtheater: From Heinrich Anschütz to Josef Kainz," *Shakespeare Survey*, 35 (1982), 21-29. Reprinted by permission of Cambridge University Press.

with a constitution and a generous subsidy. Henceforth, the actors were the emperor's personal employees and servants of the state.

The establishment of the Burgtheater as a national theatre was part of a wide-ranging reform by which Josef attempted to liberate his subjects from a feudal social order. The theatre was to be a "moral institution" to refine the taste and further the education of its audiences, an ambition underscored by Josef's abortive attempt to hire Lessing as his new theatre's dramaturg. Naturally, the drama to be offered was not to arouse disquieting or refractory emotions, but was to be restrained, appealing to the rational sentiments and perceptions of the audience members, leading them to a wholesome understanding of the world around them. This was to be a theatre of moderation in which tragedy "arouses pity and fear, but not disgust and terror . . . phrased in a high, noble diction with no fantastic verbiage."[1] In sentimental comedy, emotions aroused were to be "pleasant without being deeply moving," while conventional comedy was to excite "laughter through wit and a decorous frame of mind, not through farce, indecency, or unnatural events."

In such thinking, Josef was a true man of his time, but as an administrator he had unusually advanced ideas. Instead of appointing a director who would have absolute powers, he instituted the *Ausschuss*, a managerial board consisting of five senior actors who were to carry responsibility both for the regulation of the theatre's day-to-day affairs and for artistic policy. Although this progressive arrangement was not to last for long, it did emphasize that priority in artistic matters was to be given to standards of acting. It also elevated the social standing of the actor in Vienna to a level previously inconceivable. Not that the actors automatically deserved it. One of the founding members of the *Ausschuss*, the popular Stephanie the Elder (1733-1798), practiced a debased form of the Leipzig style. He was also capable of the most deplorable lapses in taste, as, when playing Odoardo in *Emilia Galotti,* he licked blood off the dagger with which he had just stabbed his daughter. Few Viennese actors of the time were able to fulfil Josef's ambitions for the Burgtheater. So, when he sent J. H. F. Müller, a member of the *Ausschuss,* on a tour of German theatres to hire suitable actors, he instructed him to look not only for mimetic abilities, but also for evidence of education and fine deportment. For the *Fach* of the Young Hero and Lover, Müller should chose a man "superior in youth and maturity, with easy, noble manners and pure idiom. He must not be too tall, not have a protruding stomach, his eyes must be expressive, large, round and not far apart, his gait firm and not shuffling. Through the grace of his youthfulness, he must produce the warmth that one seeks in the drama.''[2] Only Johann Brockmann, whom Müller managed to lure to Vienna, came up to these standards. Nevertheless, a flexibility that became characteristic of the Burgtheater manifested itself when, by special permission of Josef, Schröder was hired as a member of the company and of the *Ausschuss* in 1781. Both grace and realistic characterization were, therefore, to be part of the Burgtheater style. Schröder, with Brockmann, helped create a quieter, more self-possessed manner in the company's actors, though Schröder, worn down by intrigue, returned to Hamburg in 1785, Brockmann continuing as a mainstay of the Burgtheater for several years. When Josef's interests were diverted by more pressing political and military concerns, the company entered a period of decline that lasted well into the nineteenth century.

THE TRADITION OF ENSEMBLE

The revival of the Burgtheater was due primarily to Josef Schreyvogel (1768-1832), a Viennese journalist, critic, and art dealer, who, as secretary of the theatre from 1814 to 1832, created a company close to Josef II's original concept. Some years prior to his appointment, during the conservative reaction after Josef's death in 1790, Schreyvogel had spent time in exile at Jena, where he had associated with Schiller and attended the Weimar theatre. When he took over responsibility for the Burgtheater, the *Ausschuss* by now having been dissolved, Schreyvogel adopted some of Goethe's ideas. For a start, he tried to create a repertoire that depended more heavily than usual on the classics, especially Shakespeare, though in modified form to suit the rigid censorship, and the great Spanish dramatists. He gave prominence to the works of the already classic Lessing, to Schiller and Goethe, and championed the young Viennese playwright Franz Grillparzer. The more everyday drama was represented primarily by the pleasant comedies of Viennese life by Eduard von Bauernfeld. All in all, Schreyvogel established a repertoire that has served as a model to later national theatres, one that includes plays that define a national culture, the most important plays from foreign cultures, and the best work available from contemporary playwrights, as long as it passes the censor or meets with public taste.

Schreyvogel was not concerned solely with repertoire. He also worked toward realizing an idea of ensemble that had first been posited by Sonnenfels in his *Briefe über die Wienerische Schaubühne* (*Letters on the Viennese Stage*—1768), where it had been argued that the play rather than the performer should be the center of the audience's attention. Hence, the actor must not study the role in isolation, nor execute it with disregard for others, but should pay close attention to the whole of which the role is a part. "Each actor must establish from the contexts of the play he has in hand the character of the whole, through which it differs from all others."[3] Once the "character" of a play has been established, then "unity of tone" in performance is guaranteed. In developing the necessary ensemble to achieve "unity of tone," Schrey-vogel was aided by a decree of 1812 that, unique for its time, legislated opera and drama be performed by separate companies in separate theatres. He could, therefore, concentrate solely on the spoken drama. In so doing, he evolved an idealist style of acting midway between the formality of Weimar and the decorous realism of Mannheim, in which attention was paid more to the whole, than to the individual. As Bauern-feld observed, the actors "realized a harmonious concurrence with the sense and style of the author, without becoming involved in petty details."[4] But this did not mean actors were blindly subject to the whole. Schreyvogel encouraged them to discover the traits that made up the characters they played, then to realize these, not in isolation, but through paying close attention to how these traits show themselves through intercourse with other characters. The actors' delivery was modelled upon conversation in aristocratic circles, with special care being taken to highlight musicality in speech. The comparatively subdued style of acting that evolved was also determined by a close rapport between performers and spectators, due to excellent acoustics and the relative intimacy of the theatre. In this context, actors trying to represent the superhuman dimensions of suffering would strike the audience as exaggerated and strident. Yet they could captivate them by inviting their sympathy for the noble figure represented. So harsher aspects of character were toned down, warmer traits accentuated, and passages of potentially great power given in unusually muted tones.

Schreyvogel gathered around him actors all chosen to create a harmonious ensemble of "types, temperaments, figures, and voices."[5] In addition to Sophie Schröder, these included the cultivated comic actress Julie Löwe (1786-1849), the heroic actor Maximilian Korn (1782-1854), the versatile comedian Karl Costenoble (1769-1837), whose diaries give a vivid record of the theatre's life, the poetic young lover Karl Fichtner (1805-1873), and the robust Ludwig Löwe (1795-1865). But no actor was so closely associated with Schreyvogel's ideals as Heinrich Anschütz (1785-1865), who was a mainstay of the company from his first appearance in 1820 until his death.

Before coming to Vienna, Anschütz had observed performances at Weimar, following which he had striven to give his acting formal dignity. Schreyvogel managed to wean him from the woodenness of the Weimar style, ennabling him to endow his massive bearing, grave presence, and measured speech with greater warmth, so that he became symbolic for the solid human worth that the Burgtheater actor attempted to project. Lear, which he first played in 1822 when he was only thirty-six years old, was his most famous role. In it, both the strengths and weaknesses of the Burgtheater style were apparent.

Anschütz's Lear appealed not by revealing the power latent in the role, but by imbuing it with pathos. Ludwig Speidel, who saw him act it late in life, was moved by his Lear's descent into madness as "the anguish and outcry of a beautiful world on the downfall."[6] There were no pathological outbursts or disquieting moments, such as Ludwig Devrient had created. Also, Anschütz made little of Lear's being, or having been a king. It was the distressing sight of the old man become a child again, of a father abandoned by his ruthless daughters, that wrung audiences' hearts. Rarely in his outbursts was Anschütz the irate monarch, incensed by his discovery that he has dispossessed himself. Rather, familial betrayal was highlighted; the political aspects of the king excluded from the authority he still thinks his and the resulting social debacle were never explored. But, despite popular acclaim, there were some, especially in the early years, who found Anschütz's Lear incomplete. Costenoble, for example, was far from happy with it, finding it patchy. Granted from the start there were great moments, the curses on Goneril and Regan and his awakening in the presence of Cordelia; at this point, wrote Costenoble, "our Lear would have been able to draw tears from hearts of marble."[7] But despite his maturing in the role, he could never manage the mad scenes satisfactorily. Costenoble found them "reminiscent of the tomfoolery of the ballet" (Costenoble, *Burg* I, 174) and observed that Anschütz was never able to indicate where "madness ended and sanity returned" (Costenoble, *Burg* I, 298). At best, his madness was little better than theatrical rant. Anschütz, the supreme Burgtheater actor, was unable to explore with any conviction the extremes of human experience or those phases of behavior when the psyche is open to forces it cannot control.

Schreyvogel was summarily dismissed in 1832, due to a petty altercation with a court-appointed official. The next two directors of the theatre, Johann Deinhardstein and Franz von Holbein, did little but preside over the deterioration of Schreyvogel's ensemble. But, after the revolution of 1848, new vigor was injected into the company by the appointment of an artistic director who proved in his day to be the finest *Regisseur* in the German theatre, Heinrich Laube (1806-1884). Like Schreyvogel, Laube came to the Burgtheater with a political past that should, it would seem, have excluded him from an appointment to a court theatre, but, once again like Schreyvogel, he also had a keen appreciation of the values that informed Josef II's original foundation. In him were united desires to reinvigorate the repertoire and to maintain the egalitarian nature of the ensemble in service of the play.

When Laube took over, there were scarcely more than thirty plays in the theatre's repertoire, a deplorable circumstance, as plays changed almost nightly. Furthermore, the repertoire contained little of vitality and interest. Laube's intention was to expand it to include all major German plays and those plays of Shakespeare and the great Romance dramatists that still were stageable. "My ideal was, after some years, to be able to say to every guest to the city, 'Stay a year in Vienna and in the Burgtheater you will see everything that German literature has created for the stage that is classic or still has life. You will see what Shakespeare has bequeathed us Germans, will see whatever can be appropriated from the Romanic people to suit our way of thinking and feeling' " (Laube, 177). Although Laube did not achieve as broad a repertoire as initially he had hoped, Shakespeare came to be seen more frequently, in Laube's rigorously adapted versions, as did Schiller's major dramas. But, most importantly, he established, first against opposition from administrators and audiences alike, the French well-made play as a staple of the theatre's repertoire.

These changes had important implications for the Burgtheater actor. When Laube arrived, dominant figures in the company were still Schreyvogel's actors—Anschütz, Ludwig Löwe, and Fichtner, and Karl LaRoche (1794-1884), who had joined in 1833. But the new repertoire Laube envisaged, both classic and modern, was to involve an acting qualitatively different from the warm, poetic style Schreyvogel had cultivated, though with no less ensemble work. "Our time," Laube claimed, "is more egalitarian and therefore has fewer original characters, but it has greater intellectual life" (Laube, 274). He suspected anything on stage that was superfluous, overelaborate, or designed solely to reflect upon an individual character. In his versions of Shakespeare, he stripped away the poetry, and cut extended passages of introspection in order to point up the action. There was a corresponding simplicity in the settings he used, as, against the general tendency toward lavish spectacle, he insisted that only those properties essential to the progress of the action be introduced on stage. This meant the actor became almost the sole medium for the play. But the actor also developed simplicity and economy of expression. Although Laube managed successfully to incorporate older actors into his new company, his efforts to create the sparser style of performance were spent mainly in training the several young actors he hired during the 1850s. He encouraged them to avoid all temptation to indulge in poetry. "The poetic language of the higher drama does not suit them," he wrote, "they must sustain simple language" (Laube, 292). For them, ideal vehicles were not the classics, even when pared down, but the conversation pieces of Scribe, written in a dialogue that was colorless in comparison to the fuller, more vigorous, and peculiar style of earlier drama. In Scribe's plays, many of which Laube translated and staged, characters, although given distinct traits, function not as beings of interest in themselves, but as agents of the action and as types representative of various strata in society and the professions. Accordingly Laube encouraged his actors to master the manners, gestures, and patterns of speech current in Viennese society, and, ignoring the *Fach* system, cast according to how an actor suited certain social types. But he was too sensitive an appreciator of acting to argue that the performer should be merely a puppet. Instead, he trained his actors to achieve a fine balance between the general and the individual, always ensuring that the socially typical had its origins in the personality of the character.

Laube, like Sonnenfels and Schreyvogel, believed that the play, not the actor must be at the center of audience interest, even though standards of acting continued to receive particular attention in the Burgtheater. "For us the final goal of the actors' endeavors is the whole picture, not the single figure" (Laube, 233). He therefore had an ineradicable suspicion of anyone who attempted to stand alone in the company, whose virtuosity threatened to ruin the harmony of the whole. This was apparent early in his tenure at the Burgtheater, when Bogumil

Dawison's ambitions to shine disrupted Laube's attempts to form a cohesive company. Such behavior, Laube argued, was inexcusable, and he dismissed Dawison as one "without moral or artistic backbone" (Laube, 233). Despite appreciation expressed in his historical writings for Ludwig Devrient, he also disliked the *Nervenschauspieler*, who unsettled the audience and failed to create a wholly beautiful and reassuring figure. This accounts for his rather testy judgment of Marie Seebach (1830-1897), who was briefly a member of the Burgtheater ensemble.

She lacked peace of mind, the capacity for which is indispensable in the passion of the tragic art, because from this peace springs the energy that stamps the tragic figure with certain marks of eternity. Many spectators' complaints were caused by this failing: "Seebach makes me nervous!" She did not elevate her role above nervous irritation to peaceful beauty, which even makes death artistically satisfying. Hand in hand with this failing was a painful style of delivery that had a depressing effect on the listener. She "nagged," as they say in Vienna; in northern Germany, they say she snivels. (Laube, 234-35)

Despite Laube's caustic judgment, the nagger and sniveller went on to a critically successful career as a virtuoso. His opinion of Seebach does, however, suggest that even though Laube was widely regarded to be a "realistic" director, a distinctly idealist demeanor was intrinsic to the style he developed at the Burgtheater.

The high esteem in which the Burgtheater actor had been held was intensified under Laube's regime. Although he prized highly those actors who were resourceful mimetic artists, his affections were extended most strongly to those who expressed loyalty to the theatre as an institution. For example, Louise Neumann (1818-1905), not the most talented member of the company, left to get married in 1856. She was, Laube considered, an irreparable loss to the company, both because of her loyalty and for her ability as a society lady and artist to help create a bond that maintained the theatre as an integral part of Viennese life. She displayed

the most honorable, most simple devotion to her profession. She was not only *most sincere* in performing her duties, but also *most amiable,* as she never refused to sacrifice herself if the well-being of the whole demanded a sacrifice. Besides [she was] a representative of good society, a representative of cultivated manners, of decorum, and [was] therefore a jewel for the Burgtheater. She had been raised in a good family, and that produced the richest results both for her and us, as her appearance was always welcome to the good society of Vienna. [She was] a sensitive, fine link between the auditorium and the stage. (Laube, 275)

Under Laube, the Burgtheater actor became the new setter of fashion in Vienna, a social celebrity whose company was eagerly sought for at the various soirees, balls, and receptions of higher society. As the influence of aristocratic families gradually declined under the bureaucratic rule of Franz Josef, the actor became the new aristocrat to a degree unparalleled in Germany or, indeed, elsewhere in Europe.

By the time Laube was forced to retire from the directorship in 1867, mainly because his liberal policies did not sit well with conservative elements in court, he had assembled a company that, because of the peculiar longevity of its members, was to sustain his particular style of ensemble until the early years of the twentieth century. Most prominent among these were the great tragedienne Charlotte Wolter (1834-1897), the master of villainous roles Josef Lewinsky (1835-1907), the robust and reassuringly solid Bernhard Baumeister (1828-1917), and the elegant interpreter of tragic roles Josef Wagner (1818-1870). But no actor aroused such admiration and sheer love in his audiences as Adolf von Sonnenthal, universally regarded as "the living embodiment of the Burgtheater tradition."[8]

ADOLF VON SONNENTHAL

Sonnenthal was born into a Jewish family in the Hungarian city of Pest in 1834. He was trained to be a tailor, but soon after his arrival in Vienna as an apprentice, he determined to become an actor. After playing supernumary roles at the Burgtheater for no pay, he entered on a series of engagements with theatres around the Austro-Hungarian Empire and Germany until, in 1856, he was invited back to the Burgtheater as a guest. Despite some initial critical coolness, Laube offered him a permanent contract. His first appearance as a company member was as Romeo on 1 June 1856. He was to remain with the Burgtheater until his death fifty-three years later, on 4 April 1909. Over this time he acquired a unique popularity. His devotion to the company was exemplary, as was his energy. He appeared on average over 170 evenings in each of the theatre's ten-month seasons. His elegant bearing and tasteful dress made him the foremost setter of fashions. "If one looks for a type to embody the ideal of the elegant man in the Vienna of the seventies, then it was undoubtedly Adolf Sonnenthal.''[9] So celebrated a figure did he become that his twenty-five-year jubilee with the Burgtheater was marked by his elevation to hereditary nobility. In the interregna that, at the Burgtheater, inevitably occurred between the departure of one artistic director and the appointment of the next, he often directed the theatre's affairs. Until his death, he paid regular guest visits to major cities, so that, by the time of his twenty-fifth anniversary with the Burgtheater, he could justly be acclaimed as "the first actor in Germany" (Speidel, 256). Although his reputation was losing its lustre when he died while on tour in Prague in 1909, he was still among the most highly regarded of German actors.

No other actor realized so successfully the simplicity of speech and urbanity of stage-presence that was so intrinsically part of Laube's theatre. Both on stage and off, Sonnenthal also cultivated an image of himself as one who incorporated only positive traits of human nature. His simple delivery implied modesty and straightforwardness, while his refined manners indicated gracious habits, education, and ease with the world. These ingratiated him to his audiences. Almost everyone who wrote about him praised the warmth of his heart, his sensitive feelings, his generosity, and his ability to radiate "beautiful humanity," kindness, and sincerity. Typical of the endless panegyrics is the following.

In ... Sonnenthal ... all good qualities are combined and create a delightful picture, like the different yet complementary colors of the rainbow. He possesses as much sensitivity as he does understanding, he has been endowed with as much taste as imagination, he is as talented as he is diligent. He is an incorruptible critic of himself and an amiable, good man, who can ever refresh himself from the rich life of his soul, as if from an inexhaustible well.[10]

Not even Iffland could have imagined a more perfect actor! But Sonnenthal, unlike Emil Devrient, was no Adonis, and this was crucial to his appeal, for there was about him a comforting normality. "As far as I can remember," wrote Jakob Minor, "his soft, rounded features always had something puffy about them, and the tear-sacks beneath his eyes stood out prominently. His eyes were not attractive either in color or brightness; only through enlargening or contracting them artificially could he extract eloquent expression from them.''[11] He made his impression on stage by his well-built frame and noble gait, from which exuded an air of moderation. Nothing was in excess, his voice was perfectly modulated and his gestures all in harmony. For this reason Minor called him the ideal "formative artist" (Minor, 59) in that he realized the playwright's text without awkwardness stemming from unfinished technique or the intervention of his personality. From this arose the general opinion that all he did on stage was "true" and "pure."

There was a connection between the roles he played and his personality. He refused to represent any character he considered morally questionable, as for him acting consisted in establishing an identity between the character and the image he had created of goodness and integration. Furthermore, he considered the essence of performance to lie in the creation of a warm bond of sympathy between him and the audience, as if the actor were the greatest friend of all who saw him. He was, therefore, perfect as the "salon hero," the man of the world who is a paragon of good breeding, and who was a recurring figure in the plays of Scribe, Dumas, Augier, and other dramatists from the school of the well-made play. So successful was he in these roles that Laube's expansion of the repertoire may not have been possible without him. But the world of these plays is circumscribed, not only in their predominantly upper-middle-class and upper-class settings, but also in the presentation of character. As character serves primarily as a function of action, figures in the well-made play have little inner life. Surface credibility, illuminated with a generalized warmth, was sufficient to give them stage presence. When it came to the representation of inner conflict, Sonnenthal, for all his surface realism, was deficient.

Helene Richter, in writing of Sonnenthal's Shakespearean roles, described his "way to Shakespeare" as "long and wearisome."[12] The wholeness and simplicity of his acting could not encompass Shakespeare's intricate and contradictory characters, neither was he able to unleash seemingly uncontrolled "storms of passion and . . . outbursts of molten feeling" (Richter, 37). For many this simplicity was welcome. His Hamlet, reminiscent of Wolff's, was praised for its clarity, in contrast to Dawison's often perceived incomprehensibility. This was basically a healthy young man, coping with particularly unhealthy circumstances. When he appeared in the role in Munich, he seemed to be the one man "who always holds his body under the mastery of his spirit, who has naturally come to this conscious mastery."[13] But as Minor pointed out, Hamlet is not entirely healthy, the need to act reveals to him unexpected sources of inaction within himself. Sonnenthal's

failure to realize this aspect of the character meant that sentiment re-
placed resentment, and delay was caused not by lack of self-assurance,
but by Hamlet's too warm feelings toward the world. (See Figure 9.)

Richter found that Henry IV and Lear were his only two successful
Shakespearean roles. But even in these he was limited. His Henry was
a truly good, repentant man whose irregular past no longer seemed part
of himself. His attitude to Hal was solely that of a father disappointed
at his son, not of a king worrying over his heir. Pity, therefore, was
the audience's response to him, harsher aspects of Henry's character
and the issue of the legitimacy of his rule being avoided. He was
touching—of his death scene it was written, "seldom has such a moving
and artistically pure impression been realized on stage with such slight
means" (Richter, 41)—but he was no tormented being. His Lear too
was a softened representation. He lacked entirely the "wild, heartless
egoism and haughty tyranny" (Richter, 42) that dominates Lear's character and accounts for Goneril and Regan being his daughters. Instead
only Cordelia seemed related to him. Throughout the first half of the
play, Sonnnenthal's Lear was downtrodden, vulnerable to Goneril to
whom he behaved like a spoiled child. Not surprisingly the curses were
muted, given "with difficulty, with long pauses, with suppressed tears,
drawn up strangled from the exhausted breast with obvious strain"
(Richter, 44). Any fury beginning to swell inside him was subdued, as
he reached exhaustion and collapsed in tears. In the storm scenes, there
was a brief rallying of energy, Ferdinand Gregori referred to him as
"Jupiter shedding lightning,"[14] but when madness came it acted as a
balm, releasing the tension, and Sonnenthal called again on his audience's pity as he relapsed into childishness. The reconciliation with
Cordelia was, of course, his highest moment, so affecting that through
to the end one experienced "an exalted compassion rather than violent
emotion" (Richter, 45).

In classic drama, Sonnenthal was more successful as the "half-tragic"
figure, as "the dangerous and irresistible man whose magic lies not in
rugged manliness but in his delicate and sensitive being" (Minor, 65).
As Othello he was inadequate, but he was a superb Cassio. "Cassio
represents lack of passion, balance and harmony in human nature. . . .
He has nobility of soul, is brave without swaggering, sincere without
being choleric; in contrast to Othello, [he is] a European saturated with
culture. Herr Sonnenthal represents this splendidly."[15] His most noted
half-tragic figure was Clavigo, in his repertoire for decades. Sonnenthal

9. Adolf Sonnenthal as Hamlet. Reproduced by permission of Theatermuseum der Universität zu Köln.

made this difficult character credible as, by having him all affection, trust, and mildness, he could win everyone's love and still retain sympathy when he wavers in his attitude toward Marie. This meant the catastrophe was caused not by any deliberate act of callousness, but by the impossibility of his being able to control the natural flow of his feelings toward different points of gravity. As he normally played opposite Josef Lewinsky, who humanized Carlos even more than Seydelmann had done, Marie's death appeared as the unavoidable consequence of a natural chain of events.

In 1891, Sonnenthal gave one of his numerous Berlin guest performances at the Residenztheater. He was seen by Otto Brahm, the leading advocate of naturalism. Brahm was not close-minded; he recognized the quality of Sonnenthal's acting, the certainty with which he realized each emotion, his command over every movement. But, from the point of view of a man in the forefront of theatrical change, the Viennese actor seemed out of place, "like a lovely ornamental plant that knows only how to live in raised temperatures."[16] He belonged to a style of play that, after Henrik Ibsen, seemed no longer of relevance in the theatre.

It fabricates a world that does not exist, in which one loves but never goes hungry, in which concern for society is killed dead and purely erotic play seems to dominate man's existence. It fabricates toward the mind a frivolous attitude, which flies in the face of all our knowledge of psychology. It allows its characters to exchange ideas like gloves and executes sudden, radical "improvements"; the facetious man becomes reasonable, the extravagant economical, the hardhearted yielding, and the uncouth fellow polite. (Brahm, 104)

Although Brahm, thinking of a theatre in which character was a changing, flexible entity, did not at the time represent majority opinion, his comments were apt. The pervasive theme of the new drama of Ibsen and others influenced by his work was the maladjustment of the individual both to himself and society. This drama could not be fully realized by the ethos of integration Sonnenthal's acting exemplified. Not that he had not appeared with some credit in Ibsen—as Peter Stockmann in *An Enemy of the People* in 1890 and as Dr Wangel in *The Lady from the Sea* in 1902—and in the lead of Hauptmann's *Fuhrmann Henschel* (*Drayman Henschel*) in 1899, but in this drama, as in Shakespeare, he was unable to represent credibly the psychological uncertainties that mark its characters. But if Sonnenthal in his old age was unable to adapt to the new drama, the Burgtheater could.

The change was not, however, easy. To be effective, the naturalist plays of Ibsen, Gerhart Hauptmann, and the young Viennese dramatist Arthur Schnitzler needed to be performed in an intimate environment so that details of gesture, facial expression, and vocal inflection could easily be grasped by the audience. The closeness between stage and auditorium of the Burgtheater would seem to have been ideal for such acting, but, in October 1888, the company moved from these quarters into a palatial, neo-baroque edifice on the Ringstrasse. Spatially and acoustically the new theatre, with its enlarged stage and impersonal auditorium, seemed to threaten the quiet nobility of the ensemble's acting as well as the viability of performing the new naturalist drama, to which the ensemble, like Sonnenthal, was not attuned. Nevertheless during the energetic directorship of Max Burckhard, between 1890 and 1898, the plays of Ibsen, Hauptmann, Schnitzler, and other naturalist dramatists began to appear in the Burgtheater repertoire. Despite the inhospitable environment of the theatre on the Ringstrasse, the company began to accommodate themselves to the new drama.

Sonnenthal was uneasy over these changes, as he stated in an open letter published in the *Neue Freie Presse* in 1896 on the occasion of his fortieth anniversary with the company. For Sonnenthal, the Burg-theater had reached the apex of its development in the days of Laube when actors, performing with "truth, nature, and . . . simplicity"[17] had drawn empathetic responses from the audience. Now actors were, he claimed, "raw and brutal" at the cost of beauty.

The threads of the old Burgtheater tradition separated irrevocably at about the beginning of the nineties. This certainly was not by accident nor as a conse-quence of the natural development of things, but it was done intentionally and by force. This tradition was broken with because the conviction had slowly spread that it was out of date, due to the powerful flow of the so-called realistic-naturalistic tendency. Hence, no longer did one refer young, aspiring talents back to models. On the contrary, one taught them to do otherwise, as if the "old school" had outlived itself and was already a defeated notion. (Haeus-sermann, 53)

Sonnenthal, idealist to the core, concluded that nothing would come of this new acting. "The new seeds will not flourish properly, the new sprouts put forth no roots" (Haeussermann, 54). That he was wrong was demonstrated by the popularity enjoyed by the new pillar of the Burgtheater community, Friedrich Mitterwurzer.

FRIEDRICH MITTERWURZER

Anton Friedrich Maria Mitterwurzer was born in 1844 in Dresden. His father was one of the most accomplished Wagnerian baritones of the day, and his mother was an excellent actress. Both were members of the Dresden Court Theatre, and, through them, Friedrich as a child met both Emil Devrient and Dawison. His parents tried to dissuade him from the theatre, but he resisted all their protests, making his debut in Meissen in 1862. The next years he spent wandering from company to company, deeply lacking in self-confidence, frequently on the verge of despair as to whether he would be a successful actor. Recognition of sorts came in 1866 when he was hired to play the Young Lover in Graz. Critics praised him for his elegant demeanor and his correct delivery, comparing him to Emil Devrient. His marriage to the young Berlin actress Wilhelmine Rennert, who was also hired at Graz, indicated he might be settling down. In September 1867, he gave four guest performances at the Burgtheater, but, due to a mixed critical reception and Laube's imminent departure, nothing came of them. He remained in Graz until 1869.

After his resignation from the Burgtheater, Laube took over the Leipzig City Theatre and invited the Mitterwurzers to join him there. They quickly became mainstays of the company, despite Friedrich's lack of polish, his eccentricity, and intense earnestness. But Laube had little chance to foster his talents, as in 1870 he returned to Vienna to set up a new City Theatre there, his post in Leipzig being taken over by Friedrich Haase. Mitterwurzer had little patience with Haase's "French salon" manners, so when, in February 1871, his wife was hired by the Burgtheater, he looked once again to Vienna. He joined the Burgtheater ensemble in Autumn 1871, but was not at ease in it. In the three years he stayed there, he played only one major role, Schiller's Fiesko. But as soon as he left, his fortunes improved. After guest appearances in Graz, Stuttgart, and at the Theater an der Wien, the director of the Burgtheater, Franz von Dingelstedt, rehired him, this time to play leads in alternation with Sonnenthal and Lewinsky. But once again Mitterwurzer failed to fit in. His Shylock, Iago, Richard III (all 1875) and Macbeth (1877) attracted interesting, though often uncomplementary notices, and soon he was confined once more to small roles. At his own request, he was released in 1880.

He remained in Vienna, acting at the City Theatre, and, for a few months in 1881, at the Ringtheater, until it burned down. In 1884, the City Theatre also burned, so Mitterwurzer turned briefly to management, running the Carltheater at serious financial loss. The next ten years were spent on the road as a virtuoso in German and Dutch theatres and, for two years, in the United States. Strangely enough, his acting matured rather than declined over this period. When he returned to Vienna in 1890 and 1892, as a guest of the Deutsches Volkstheater, he won critical aclaim for the strength and accuracy of his performances. Burckhard, firmly entrenched as director of the Burgtheater, saw him as the ideal actor for the new repertoire and, against official protests, in 1894 hired him for a third time, an event unprecedented in the history of the Burgtheater. Mitterwurzer's graphic acting filled the empty spaces of the new house, and he quickly became the star actor of the company, his presence on stage being the prime factor that drew in audiences. He enjoyed widespread critical and popular support. But his success was short-lived. In February 1897 he contracted a chill. To counteract it, he used a chlorine mix as a gargle. By accident he swallowed it, and died of poisoning a few days later, still at the height of his powers.

Mitterwurzer was the antithesis of Sonnenthal. A restless misfit, even when he finally won recognition at the Burgtheater, he was constantly struggling to be free from the restraints imposed by his contract. His colleagues, as if to defend themselves against his often disquieting personality and his wild outbursts of anger, considered him to be slightly *verrückt* (deranged). There may have been some truth in this, as both his parents had ended their lives with minds sadly unbalanced, and Mitterwurzer always had unusual trouble in adapting to the world. Torn between strong affection for his parents and his feelings for his wife, his private life was vitiated by an intense idealization of Wilhelmine that she quite naturally could not fulfil. Despite her common sense in dealing with him, she could not tie him down to a regular domestic life. He was also deeply religious, a quality not especially compatible with the theatrical profession. He spent hours in prayer before a group of wooden saints in his room in Vienna, and was quite capable, when on a walk in the countryside, of falling to his knees to offer up thanks for the beautiful scenery. This somewhat fundamentalist attitude meant frequent crises of conscience over his choice of the theatre as a living, and he used it to justify the small roles in which he was often cast. "It is good that the role is so small," he would say, "all acting is sinful— therefore the smaller the role, the smaller the sin."[18] Naturally, such convictions caused bouts of self-recrimination and a consistently ironic view of himself. Nevertheless, like Seydelmann, he had those who were deeply atached to him. Rudolf Tyrolt, who knew him from Graz, wrote, "I found in Mitterwurzer one of my dearest, most devoted colleagues, who, for more than thirty years, proved to me his sincere good will and his friendly disposition, not only through words but through deeds."[19]

As an actor, Mitterwurzer was highly unorthodox. His first biographer, Eugene Guglia, divides his career into three distinct phases. The first, up to his second Burgtheater contract, was marked by an obsession with originality, similar to Ludwig Devrient's. On stage, he was noted for nervous movements of arms and hands, and in comedy he was often awkward. "He came close to the grotesque, his figures having something of the wood-engraving about them; they were characterized by angular movements and grimaces."[20] The middle phase, comprising his second Burgtheater contract and the touring years saw him possessed by "feverish excitement" and "demonic exaltation" (Guglia, 59), acting with an energy bordering on the hysterical, interpreting his roles by fastening on psychotic aspects of character. But he could not easily be accused of self-indulgence, as he always paid scrupulous attention to details of characterization. He could easily be thrown by incidental shortcomings in the production. Furthermore, in longer roles especially, he was inconsistent and contradictory for no apparent reason. The final phase was from his first appearance at the Deutsches Volkstheater in 1890 through to his death. This was a time of maturity, when contrasts were not so strong, contradictions were understandable, and his quiet presence suggested self-containment that added to rather than detracted from his power. Guglia writes of a superhuman quality radiating from him that at times, as in his performance of Alfred Allmers in *Little Eyolf,* could be transformed into supreme resignation. "Now he crosses to a new sphere, a new chord begins to ring within him. . . . He becomes one who renounces, who seeks holiness. He turns his eyes away from earth 'toward the stars' and 'toward the great stillness.' He tries to release himself from the magic world of the senses; the Nietzschean man goes over to Schopenhauer" (Guglia, 103).

The difficulty of determining exactly Mitterwurzer's development is highlighted by Jakob Minor, who, reviewing Guglia's book, saw no such final phase. Instead, recalling Laube's oft-quoted judgment that Mitterwurzer could only play "fissured characters" (Minor, 169), he claimed that this was still so, only it was done with far greater completeness. Max Burckhard also denied the transformation, arguing that Mitterwurzer had just "become greater, more mature, his creations more balanced, and his art now benefits richly from anything his heart has learned about the human species."[21] But this did not make him new. Instead, Burckhard posited, audiences had changed. In the 1870s Mitterwurzer had been victim to an idealist mentality that was unwilling to sanction any interpretation not hallowed by Burgtheater tradition.

Critics and . . . audience members became irate and irritable when Mitterwurzer, following the innermost promptings of his being, attempted to build the new upon what clearly stood in the imagination of the spectator as if sculpted in eternal lines. Above all [they disliked] him for playing one of the great roles of the classic repertoire in a way entirely different from what they were accustomed to. The inner unity of the figure seemed to be lacking because unity with beloved tradition was lacking. (Burckhard, 103)

By the 1890s, however, "the rejection of every tradition, the absolute freedom of each artistic creation" was, Burckhard argued, becoming widely prized. "The musician, the painter, the poet, each one wishes to begin in opposition, to annul the prevailing artistic form, to be entirely independent and to appear entirely original" (Burckhard, 104). Although Burckhard might not have sufficiently credited the dependence of artists such as Mahler, Klimt, and Schnitzler upon the traditions of the city, it is clear that Mitterwurzer's success was due in part to changes occurring in the cultural life of Vienna.

But Mitterwurzer's significance was not only Viennese. Otto Brahm saw him in Berlin in the 1880s and welcomed him, along with Josef Kainz, as the actor who could free German theatre from its still widespread dependence on the Weimar style. His influence on the classic theatre would, Brahm claimed, be as potent as Ibsen's influence on the theatre as a whole. That this was possibly an exaggeration even Brahm knew. Among Mitterwurzer's more peculiar traits was his unwillingness to read anything but plays and his indifference to the quality of those plays. As a self-absorbed man, he looked mainly for good roles. This lead Brahm to qualify his approval by questioning Mitterwurzer's virtuoso nature, "which, like the central sun, craves for domination, that arranges others according to its will, even at the cost of the poetry, and whose struggle with the role is not of value for the play. But he enters into the innermost part of the work of art with all his soul, fearing no heated struggle in order to solve the last word of the puzzle"(Brahm, 103). The intensely personal interests of Mitterwurzer must therefore remove him from being considered an active creator of the new theatre. His final ascendancy was due more to fortunate circumstances than to any carefully planned strategy of his own.

Nonetheless, Mitterwurzer was not entirely indifferent to the quality of theatre. In an essay entitled "Style," published in 1881, he recounts a conversation between a young actor and an audience member in which the latter accuses the actor of not being "stylish" enough as Shylock. The actor, who clearly articulates Mitterwurzer's views, launches into an attack on "style," which is, he claims, nothing but "roundness, evenness in gesture, imitation, and speech—smoothness."[22] "Stylists" are nothing but "polite actors."

They wish to offend nowhere, to insult no one, everything has to flow in quiet channels. The most passionate gesture, the most significant speech, they glide over prettily and without attention. Only no impoliteness! When such an artist receives a role, it is polished up, kneeded, and chiselled so long that the whole characterization goes to the Devil. In the end nothing remains but the honorable Herr So-and-So, who simply puts on a strange costume, which he possibly doesn't even understand how to wear properly.... Whether it's a king or a beggar, in a red or a white coat, it's still only the face of Herr X staring, often miserably, out of the fool's jacket at the audience. (Mitterwurzer, 183)

The actor then discusses Wurm in *Intrigue and Love* and Shylock, not a nobly suffering figure he contends, but "the common moneypeddling Jew, rich beyond all measure, greedy and mendacious" (Mitterwurzer, 184), filled with malice and the desire to murder (see Figure 10). He concludes by returning to his attack on style.

To my mind, life is sharp and angular, and our art is called the representation of mankind. Working out and representing all those edges and angles completely and strongly, [this] first gives the represented figure character, sets it in a proper light. To polish, to dampen down, to suggest, to soften—those beloved terms of the stylist—seem to me idle and false. It is often the result of a peculiar faint-heartedness, even though they imagine themselves heroes!! (Mitterwurzer, 186)

10. Friedrich Mitterwurzer as Shylock. Reproduced by permission of Öster-reichische Nationalbibliothek, Vienna.

The essay is violently hostile to the values Sonnenthal and the Burgtheater stood for.

Physically, Mitterwurzer became well suited to the type of acting
described in the essay. When young his good looks drew comparisons
with Emil Devrient, but as he aged his face registered experience and
strain. Maximilian Harden caught the ambiguity of his appearance well.
"A face withered and ruined early in life, with broad, empty surfaces,
loose and shallow cheeks, a sensuous, desiring mouth that has nibbled
at all dainties, is always restless for new pleasure—and above this
devastation of a once noble face, a wonderful eye, the eye of an inflexible
master that enforces obedience, love, will-less surrender, and near-
adulation from the weakest."[23] The antithetical traits Mitterwurzer represented in the theatre were not always those of defeat and dominance,
but the ambiguities of his personality and appearance caused wide disagreement among critics as to what they actually saw. Burckhard cites
three widely ranging opinions on his performance as Macbeth in 1877:
Ludwig Speidel, who found him utterly unheroic, "so tearfully disposed
that one well believes he could not inflict pain on a fly"; Josef Bayer,
who found him interesting and imaginative though too nervous and
excitable; and Friedrich Uhl, who saw his Macbeth grow from a man
"too full of the milk of human kindness" to a giant of despair at the
end of the play (Burckhard, 79-83).

But perhaps the real clue to Mitterwurzer's enigmatic, uncomfortable
acting lay in his denial of a central point of identity to his characters.
In the classics, this could open up disturbing meanings. Guglia describes
his Julius Caesar, played until 1877 at the Burgtheater by Ludwig
Gabillon (1825-1896), who represented Caesar as a witty, Olympian
ruler. Mitterwurzer made of him a man deeply unsure of himself, crippled by superstition and paranoia (see Figure 11). He was also supremely
ambitious. This gave a disturbing ambivalence to the scene where Caesar
ponders whether he should go to the Senate or not. Despite denying his
belief in Calpurnia's dream, his voice and body indicated he did believe
in the portents she had seen. At the same time, a light in his eyes showed
that the hope of being offered a crown was still potently alive in him.
It was the overwhelming desire for power, not fear that the Senate
would laugh at him, that drew him to the chamber. But he went, fully
aware of what lay in store for him. In the chamber, his speech "But I
am constant as the northern star" was addressed not to the senators but
himself, "the words freeing themselves slowly and quietly from his

11. Friedrich Mitterwurzer as Julius Caesar. Reproduced by permission of Österreichische Nationalbibliothek, Vienna.

lips'' (Guglia, 49) as if he were questioning himself. Confronted by the assassins, he showed no surprise but, resigned to his fate, covered his head to await their blows, dying unheroically "as if blown away by the stormy winds of history." Mitterwurzer had deprived Caesar of nobility and strength, making him as much a man destroyed by his inability to resolve antithetical compulsions within himself as a victim of others' ambitions. The drama was within as well as between characters. Furthermore, in an institution that was still a court as well as a national theatre, he had broken the decorum of the stage that in the acting of Sonnenthal, Gabillon, and others had always posited identity between personal worth and public responsibility.

By the mid-1890s, when he was hired for the third time, not even the Burgtheater could deny the changing view of human nature in contemporary drama, where human actions and statements were not seen to have absolute value but as indications of hidden, often unconscious motivation and of social and biological conditioning. Mitterwurzer was the ideal "modern actor" who could make clear this view of human behavior as evasive and deceptive. Unlike other actors of the time, Minor observed, he could never express pure, unadulterated passion, but was best in portraying mixed characters, whose passion was in conflict with their understanding, whose seriousness was undermined by cankerous humor or self-irony and, on the broadest scale, whose aspirations for personal fulfilment were destroyed by weakness and fallibility. His ability to embody these contradictions, at the time widely considered to be unique to man of the late nineteenth century, had created for him a reputation as the foremost interpreter of "problematical characters." He was above all a fine actor of Ibsen.

Mitterwurzer played three Ibsen roles—Consul Bernick, Hjalmar Ekdal, and Alfred Allmers. Of these his Hjalmar was the most widely admired. The widespread popularity of *The Wild Duck* was due to a common conception, repeated by several critics, of Hjalmar as a modern Everyman. "There is no figure in the whole of world literature who is so important to us men of the present, who so touches on all sorts of secret wounds that each person feels within himself and none wishes to show. In everyone there is at least something of Hjalmar—a character trait, an inclination, an instinct."[24] Hjalmar, who colors the most mundane of events with a romantic hue, who avoids all responsibility through adopting an outdated rhetoric, who explains his vacillating moods as evidence of unswerving will, might also, from the theatrical point of

view, be regarded as a figure through whom the values of idealist art
are questioned. The play's very presence on the Burgtheater stage indicated the company's own questioning of the values upon which it had
been built.

Helene Richter wrote an exceptionally detailed description of Mitterwurzer as Hjalmar.[25] From this it is clear that his acting was the
antithesis of that practiced by Sonnenthal. He was never at rest; the
nervous play of his hands, his voice jumping from register to register,
his tonal vibrations and shifting movements, all created the impression
of a man not self-possessed but open to the slightest of stimuli. He was
also one who had failed to fulfil his promise.

The overall impression of his Hjalmar was of a rootless, half-grown person, a
highly problematical creature, divided between his latent possibilities and his
actual being. This Hjalmar was born to be something infinitely better than the
miserable wretch he had made of himself. Beneath the ashes of humdrum trash,
there still gleamed a spark of the gifted fellow he could have become. This
never-realized nobler self formed the unconscious background of his inner life.
(Richter, 141)

Later, his Hjalmar developed into ''a parody of the artist [whose] tragedy
was the bankruptcy of a productive spirit'' (Richter, 143). But there
was no caricature to his performance, as Hjalmar's adoption of faded
heroic poses was seen to be necessary, as an expression of the potential
he could never fulfil. The fulsome cliches, delivered with a declamatory
flourish—''perhaps Hjalmar could have become a splendid actor'' (Richter, 143)—were an attempt to deny his failure. Mitterwurzer also
avoided realizing any aspect of character fully enough for it to be seen
as fixed. This meant he defused any possibly judgmental response by
the audience and maintained their fascination with the character. ''He
[was] banal, but not boring, shallow but not frivolous, grotesque but
not ridiculous, blameworthy but not repugnant'' (Richter, 141). He
remained interesting and likeable, thus making credible Gina's and
Hedvig's attachment to him and Gregers's respect. One unambiguous
quality that developed consistently was his love for Hedvig; as the
dialogue at the end was pruned at the Burgtheater to allow for a more
purely tragic tone, Mitterwurzer's Hjalmar ended the play in a state of
genuine desolation. ''He sobbed and clenched his trembling hands.
However right Relling may have been with his prophecy for the future,

at that moment he was undergoing a shattering experience" (Richter, 147). While such a distinct closure is questionable, Mitterwurzer's performance demonstrated acting analogous to Ibsen's dramaturgy. As Ibsen used familiar aspects of the nineteenth-century stage to elicit from the audience a response opposite to what they might have expected, Mitterwurzer's sustaining of ambiguity never allowed the audience to rest in their perception of Hjalmar, so they were never able to respond to him in terms of approval or disapproval. Some found this made a difficult play remarkably clear. "Everything was represented with thoroughly unforgettable obviousness, with a simplicity that as a rule was not typical of Mitterwurzer. Everything corresponded and was complete" (David, 63). In Ibsen, Mitterwurzer seemed to have found his counterpart.

For Guglia, Alfred Allmers was his most compelling Ibsenesque creation. Initially, in an interview, Mitterwurzer had expressed serious doubts about Allmers' character, referring to him as "a pretty poor fellow who could no longer gratify the sensual passion of the man-hungry Rita; one who can do nothing, only wishes to; a decadent philistine!" (Guglia, 129). On stage, while Mitterwurzer captured Allmers' self-deceptive nature, as with Hjalmar he might have ended on a note of resolution that implied integration. He first appeared quietly cheerful, as if recovering from a long sickness, and mild, as if he had reached an unfamiliar level of religious awareness. But his serenity was undercut by sudden flashes of anger and passages of coldness that cast an ironic light on his serenity. Here Guglia drew a suggestive parallel with Sonnenthal. "Sonnenthal would have spoken more rapturously, with greater spirit, more poetically. . . . With Mitterwurzer there was always a brittle ring. . . . Sonnenthal would have appeared like one born into light, Mitterwurzer is like one who struggles painfully out of night into day" (Guglia, 130). The darker strata of Allmers were exposed at the end of the act as he became "coarse, unruly, and wild" (Guglia, 131). This carried over into the second act when the internal conflict of Act 1 was directly worked out on Rita. At moments, he was ready to assault her, only to draw back in fear as to what he was becoming. As the act progressed, his disordered nerves grew composed, the ponderous thinker came to the fore as he admitted his humanity. But there was no pathos in this change. It was deeply depressing. "Sonnenthal would have spoken everything more softly, in a more melancholy tone, more lyrically; but . . . with Mitterwurzer everything [was] heavy and hard"

(Guglia, 134). In the last act Mitterwurzer's Allmers began with "a heavy, dark residuum in his soul" (Guglia, 134), but as Rita explained her plans, he became milder, at the end reaching a state of mind equivalent to that at the play's opening, only with greater body and certainty. "Now everything is pure in his soul, the earthly rolls aside like heavy clouds, leaving him in a mild, radiant light. And with his great, broad, misgiving look, he now stares no longer into a desolate, formless distance, but upward—to the peaks, to the 'stars and to the great stillness' " (Guglia, 135). Minor disagreed with this reading of the performance, finding to the end that Mitterwurzer's Allmers exhibited pathological tendencies and that this "conversion" was merely another manifestation of them. From this division of opinion one can speculate that Mitterwurzer might not have fully resolved the character and so maintained the irony of viewpoint encouraged by the text.

Mitterwurzer's repertoire was extensive. As a guest actor, he had played most major classic roles. He was noted for his "Jewish Hanswurst" of a Shylock, for a bestial and craven Caliban, for a Richard III that degenerated into wild fury while maintaining a certain defiant heroism. In the modern repertoire he turned the lead role in Brachvogel's *Narcissus,* normally played sentimentally, into one of elemental power, as the betrayed husband oscillated between convulsions of despair and outbursts of violent cynicism. He was also a disturbing Copeau in the stage adaptation of Zola's *L'Assommoir.* In the German classics, as Mephistopheles he was "beautiful and ugly, attractive and repulsive" (Guglia, 129), while as Wallenstein he stressed the general's superstition, throwing it sharply into contrast with his arrogance. Never was he the noble, humane hero Sonnenthal had made of Wallenstein. But his two greatest roles from Schiller were Franz Moor and King Philip.

His Franz was not on first appearance overtly malign, though he was not the seemingly acquiescent creature Ludwig Devrient had made of him. Instead he was disquieting, "an insipid, childish wastral, a spiteful boy, who in younger days had probably impaled butterflies and plucked feathers off helpless little birds and who had slowly matured to great villainy" (Harden, 375). To the end, he was a child, delivering the speech on the Last Judgment as if he were a boy afraid of ghosts. This was strangely unsavory. His malevolence was never titanic, everything was reduced to petty scheming. He was not driven by an eagerness to possess Amalia, but his lust, as can be the case with undeveloped natures, made itself apparent through sarcasm, as though he were unable to accept his physical growth. All feeling was absent. With a childlike coldness, Mitterwurzer's Franz delighted in the chaos he caused, as if it were an experiment, and congratulated himself on his power over others. As the fear of death infiltrated him, he became evermore a whimpering child. Perhaps no character he played was as unsympathetic as his Franz Moor.

In total contrast was his King Philip, generally regarded as the finest creation of his later years. When he first played the role at the Burgtheater in 1879, critics commented that he created two characters in one figure. At a time when he was concerned with the "angularity" of the human condition, he failed to unite the aloof monarch with the wildly excitable man who suspects his wife. In the last Burgtheater performances, this union had been achieved and the figure given credibility. He was a man who suffered. "A tall, thin gentleman stood before us. His face faded, bloodless; his eyes deep and sleepless, his hands very thin, almost waxen, and extremely mobile. A man whose solemnity of movement and self-control necessarily developed from the feeling of highest responsibility, who knows each of his words carries weight and, under certain circumstances, portends destiny" (David, 67). He was deathly pale. Hermann Bahr wrote of his Velasquez-like head, "pale, full of pain, dark, the anemia of the old race."[26] Nevertheless, in contrast to his exterior, Mitterwurzer made mildness the basis of the king's character and his love for Elizabeth the center of his life. In his dealings with Carlos, he was too unsure of himself to come close to him, timidity rather than hidden resentment seemed to dominate him. His attitude toward Posa arose from his being able to overcome this timidity, which meant that Posa's liberal idealism touched him emotionally and did not remain at the level of ideas. "In the conversation with Posa, from the very first look at the young man, he showed he was fettered, as if enchanted. He hardly turned his eye away from him. Sometimes he lost himself entirely in deep contemplation of his features. . . . Rich, full trust flowed from his speeches, trust and happiness" (Guglia, 137). Ironically this trust made him more vulnerable, as while his experience as king taught him to reject the ideas, as an expression of Posa's personality they moved him, and opened up a rift between the private man and his public position. This also exposed the darker side of his character. Facing Elizabeth's accusers, then Elizabeth herself, Mitterwurzer's Philip exploded with jealousy, in total contrast to his earlier mildness. From here on, his iron control began to slip, and he became a tormented figure, struggling in vain to maintain some vestige of equilibrium. This led to his final decision, after Posa's "betrayal" of him, to sacrifice his son to the Inquisition and lay waste to the Netherlands, an act of sheer desperation and self-defense. At this point, he regained control of himself and reappeared as the initially calm monarch, only older, deeply embittered, and on the verge of collapse. His iciness was now only a mask. "His lips twitched, his grey hair hung dishevelled over his forehead, his limbs had grown yet more tired" (Guglia, 139). Through his focus on the personal life of the king, Mitterwurzer had shown not how tyranny operates but how, through a personality that is not integrated, it is generated.

Mitterwurzer's contribution to the Burgtheater and to the development of German acting as a whole was considerable. Despite the widespread respect accorded Sonnenthal and, through him, the Burgtheater style, by the 1890s audiences and critics in Vienna, Berlin, and elsewhere were beginning to recognize the outdated quality of Laube's school. This indicated an even broader suspicion of the idealist approach to acting that, after a hundred years, was beginning to loosen its hold on the German theatre. In Berlin, actors such as Emanuel Reicher (1849-1924) and Rudolf Rittner (1869-1943) were drawing attention by the unvarnished quality of their acting, which suited well the plays of the naturalists. Mitterwurzer, whose acting was more pronounced than the Berliners', fulfilled a similar function in Vienna. He was an invigorating influence. Ludwig Speidel, who had mercilessly attacked him in the 1870s, belatedly came to recognize this in the 1890s. For him, Mitterwurzer introduced a harshness and lack of sentimentality that accorded well with an age that was becoming indifferent to the gracious values for which the Burgtheater stood. In Mitterwurzer, there was a lack of idealism and a fascination with reality that lead Speidel to draw, somewhat improbably perhaps, comparisons with Bismarck. For all his personal confusion, Mitterwurzer was a man who suited the hard-headed mentality of the time and, however much one disliked him, like Bismarck, "after his successes one saw and heard only him. From the most detested man he was, he became the most popular" (Speidel, 287).

Not all were happy with this change. Minor, who believed deeply in the Burgtheater tradition, felt that in the performance of classic roles he "changed the relationship of the actor to the poetry" (Minor, 173). Indeed Mitterwurzer did not always embody his roles but often stepped outside them, as if "standing above the role from the standpoint of the playwright" (Minor, 173). If this sounds reminiscent of Seydelmann, so too does the comment that at times he acted against the meaning of the text. "Mitterwurzer was the first [in the Burgtheater] to take the dangerous road, incalculable in its consequences, of playing against the intentions of the poet, forcing upon him, even in the simplest and clearest of places, false intentions" (Minor, 175).

Others, however, welcomed Mitterwurzer for the very reasons Minor suspected him. Bahr acclaimed him for his refusal either to act ideal-istically or to be worried about the social worth of the actor. Mitter-wurzer acted, Bahr wrote, because he had to. This enabled him to return to the Burgtheater a love of acting for itself alone. "He played theatre in order to play theatre, as the bird sings because he must sing and because it pleases him."[27] The salutary effect of such freedom was better explained by Hugo von Hofmannsthal, who disliked both the style and eminence of the Burgtheater as, despite the old ambitions of Schreyvogel and Laube, the worship of the actor, which had arisen partly as a result of their efforts, tended to withdraw attention from the theatre as a place where plays are performed and set it up as a model for a vast social game. Partly through the emulation of the Burgtheater actor, Hofmannsthal argued, all Vienna had become a society of bad actors. The Viennese played the appearance of an appearance, using words for purposes that deprived them of their elemental meaning. Meanwhile, actors themselves aspired to be "interpreters of the poet, orators, educated citizens, and God knows what offensive stuff . . . [who] carry their roles like clothes to be greatly cared for, obviously stolen clothes."[28] In this highly artificial world, Mitterwurzer gave back that elemental meaning and, in his knowledge that he was an actor and nothing but an actor, reinvigorated the theatre with its own truth and life.

NOTES

1. Quoted in Heinrich Laube, *Das Burgtheater,* in *Schriften über Theater,* ed. Eva Stahl-Wisten (Berlin: Henschel, 1959), 99-100.

2. J. H. F. Müller, *Abschied von der k. k. Hof- und National-Schaubühne* (Vienna: Wallishausser, 1802), 100.

3. J. von Sonnenfels, *Briefe über die Wienerische Schaubühne* (Vienna: Konegen, 1884), 150.

4. Eduard von Bauernfeld, *Aus Alt- und Neu-Wien,* in vol. 12 of *Gesammelte Schriften* (Vienna: Braumüller, 1873), 166.

5. Friedrich Schreyvogl, *Das Burgtheater: Wirklichkeit und Illusion* (Vienna: Speidel, 1965), 43.

6. Ludwig Speidel, *Kritische Schriften,* Klassiker der Kritik, ed. Julius Rutsch (Zurich & Stuttgart: Artemis, 1963), 278.

7. Karl Costenoble, *Aus dem Burgtheater* (Vienna: Konegen, 1889), I, 174.

8. Joseph Handl, *Schauspieler des Burgtheaters* (Vienna & Frankfurt-am-Main: Humboldt, 1955), 36.

9. Rudolf Lothar, *Sonnenthal,* Das Theater 8 (Berlin & Leipzig: Schuster & Loeffler, n.d. [1904]), 39.

10. Eugene Zabel quoted in Hermann Bartsch, *Adolf Sonnenthal: Schilderung in Wort und Bild* (New York: Bartsch, 1885), 68.

11. Jakob Minor, *Aus dem alten und neuen Burgtheater* (Zurich: Amalthea, 1920), 54.

12. Helene Richter, "Adolf von Sonnenthal," *Schauspieler-Charakteristiken,* TF 27 (Leipzig & Hamburg: Voss, 1914), 39.

13. Johannes Lepsius, "Adolf Sonnenthal als Hamlet," *Schauspiel und Bühne* I (1880), 75.

14. Ferdinand Gregori, "Adolf von Sonnenthal: König Lear," *Jahrbuch der deutschen Shakespeare-Gesellschaft* 40 (1904), 87.

15. Michael Knapp quoted in Ludwig Eisenberg, *Adolf Sonnenthal* (Dresden & Leipzig: Pierson, 1900), 118.

16. Otto Brahm, *Theater, Dramatiker, Schauspieler,* ed. Hugo Fetting (Berlin: Henschel, 1961), 103.

17. Letter quoted in Ernst Haeussermann, *Die Burg: Rundhorizont eines Welttheaters* (Vienna, Stuttgart & Basel: Deutsch, 1964), 47.

18. Julius Bab, *Kränze der Mimen* (Emsdetten: Lechte, 1954), 267.

19. Rudolf Tyrolt, *Aus Lebenswege eines alten Schauspielers* (Vienna: Schworella & Heick, 1914), 14.

20. Eugene Guglia, *Friedrich Mitterwurzer* (Vienna: Gerold, 1896), 24.

21. Max Burckhard, *Anton Friedrich Mitterwurzer* (Vienna & Leipzig: Wiener, 1906), 10l.

22. Friedrich Mitterwurzer, "Styl," *Vor den Coulissen,* ed. Josef Lewinsky (Berlin: Hofmann, 1881), 183.

23. Maximilian Harden, *Köpfe,* 22d ed. (Berlin: Reiss, 1910), 369.

24. J. J. David, *Mitterwurzer,* Das Theater 13 (Berlin & Leipzig: Schuster & Loeffler, n.d. [1905]), 61-62.

25. Helene Richter, "Friedrich Mitterwurzer: Hjalmar Ekdal," in *Schauspieler-Characteristiken.*

26. Hermann Bahr quoted in Guglia, 136.

27. Hermann Bahr, *Kritiken*, ed. Heinz Kindermann (Vienna: Bauer, 1963), 349.

28. Hugo von Hofmannsthal, "Eine Monographie," in *Prosa* I, *Gesammelte Werke in Einzelausgaben* (Frankfurt-am-Main: Fischer, 1950), 269-70.

Chapter 6

THE LAST HEROES, 1875–1910

In 1870, as Germany was united under the Prussian kaiser, freedom of competition for the theatre was declared. Until then theatres could only operate under licenses granted by the police or governmental authorities. Now, whoever wished to found a theatre was entirely free to do so. Consequently, the expansion that had occurred after 1848 accelerated, so that by the end of the century there were an unprecedented number of theatres and a vastly increased acting profession. "In the area of the present German Empire before 1870," wrote Martersteig, "there were about two hundred real theatres with about 5,000 artistic employees; by 1896, the number of theatres had tripled as had performers of all types."[1] Not all these new performers were, of course, actors; neither were all the theatres devoted to the production of classic or serious contemporary drama. As with the previous decades, musical theatre, be it Wagnerian opera or Viennese operetta, was considerably more popular than the legitimate drama, while institutions of light entertainment—circuses, café theatres, *Tingel-Tangel* (music hall)—flourished in the major cities. No special training or qualifications were needed to enter the profession, despite constant demands by theatrical leaders that acting schools be established with governmental funding. Given a substantial degree of luck and suitable contacts, anyone with a modicum of raw talent could become an actor. As Adolf L'Arronge observed,

Whoever had straight legs and knew how to wear a black suit with tolerable dignity was a Young Lover with a monthly wage of 150 to 200 marks. A youthful, slender girl, who until now had scraped her living with her scissors and needle and whose only view was the garret window across the way, trod the boards as a Lover and, in an aura of "art," quickly made her fortune through her sympathetic appearance. A pretty young snub-nosed thing with a dainty little voice was immediately a soubrette.[2]

Not surprisingly, the general level of performance was low. Even though there was a public who appreciated serious drama, L'Arronge argued, they stayed away from the theatre as the actors, "dressed in particolored rags from various centuries, with bedaubed faces, move about awkwardly and often can't even speak German properly, let alone deliver verse" (L'Arronge, 40). Of course, the artistic wasteland of this vastly increased theatre was fertile ground for talented virtuosi, and actors such as Friedrich Haase, the robust and heroic Ludwig Barnay (1842-1924), and the fine rhetorical actor Ernst Possart (1841-1921) earned handsome fortunes from their various tours of Germany and the United States.

Nevertheless, commonly low standards and the prevalence of the virtuoso gradually came to be challenged by the advancement in the theatrical hierarchy of the *Regisseur,* who, assembling around him a company of actors, attempted to create some stylistic unity within his ensemble, with greater attention being paid to the interpretation of the play than had been the case with his forebears earlier in the century. Three different lines of development can be distinguished in the rise of the stage director over these years. First there was the "pictorial" director, such as Franz von Dingelstedt, who led the Burgtheater from 1870 to 1881, and the widely influential Duke of Saxe-Meiningen. Such directors tended to place major emphasis upon stage spectacle and on historical accuracy in costumes and sets, so that the actor often served more as a component in a picture than as an independent artist in his own right. Then there was the "ensemble" director, whose work had been anticipated by Karl Immermann during the 1830s in Düsseldorf and by Laube at the Burgtheater. As has been seen, his energies were devoted to evolving interplay between actors, and allowing each to develop as an individual to the extent that he did not destroy the harmony of the whole. Although he claimed to have been inspired by the Meiningen, Adolf L'Arronge was a director of this tendency. He founded the Deutsches Theater in Berlin in 1883 in an attempt to provide the city with a regular repertory theatre that offered an alternative to the dreary pomposity of the Royal Theatre. L'Arronge's Deutsches Theater was surprisingly successful, laying the basis for an ensemble that was brought to full fruition by Max Reinhardt early in the twentieth century.

Between L'Arronge's and Reinhardt's directorships, from 1894 to 1904, the theatre was directed by the prime example of the third type of director, the "naturalist," Otto Brahm. While Brahm paid little attention to stage decor, he encouraged his actors to develop a naturalistic style of acting that would create as complete an illusion of everyday life as possible. Such an approach was, at the time, seen as the ideal way to present the plays of Ibsen and Hauptmann. It also challenged decisively the Weimar style of acting. In the words of one of Brahm's leading actors, Emanuel Reicher, members of his ensemble

wanted to be nothing other than people who, through the simple, natural sound of human speech, determine from the inside out the feelings of the person presented, quite unconcerned as to whether the voice is beautiful or resonant, or the gestures gracious, or whether this or that is suitable to this or that *Fach*. [We are concerned] as to whether [our acting] is consistent with the simplicity of nature and whether it displays to the spectator the image of a complete human being.[3]

The prominence of the stage director, the gathering together of many distinguished actors at the Deutsches Theater, and the new repertoire of the naturalist and later the symbolist or neo-romantic dramatists meant that, in the closing decades of the nineteenth century, the focus of German theatre shifted from Vienna to Berlin. And above all this theatrical ferment stood two remarkable actors, both of whom, in radically different ways, united the opposites that had provided German acting with its distinctive stamp for the last hundred years, Adalbert Matkowsky and Josef Kainz.

ADALBERT MATKOWSKY

Adalbert Matkowsky was born in Königsberg on 6 December 1857, the illegitimate son of an impoverished seamstress. Despite hardships, when he moved with his mother to Berlin in 1867, he acquired a reasonable degree of schooling, though he was mediocre in all but gymnastics. After seeing a performance of *Hamlet* in 1874, his heart was set upon the theatre, though he still had to suffer two more years at school. His subsequent career as an actor was effortless. In 1877, he was hired by the Dresden Court theatre, then still a bastion of the Weimar style. For the next nine years, his powerful stage presence and uncom-

monly good looks brought him an enthusiastic following that verged
on idolatry. However, his irregular habits did not sit well with the
conservative administration of the theatre and, after missing some performances due to an emotional crisis, he was dismissed in February
1886. After some months out of work, he was engaged by Bernhard
Pollini, the highly successful entrepreneur who led Hamburg's two main
theatres. Matkowsky remained in Hamburg until 1889. He was then
hired by the intendant of the Royal Theatre in Berlin, Bolko von Hoch-
berg, who was attempting to reinvigorate the theatre after thirty-five
years of stagnation under the previous intendant, Botho von Hulsen.
Matkowsky alone could not transform the Royal Theatre and even after
his death in 1909 it remained a boringly pretentious, nationalistic institution. Nevertheless, the archaic scenery and old-fashioned repertoire
provided a curiously apt setting for Matkowsky's rather dated art. When
he died, at the age of fifty-two, possibly as a result of years of sleepless
nights and defiant dissoluteness, he was deeply mourned in Berlin. ''The
last living example of the romantic actor''[4] had passed from the German
stage.

Matkowsky reminded his contemporaries of an earlier, by then legendary age in the German theatre. His inability to adapt to the regular
habits of bourgeois life, then *de rigeur* for most actors who wished to
succeed, gave him the reputation of being a ''demonic'' personality.
This, coupled with his frequent carousels in Lutter and Wegner's tavern,
automatically gave rise to comparisons with Ludwig Devrient, while
on stage Matkowsky's refulgent personality and striking appearance put
people in mind of Fleck. Ludwig Barnay, who acted with him in Dresden
in 1884, caught this quality well. ''In this youth . . . were united everything that the most demanding connoisseur of art may demand and
expect of the Young Lover and Hero. A slender, well-proportioned
figure, a most beautiful head, great expressive eyes, a splendidly resonant voice, blazing fire, and thrilling passion, and with them the most
assured mastery of diction and of the text.''[5] At the same time, the
sense of mastery that emanated from him could be ambiguous. While
Fleck had transported his audiences by the rush of powerful feelings,
Matkowsky was less abandoned, so he could hold both himself and his
audience's response in check. Pictures of his early roles—Sigismund
in *Life Is a Dream,* Romeo, Prince Hal—suggest a herculean innocence.
There is about him a chubbiness of feature, hinting that here is a man
who has possibly grown too quickly, whose splendid physique incor-

porates a mentality not fully developed, not attuned to the world around him. Yet he has none of the more disquieting features of a Mitterwurzer. Instead these pictures suggest a pristine quality of mind, untouched by corrupting contact with the human world. They are not, however, devoid of a certain flamboyance, detectable not only in Matkowsky's poses, affected even by the standards of a time when artificiality was common in portrait photography, but in the Makart-like luxuriance of costume he wears. The contrast between natural strength and theatrical lushness also applied to his voice, described even by his fervent admirer Max Grube as "sonorous and mighty, but . . . of the sweetest harmony" so that passages of heroic assertion often verged perilously close to "the sentimentality of the jasmine bower" (Grube, 17). No doubt Matkowsky, who was an uneven actor, highly dependent on his moods, relied upon a somewhat cloying appeal when his energy was low. On good nights, however, he eschewed sentimentality to realize figures that were models of heroic conduct in extreme circumstances.

His Ferdinand and Carlos, his Romeo and Prince of Homburg, are performances of rare energy and fire, of natural nobility in bearing and truly overwhelming feeling, issuing from the accelerated beat of a heart that still believes in the ideal and holds honor and love as the highest qualities on earth. . . . Matkowsky is a whole, masculine personality, a heroic personality, a complete fellow, who only feels at ease when the storm of passion is gathering and the path is struck out before him by flashes of lightning.[6]

Later in life, when stoutness had given him a solid presence on stage, Matkowsky's evident mastery of both voice and body strengthened, and he took on mature, heroic roles. These either required titanic defiance, such as Karl Moor and Coriolanus, or the expression of vehement emotion, such as Othello or Macbeth, or the realization of qualities of rugged worth and fearless honesty, such as Götz von Berlichingen. What gave these roles their unique stamp was that even when the character disintegrated in the course of the action, Matkowsky would always at the end return him to oneness, to a "unity between will and thought."[7]

It is clear then that if Matkowsky was "the last living example of the romantic actor," this was a very different being from Ludwig Devrient. In fact, Matkowsky may better be considered as one who combined the opposites in German acting. His ability to portray the human being as complete and unbroken, as controller of the world, was distinctly idealist in tendency. Yet the means used to achieve such a figure were diametrically opposed to those of the Weimar style, even though, as he admitted, in his Dresden days he used at times to fall back into a sing-song pattern of speech and, as pictures suggest, into mannered poses. In his approach to a role, he was entirely original, playing from instinct rather than by predetermination, never entirely hiding his personality behind the mask of character, but still infusing the character with himself. Unlike most actors of the time, he was happiest when playing a role he had never seen anyone else play. Indeed, partly to cherish this necessary ignorance, he would only enter a theatre for rehearsals and on nights when he performed. Otherwise he knew nothing of the theatrical world around him.

Matkowsky was an isolated man, and welcomed it. Actors, he claimed, have little to offer society. They belong nowhere, they "remain pariahs, homeless, without property, wandering as outcasts through varying dreams, dying, none too old, on the highway" (Harden, 452-53). He cannot, therefore, be regarded as representative either of a stratum of the theatre of the time or of a particular artistic tendency. As everybody observed, he was the antithesis to naturalism and unsuited to the ensemble approach developing in other theatres. Yet, strangely enough, although like other actors he was always giving guest appearances, he was never regarded as a virtuoso, due mainly to his overt lack of dependence on technique and to his ability to dominate any performance in which he appeared by harnessing the energies of his colleagues to his view of the play. In this way he alone appeared "to modify the tempo and temperament of the whole performance" (Zabel, 559). Ironically this led some critics to see him as "a thoroughly modern personality," as if he were the incarnation of individualism. This was not, however, the sole appeal he had for the conservative theatre critic Julius Bab. For Bab, the new, industrialized Germany was not a welcome phenomenon, as in it the individual no longer seemed to be of significance. Meanwhile, modern literature took a reductive view of his potential for coherent action. "Heroes," wrote Bab at the start of his biography on Matkowsky, "were needed to give a new image to modern man whose potency of will is broken by a feeling of thousandfold dependency."[8] The individual is effectively nothing but "the limb of a mass," Bab argued, subject to influences he or she is helpless to control. The mass must always in the end be dominated by one person, the hero. Bab saw Matkowsky as that hero, indeed his biography is subtitled *Ein Heldensage* (*A Hero's Saga*). In view of the subsequent history of Germany—and Bab's book was published in 1932—the attraction Matkowsky held both for his audiences and actors can be seen to have dangerous implications. Retrospectively there now appears to be much justice in the opinion delivered by Theodore Fontane, who, on reviewing Matkowsky's guest appearances in Berlin before he joined the Royal Theatre, declared himself to be "anti-Matkowsky." Fontane did not deny the actor's power, acknowledging that his "manner of playing is superior in strong, external effects"[9] from which it was difficult to detach oneself. All the same, he found his acting too general and haphazard, and Matkowsky's roles like a kaleidoscope of colors arranged by chance, not characterizations worked out with accuracy and precision. Matkowsky's heroic image seems to have had little purpose and little direction beyond itself.

Bab provides detailed reconstructions of some of Matkowsky's most famous roles. As Karl Moor, he was able to give expression to the most elemental of emotions, ranging from determined, heavy anger at the beginning, through the most profound declaration of love for his homeland, to an extended outburst of despair as he sees his father near death. "Matkowsky screams, he screams almost for a minute. . . . He screams with utmost and final power, actually wails like an enraged animal. . . . Everyone feels . . . that this scream is a physical necessity, that it arises from the most complete experience of the situation. . . . This man screams simply not to suffocate!" (Bab, 221). After the tumultuous events at the end of the play, Matkowsky's Karl Moor sank into "a great, gruesome calm" (Bab, 224). His Macbeth was a figure of equal extremes, oscillating between periods of brooding introspection and outbursts of wild defiance, ending, predictably given Bab's thesis, as a hero who finally redeems himself by sheer bravery (see Figure 12). His Othello moved from a condition of relaxed confidence in his own strength to a single climax of demented hysteria during the oath scene with Iago. From then on he was quiet, unswervingly determined, only once erupting into anger, during the visit of the ambassadors. After the murder of Desdemona, he returned to the Othello of Act 1, "standing at the end once more as he stood before Brabantio, the general and hero full of restrained power, towering over everyone, and again a smile of superior mastery on his lips" (Bab, 232). But no Shakespearean role so suited his temperament as Coriolanus. Max Grube, perhaps putting

12. Adalbert Matkowsky as Macbeth. Reproduced by permission of Theatermuseum der Universität zu Köln.

too much faith in the supposed democratic instincts of the Berlin audiences, attributed Matkowsky's success in the role to his persuasively
human portrayal of the aristocrat, who, Grube speculated, should have
been inimical to their sentiments and instincts. Bab, however, found
the strength of his performance to be the extrahuman dimension he gave
the character and his revelation of the inner heart of the tragedy, which
is that though people are capable of being totally free, the world will
not allow them to live outside the bounds of society, as if *Coriolanus*
were a commentary on Bab's view of a world in which all individualism
is of necessity denied. Coriolanus's death once again asserted the heroic
man, representing as it did ''a demonic, a shattering, a suicidal triumph''
(Bab, 251).

The excitement Matkowsky aroused in his audience was caused partly
by his overwhelming physical and vocal powers, partly by his ability
to create within and around him a world that was complete to itself.
He projected an impression of ideal unity. In essence, he was a simple,
uncomplicated actor, whose work showed to best advantage in the
somewhat timeworn ambience of the Royal Theatre. This was not so,
however, with his greatest competitor for public attention, the Austrian
actor Josef Kainz, whose career, both as a standard-bearer for the new
and as guardian of the old, made him the most discussed actor in the
German theatre of his day.

JOSEF KAINZ

Josef Kainz was born in the Hungarian village of Wieselburg on 2
January 1858, the son of a petty official of the Habsburg state railways.
When he was eight years old, his family moved to Vienna, and soon
both he and his father, who had once had theatrical ambitions, were
habitués of the fourth gallery of the Burgtheater. There was no question
in either of their minds that Josef would become an actor. After appearing as an amateur at the Sulkowskytheater in the Viennese suburbs,
at the age of seventeen Kainz was hired as First Hero and Lover at the
City Theatre in Marburg (now Maribor, Yugoslavia), where in six
months he learned over fifty roles, including Mortimer in *Maria Stuart*
and Goethe's Faust. In July 1876, he became a member of the Leipzig

Portions of the section on Josef Kainz in this chapter appeared earlier as Simon Williams, ''Josef Kainz: A Reassessment,'' *Theatre Research International*, 6, 3 (Autumn
1981), 195-216.

City Theatre, whose director August Förster was later to be instrumental in founding the Deutsches Theater and would briefly direct the Burgtheater. Förster recognized Kainz's unusual talents, despite his diminutive stature and awkward appearance, and, after the young actor's failure in the *Fach* of the Young Lover, gave him critical and popular acclaim by casting him as the grotesque but pathetic hunchback in Coppée's *Violinmaker of Cremona*.

Kainz left Leipzig in the summer of 1877 after differences with Förster, to be hired at once by the Meiningen company. Here he stayed for three years, studying plays under the benign guidance of the duke and his wife, and reading widely in various areas of scholarship. As an actor, he became skilled at playing characters who revealed profound, often violent contradictions. Of special note were his Ferdinand in *Intrigue and Love* and the prince in *The Prince of Homburg*, which captured the interest, if not the instant admiration of critics in Berlin and Vienna. Wider fame of a sort came to him between 1880 and 1883 when, as a leading actor of the Munich Court Theatre, he was involved in a brief relationship with the fantastical Ludwig II. Kainz was the last in a long list of artists, beginning with Richard Wagner, through whom Ludwig attempted to live out his luxuriant and morbidly romantic visions.

The turning point in Kainz's career came when he was hired as a member of the new Deutsches Theater in Berlin. On 9 and 10 November 1883, his passionate rendering of the lead role in Schiller's *Don Carlos* instantly established him as one of the foremost German actors of the new realism. "The last hour of the Weimar style had struck," wrote Otto Brahm, "and the advancing realism was preparing to shatter the old rules of Goethe."[10] This Carlos was one of the landmarks of the time. As Paul Schlenther later wrote, "In my early memories of the stage, Kainz's Carlos stands close to Salvini's Macbeth, Rossi's Othello, Booth's Hamlet and Niemann's Florestan.... [Kainz] had set right a great poet, had demonstrated the human reality behind Schiller's ideal figure."[11] For the next sixteen years, until 1899, Kainz dominated Berlin from the stage of the Deutsches Theater, with the exception of a break of two and a half years between 1890 and 1892, when he was forced to tour both in Germany and the United States, as the *Deutsches Bühnenverein* banned him from their theatres due to a contract dispute with Ludwig Barnay. But this did little to tarnish his image. Few actors have been so idolized. His delicately aristocratic good looks assured him rapturous popular acclaim, while his ability to renovate the classics by presenting characters within them as if they were modern people aroused intense and sustained critical interest.

Despite his reputation as the epitome of "modern man," Kainz's sights were set firmly upon the Burgtheater. When Mitterwurzer died, Burckhard had to look for a replacement. Kainz was the natural choice. After two guest appearances in 1897 and 1898, which were nothing less than sensational, Kainz became a permanent member of the Burgtheater in 1899. These were not, however, the happiest of years. Tensions developed between the actor and Burckhard's successor, Paul Schlenther, who was unwilling to allow Kainz the position of *Regisseur* for which he was ambitious. Furthermore, although the repertoire of the theatre was tailored primarily to suit Kainz's interests, there was a distinctly virtuosic element in his personality that at times strained his relationship with the ensemble, so he spent several months each year touring. Then, although in appearance and vocal quality Kainz seemed to be the paragon of the Burgtheater actor, against the tradition of the theatre, like Mitterwurzer, he highlighted contradictory elements within his characters. Hermann Bahr wrote of these years as a dark period in Kainz's career, when his interpretations became increasingly pessimistic, with a focus on the forces of evil and the will to power that can motivate characters' actions. If this was so, it was due no doubt to Kainz's increasing ill health through the growth of stomach cancer. This led to his early death on 22 September 1910.

Kainz was celebrated because he was "modern," but precisely *how* he was "modern" is not easy to establish. Mainly this is because his career spanned precisely the time in which idealist acting, both of the Weimar and Burgtheater kind, was being undermined by the antithetical modernist movements of naturalism and impressionism. Kainz appeared to typify both the modernist styles, but the confident manner in which he bore himself on stage and his attention to the musicality of language suggested he also recognized the values of the old idealists, even if he did not copy literally their speech and physical mannerisms. Kainz's career is truly a watershed in the history of German acting.

Otto Brahm, who was associated with Kainz from 1883 on, first as critic, then as director, always as loyal friend, found Kainz "modern" because he brought a new sense of reality to the classics, refusing to rely on traditional gestures and attitudes.

Kainz was the first to fulfil the demands of modern art in our tragedy—this is his great, his historic merit. Far from all empty doctrine, entirely out of his own nature, out of a nervous, modern nature, he grasped the problems of Schiller and Shakespeare, and filled them once again with the warm blood of life. Whatever had become dry tradition, routine, and declamation, he shaped with a realistic directness, which was lost in the others; they were fumbling epigones, he an impudent modern. (Brahm, 134)

As a director, Brahm was constantly concerned to break down the barriers between art and life; for him even the stylistically most artificial of the classics should be done realistically. From his description, it would seem that Kainz was ideal for this purpose. It suggests he approached his roles with a naturalist's grasp, searching for psychological detail and interpreting them from the basis of his own experience and observation. For many of his contemporaries, a notable feature of Kainz's acting was his ability to communicate the inner life of his characters, leaving no aspect of personality hidden, no obscure corner unexplored. Indeed, for some, this thoroughness meant he lacked the aura of mystery that made the acting of the older idealist schools so attractive. To unsympathetic critics, he was incapable of maintaining "pure poetic construction. . . . Herr Kainz, the pioneering advocate of an ultra-modern dramatic art does not bother to exercise an ennobling influence on the spectator."[12] Instead he was concerned only with "interesting patterns of pathology" (Wahr, 31).

In practice, however, Brahm and Kainz did not always agree. When Brahm took over the Deutsches Theater in June 1894, he attempted to produce the classics naturalistically. He began with *Intrigue and Love,* with Kainz playing Wurm. The production was a failure, the raw conflict at the heart of the play was dampened, and the shrill note of protest went unheard. But the muted tones and grey colors that were characteristic of Brahm's naturalism became the mark of the company. This lead to differences between Brahm, who was worried by Kainz's increasing attention to musicality and technique, and Kainz, who argued that naturalists "can only copy because they are lacking in creative imagination."[13] Also, Kainz's stage presence worked against the spirit of the naturalist ensemble. Helene Richter has described how through him the threads of the play came together, how he was the driving force of the action so that everyone else on stage stood in relationship to him. Inevitably, he seemed to stand at the top of the hierarchy, not as just one member of a company. As if to highlight this eminence, he maintained an aristocratic demeanor, regardless of the material. This was typified by his refusal, while playing Old Hilse in Hauptmann's *Die Weber* (*The Weavers*), to remove from his finger a ring given him by Ludwig II.

The increasing refinement of Kainz's acting, attributable in part to the influence on him of the Italian virtuoso Tomasso Salvini (1829–1915), who often appeared in Berlin, suggests he might be identified with the impressionist tendencies of the turn-of-the-century theatre. Almost all descriptions of his acting include somewhere the term "nervous"—Kainz's acting was the "most characteristic expression of his age, the period of nervous individualism that stressed the ego";[14] "he was the actor of "nervous impressionism" (Martersteig, 667). Naturally, such attributes call up memories of Ludwig Devrient. But Kainz, although capable of "demonic" passages, had a different appeal from the romantic actor. His technique was part of this appeal. He could exercise control over each muscle of his body with a degree of expertise normally associated with the Oriental actor, so making his body "a delicate barometer of passion."[15] In addition, he had built his originally mediocre voice into a formidably flexible instrument. His delivery could be extremely rapid; for example he only needed thirty-three seconds to deliver with complete clarity the "glove" speech from Act 1 of *The Prince of Homburg,* a passage of twenty lines that normally took actors twice as long. Furthermore he could extract musical tones from German in a way hitherto unequalled. His voice "inundated the German language with a splendor, brought to it a glitter and sparkle, the like of which had never been known before."[16] This virtuosity meant that Kainz could communicate with ease infinitesimal fluctuations of mood. He could, in the words of Siegfried Jacobsohn, "illuminate with his sensitive receptiveness the fleeting palpitations of the modern soul."[17] This, of course, limited the roles available to him. In the classics Jacobsohn felt he was best suited to portraying "pallid, romance princes, fickle, unmannerly boys, passionate and lightly restrained Renaissance youths," figures in whom the flow of emotion was scarcely covered, delicate souls whose emotional equilibrium could be displaced by the slightest shock, whose gestures were suggestions of mood rather than expressions of deep-seated emotion.

While Kainz's ability to embody new styles of acting made him the center of interest in the theatre, he himself rejected any identification with trends. With sentiments that recall Schröder, Ludwig Devrient, and Mitterwurzer, he claimed to approach each role "as part of an organic whole that is complete in itself'' (Kainz, 31). Like them, the only external consideration he would take into account was the avoidance of anything traditional in his interpretation. "Tradition," he wrote, "is the broad comfortable thoroughfare along which the great host of mediocrities noisily crowd" (Kainz, 31). Slotting Kainz into one of the characteristic styles of the early modernist theatre, or placing him close to one of the polar points of nineteenth-century acting clearly deprives any account of him of a crucial dimension.

This extra dimension is best described as the ostensible placement of the actor's personality as an interpretative instrument at the center of performance, so that he is of equal interest to the character and the play. Felix Salten, describing an evening at the Burgtheater when Kainz played Goethe's Tasso, identified it as follows. "Something wonderful happened on this evening. One witnessed an actor elevated to genuine creative power. There were intermediate spaces. There was Tasso and there was Kainz and there was Goethe and one could see how the living mediator connected with both the others, how he found the veins that once went from the poet to his work, how once again he let fresh blood flow, and again let them pulsate" (Salten, 152). Elsewhere Salten referred to this as a deliberate interpretative strategy. He found Kainz's ability to associate entities whose separation is problematic made him into a genuine artist. "Mitterwurzer was the born actor. Kainz was the born artist who became an actor" (Salten, 161). Other critics felt a distinct personal statement in all that Kainz did on stage. Oscar Fontana wrote that everything he did "was always a hymn to the joy of life,"[18] while Hermann Bang, the Danish novelist, who followed Kainz throughout his career, sensed that he struggled with his roles, as if he were not entirely at ease with them. In doing so he appeared to damage them. "In a certain sense he inflicts injuries upon [the figures he portrays], as he forces them to bend to a conception and a rhythm that are foreign to them. But while he violates them, he invests them with his *own* life. And suddenly the audience discovers in the old classics their own way of thinking."[19] This conscious distortion and critical approach to character were not, of course, entirely new. Seydelmann had often been accused of twisting the character to his own view and of not respecting the assumed intentions of the playwright. Negative comments had also been made on Mitterwurzer's tendency to stand above the character, despite Salten's assertion that he was a "born actor." But with Kainz such an approach was accepted. In the meeting between the actor and his role, the actor's personality did not need to be submerged within the role, as was the conventional assumption of acting. Instead, the personality could remain defined, inviolate, and the actor's intepretation be regarded as a critique of the role or, at times, as an exposition of a philosophy upon which the role cast light. The actor could stand alone, confident in his status, confronting the audience with his interpretation rather than wooing their sympathies or adopting conventional poses that deprived both him and his role of distinction and singularity.

Why Kainz succeeded in gaining acceptance for such acting can be attributed in part to the identity many saw between the attitudes he adopted on stage and certain attitudes expressed in the writings of Friedrich Nietzsche, which, by the turn of the century, were being widely and enthusiastically read. Joseph Handl claims that, in the final years of his life, Kainz's work was grounded in Nietzsche. The extra dimension Handl describes in his acting was the struggle to rise above the role to make a statement of absolute truth that might be neither "beautiful" nor persuasive but was far beyond the mundane truths of life. "Those who saw Kainz could never forget that over the cold, often meaninglessly strange truth that freezes the heart, there arose a purer and more beautiful truth of art."[20] Handl does not continue by defining what he means by the "truth of art," but what does emerge from his writing is the image of Kainz the artist struggling to free himself from the imprisonment of crass matter. Here the connection with Nietzsche can be made. Although Alfred Kerr in a famous epitaph on Kainz referred to him as "Dionysus from Austria,"[21] the actor should not be conceived of as one who, Dionysus-like, swept away his audience by seizing on their emotions and intoxicating them with beautiful sound. Instead, Kainz's acting referred more to the Apollonian elements of Nietzsche's thinking, to writings such as *Also sprach Zarathustra,* in which the values of form, clarity, and graceful yet disdainful domination were centered in the figure of Zarathustra, the precursor of the *Übermensch.*

Hermann Bahr's enthusiastic portrayals of Kainz suggest there was much in common between the actor's Olympian stage presence and the supreme detachment of Nietzsche's prophet. Bahr saw in Kainz the soul of healthy man triumphing over the materialism, compromises, and common meanness of heart which, in Bahr's opinion, typified the life of the bourgeosie for whom Kainz played. His acting, Bahr insisted, was a challenge to a culture in which art was merely comfortable recreation, in which the forms of the past were worshipped solely for their external beauty, not for any truths they may originally have embodied. Kainz, Bahr claimed, not only took those forms and filled them with new life, he also used them to express his distaste for the world. He felt Kainz did not act to entertain an audience, nor even to interpret a dramatist's text. Rather, he acted because only on stage could he achieve fulfilment. "In this world of taxes and trash, there was no place for the sentiments, perceptions, desires, moods, and wishes . . . of his naturally noble nature" (Bahr, 302). By the time Kainz had reached the Burgtheater, Bahr saw him as an iconoclast, pouring forth his scorn upon the world in torrents of "burning ice"!

Bahr was never the most objective of critics; more than most he idealized his heroes out of proportion to the world around them, often using them as propaganda for his own artistic passions. But, in the case of Kainz, he was not alone. While not all writers felt as acute a degree of scorn in Kainz's acting, many recognized its superhuman qualities. Among them, not surprisingly, was Julius Bab, who found that he stood for all that was regenerative in Nietzsche's thought. Kainz, Bab wrote, portrayed the sufferings of contemporary humanity, which found itself a helpless victim of natural forces with no guiding absolutes. But he also demonstrated how those forces could be overcome, so the comfort he offered meant that he was a figure of health in a post-Darwinian world. "[Kainz's] strength dignifies and explains our suffering."[22] Bab described Kainz as an energizer of audiences, as after seeing him, they left the theatre more confident and more willing to face life without fear.

Kainz's technical prowess added to the Zarathustran image. Critic after critic marvelled at his easy ability to dominate the stage and at the illusion he created, as the role developed, of gaining ever-increasing control over his physical and vocal resources, the impact of such control being intensified by his comparative smallness. Furthermore, his finely formed features, which never seemed to age, gave him the aura of perpetual youth. Perhaps the way in which Kainz combined delicacy and lightness with powerful postures of resistance in order to create the illusion of mastery over the physical world was best described by Hugo von Hofmannsthal in his memorial poem to the actor.

Wie er blieb!
Wie königlich er standhielt! Wie er schmal,
gleich einem Knaben, stand! O kleine Hand
voll Kraft, o kleines Haupt auf feinen Schultern,
o vogelhaftes Auge, das verschmähte
jung oder alt zu sein, schlafloses Aug,
o Aug des Sperbers, der auch vor der Sonne
den Blick nicht niederschlägt, o kühnen Aug,
das beiderlei Abgrund gemessen hat,
des Leben wie des Todes—Aug der Boten!
O Bote aller Boten, Geist! Du Geist.[23]

[How he stood fast! The royal way in which he resisted! How,
small like a boy, he stood! Oh small hand, full of power, oh small
head on delicate shoulders, oh bird-like eye, that disdains to be
young or old, sleepless eye, oh eye of the sparrowhawk, that does
not even cast down its look before the sun, oh daring eye, which
has measured the precipice both of life and death—eye of the
messengers! Oh, messenger of all messengers, Spirit! You Spirit!]

Although the manner in which Kainz articulated his individuality on
stage was new, and although the Nietzschean terminology used to describe it gave him a distinctly "modern" character, the values of his
acting were not at all unfamiliar to his audiences. While he typified the
present, he recalled the past. Otto Brahm, after seeing his 1883 Don
Carlos, may well have claimed that with Kainz the predominance of
the Weimar style was destroyed. But later, as the actor grew to maturity,
he revived the spirit of that style. Though Kainz never concerned himself
with mastering Goethe's "Rules," he, more than any other actor of the
nineteenth century, realized most fully the bouyancy and grace Goethe
felt was the essence of true acting but was so rarely achieved by anyone.
For Kainz, the world was to be played with, it was not imprisoning
matter. Like Goethe's actor of genius, he had the ability to determine
species of feeling, explaining them to his audience, always presenting
them as part of a harmonious whole. In Kainz, the spirit, if not the
letter of Weimar acting was fulfilled.

Kainz's repertoire in both classic and modern drama was not as
extensive as those of his predecessors. Heavy roles such as Wallenstein,
Lear, or King Philip did not attract him, or he died too young to try
them. In general, he played lighter, more youthful figures, ones who
were conventionally considered to be exemplars of determining forces,

either social or psychological. Kainz, however, reversed directly such assumptions, representing the character as achieving victory over himself and the world. Technical factors in his interpretations were sharp contrasts and sudden reversals, while contours were unusually firm and individual. Furthermore, he was always intensely deliberate so that no effect appeared to be haphazard but was executed with an eye to theatrical impact. Kainz never ingratiated himself by adopting a pleasing manner. As Helene Richter observed, "His youthful figures impressed more through sharp freshness than through charm, his men were more imposing, more fascinating than full of feeling, his heroes aroused more wonder than heartbreak."[24]

Romeo was one of his early roles, first played in Munich in 1880, remaining in his repertoire for the rest of his career (see Figure 13). Initially, he portrayed sexual passion as a debilitating force, but as he grew older that disappeared. His Romeo always began as a callow young man, one who acted out "a parody of love with empty exaggerations and quibblings,"[25] an egoist, playing with appearances. But as soon as he met Juliet, all was changed. After ambling past her negligently, he turned, caught sight of her, and reacted as if struck by a blow. At once he was filled with impetuosity and ardor, and, on discovering she was the daughter of his family's enemy, was jubilant; this was just one more obstacle to overcome, nothing more. The scenes of courtship, marriage, and consummation were remarkable for the sense of movement and inner change, though exactitude was still a dominant element in Kainz's acting. He achieved wonders of athleticism in the balcony scene, springing to the balustrade "like a wanton boy who wishes to steal ripe fruit hanging too high on the tree" (Gregori, 92). In Friar Lawrence's cell before the marriage, Romeo and Juliet were incapable of keeping their hands off each other, though the audience was distanced by a contrived delicacy of gesture.

The through-line of Kainz's Romeo was growth, from unripe youth to vigorous lover, then in the last act to mature hero. The second transition was sudden. As Romeo met Balthazar in Mantua, it was clear all was not well in Verona. His questions became "slower, lighter, more unsure, anxious" (Gregori, 93). After his fears had been confirmed, he paused, then rising slowly to his feet, on the words *"Ich biet' euch Trotz ihr Sterne!"* ("Then I defy you stars"), this Romeo was transformed into a hero at the moment of *anagnorisis*. The contrast to the earlier figure was electrifying. In the place of the confident young

13. Josef Kainz as Romeo. Reproduced by permission of Theatermuseum der Universität zu Köln.

lover now stood "a fieldmarshal giving strict orders amidst the pow-
dersmoke" (Gregori, 93). In the scene with the apothecary, Kainz
moved from monumental defiance to stoic acceptance and, with a smile,
often his hallmark for the recognition of destiny, he saw the necessity
for his death. At the end, taking his cue from his own lines "How oft
when men are at the point of death / Have they been happy," he died
willingly, completely master of himself.

Kainz's Romeo was a strong contrast to the lachrymose performances
of the role current at the time. He provided a stronger through-line and
made of Romeo a more substantial and aggressive young man. This
strength he brought to the lead role of Alfons in Grillparzer's *Jüdin von
Toledo* (*The Jewess of Toledo*), so establishing one of Grillparzer's
major plays firmly in the repertoire for the first time, as he managed to
show how Alfons's mastery as a ruler is achieved through his ability
to overcome his sexual immaturity. As with Romeo, Kainz played the
role for growth.

While Emmerich Robert of the Burgtheater had played Alfons as a
man "sickly with displeasure, phlegmatic to the last thread of his
being,"[26] Kainz began and ended brightly. He never became servant
of his passion for Rahel, his deep absorption in her being balanced by
his awareness as to how ephemeral his feelings were. In fact "fulfilment
was already satiation for Alfons."[27] To audiences of the time, his
offhand attitude toward Rahel did not seem offensive. No doubt it added
to Kainz's superhuman image, as did the dumb play in Act 3 when,
after contemplating Rahel with supreme detachment, Kainz "suddenly
springs up, seized by desire, and rushes across the stage . . . as if he
wants to ravish her—*while imperceptibly shrugging his shoulders*"
(Bang, 128).The groundwork established during the first three acts made
the last two acts not especially difficult for Kainz, as he had shown
how, despite Alfons's infatuation, his kingliness remains intact. Consequently, in the long monologue of Act 4, Kainz was able to concentrate
on charting the fluctuations in Alfons's psyche as he tries to reconcile
the demands of political necessity and erotic desire. It was his failure
to do this, rather than any arbitrary kingly anger, that motivated his
fury against the vassals who had forgotten their loyalty. The last act,
when Alfons confronts Rahel's corpse, normally required such a brutal
reversal of attitude that it eluded most actors. But Kainz made it credible
by having Alfons's physical disgust change into mental disgust against
both Rahel and his past self, logically so as throughout he had empha-

sized the purely physical nature of his attraction. Once again Alfons took on "the whole, unbroken strength of hero and ruler" (Richter, *Kainz,* 128). It was an integral and consistent performance, establishing Alfons as one of Grillparzer's psychologically richest characters.

Hamlet was among Kainz's most celebrated roles (see Figure 14). He first played it at the Ostendtheater in Berlin in 1891, during his exclusion from the stages of the *Deutsches Bühnenverein,* and then acted it regularly through to 1909. So admired was his interpretation that the last time he performed it in Berlin, in a run of eight performances at the Neues Schauspielhaus in January and February 1909, a professor of psychology from Zurich watched every performance and wrote a 276-page book in which Kainz's performance is reconstructed line by line, gesture by gesture.[28] Once again the importance of his interpretation lay in the clarity he brought to the role. "His acting," wrote Ludwig Speidel when he first performed the role at the Burgtheater, "was like a polemic against the countless commentaries on Hamlet that present him as a perpetually impenetrable wall."[29] He was not the brooding melancholic who normally passed for Hamlet on the German stage, nor Emil Devrient's "wistful child of moonlight." Instead his approach to the role was reminiscent of Wolff and Sonnenthal, though with crucial differences.

Like Wolff and Sonnenthal, Kainz's Hamlet was initially an uncomplicated young man with noble instincts who finds himself, half against his will, fighting against the corrupt spirit of the time and society in which he has grown up. However, unlike his predecessors, the charge laid upon him to murder his uncle revealed a previously unsuspected breach in his character, between a raw, Viking-like temperament that was atavistic in its demands to wreak revenge on Claudius and a more inward, self-reflective nature belonging to the Wittenberg scholar. For most of the play Kainz represented Hamlet as attempting to reconcile these two contradictory elements, and to good effect, as the mighty outburst of horror and triumph after he had heard of his father's death from the Ghost should, like critics had felt with Dawison, have instantly driven him to murder the king. But his more contemplative nature held him back. In sustaining the inner conflict, Kainz managed to give unity to the role, the soliloquies were treated as passages in which he attempted to work out the division in himself, while his haughtily, dismissive conduct toward Polonius, Rosencrantz, and Guildenstern was motivated by the lack of importance such figures had in relation to his mental

14. Josef Kainz as Hamlet. Reproduced by permission of Theatermuseum der Universität zu Köln.

struggle. There were moments in which he allowed his vehemence to break through his surface coldness or false geniality, as at the end of his scene with Ophelia, when he uttered a bitter outburst of disgust, for he realized by a movement of the curtain that they had been overheard. He also let forth a great cry of revenge and victory as Claudius revealed his guilt during the play scene. But, as the action progressed, he came to reconcile the opposition within himself, thereby becoming filled with hard determination. Richter noticed that the last phases of the play were marked by a new tension between his sense of what needed to be done and his fear that he was not strong enough to carry it through. But at the end he triumphed over any weakness, and in a characteristically Kainzian manner, this Hamlet died smiling, with "a still, pure, fatalistic serenity of soul."[30]

Such serenity also marked the final moments of his Richard II, which he first played at the Burgtheater in 1901. As with Romeo and Alfons, he gave a man who grew rather than diminished in stature. Initially his king was supremely indifferent to those around him, a totally self-indulgent, self-pitying creature. When he heard of Bolingbroke's invasion, however, he did not collapse into lamentations, but was seized by megalomania of almost monstrous proportions in which the prevalent tone was bitter scorn for those around him. Once Richard's egoism was opposed, it turned into vigorous resistance. In the sequence of humiliating events leading through the abdication to his death, Kainz's Richard was sustained by a burning sense of injustice. He was not melancholy, but angry; he wept few tears, but was possessed by withering disgust. His earlier self-centeredness turned into steadfast assurance in the face of overwhelming opposition. In the dungeon scene, this led to a process of stringent self-reckoning. When Richard died, Kainz left his audience with the impression that the king had achieved a noble balance and secure inner peace.

Kainz's greatest role was one of his last, the lead in Goethe's *Torquato Tasso*. Throughout the nineteenth century, the play had normally been considered undramatic due to its lack of action and its complex characterization. But Kainz, by revealing a sharp tension and clear line of development in the central character, established the play firmly in the repertoire. He rejected the idea of Tasso as a pale visionary. "Tasso is *the* genius," he wrote. "Genius is never tragic, but the princess is. She builds a world for herself, and when this collapses, she is completely broken" (Kainz, 64). Defeat, therefore, became a side issue, the main

action became the struggle of an artist to determine his originally confused response to a world that is indifferent to him, then to come to
terms with that world in a way that does not compromise him.

From the very start, Kainz's Tasso was a malcontent whose black
silk costume contrasted sharply with the pastel-shaded, pastoral setting
(see Figure 15), whose surliness and resentment against the Ferrarese
aristocracy was tempered neither by his being crowned by a laurel wreath
nor by his ability to escape from the world around him into spheres of
the imagination. The only warm contact he had with the court was
through the princess, with whom in Act 2 he conversed in a brighter
vein, filled with energy. The following monologue, the rebuff by Antonio, and the challenge were impelled by the life generated in the scene
with the princess, allowing for a mighty climax without shrillness or
exaggeration. In Act 4, Tasso reappeared, pale and pain-wracked. Bitterness overwhelmed him, first in the scene with Lenore, where he
indulged in vitriolic outbursts against his enemies real or imagined, then
in the interview with Antonio, where his anger and impatience grew
beneath his composure, until they burst out in the final monologue as
he broke down under the influence of seemingly insufferable pain.

Act 5 was Kainz's masterpiece. He entered composed, was distant
with the prince, and offended by the suggestion that he was ill; on the
contrary, he distinctly asserted his healthiness. In the next scene with
the princess, he was reinvigorated with the energy and enthusiasm of
Act 2, but it was stronger. The speech on his imaginary sequestration
in one of the prince's castles was delivered very rapidly, as if to emphasize the phantasmal nature of his dream, while the climax as he
declared his love and embraced the princess was so ecstatic he seemed
to lose all sense of reality. After the princess's hasty departure, there
seemed to be little chance of Kainz maintaining the high level of excitement, but, without a pause, he launched into the final scene with
Antonio by flinging himself to the ground in yet another frenzied outburst. From this, he built to a violent denunciation of the world that
had denied him the fulfilment of happiness, a climax of hatred that
seemed, literally, to be pathological. Then came the unexpected, crown-
ing moment of his performance. This paroxysm, far from crippling the
poet, had purged him. Suddenly Tasso became quiet and, with the words
"Gab mir ein Gott zu sagen, wie ich leide" (God gave me a voice to
say how I suffer"), he realized the strength suffering had given him.
Then came the famous final speech, but it was not delivered close to

15. Josef Kainz as Tasso. Reproduced by permission of Theatermuseum der Universität zu Köln.

Antonio. Instead, after an unashamedly theatrical move down to the footlights, the last two lines were delivered directly to the audience—*"So klammert sich der Schiffer endlich noch / Am Felsen fest, an dem er scheitern sollte"* ("So at last the sailor clings fast to the rock on which he would have foundered"). The rock to which Tasso clung was not Antonio, but the world itself, as the clear, confident tones of Kainz's voice unambiguously indicated. Tasso would go on to conquer the world and achieve greatness as an artist.

If Matkowsky provided audiences with an ideal image of individuals whose will, thought, and instincts were at one with each other, Kainz went further. He demonstrated the process by which such unity could come about. While Matkowsky served mainly to provide images of an imaginary lost age of romantic heroism, Kainz, through regenerating the spirit of idealist acting, also provided the German theatre with a new vigor. He did this not simply by transferring styles of acting developed in the performance of new plays to familiar classics, but also by developing the status of the actor as an independent, creative contributor who is not just an obedient servant of the playwright. Through Kainz, audiences experienced a clash between the modern experience of the actor and the historical milieu of the play he was acting in. This may frequently have seemed to distort the original purpose of the playwright, and few would claim that Kainz gave "definitive" interpretations. Indeed, his whole approach to acting challenged the very concept of "definitiveness." But in his so doing, the eminence of the German actor as an independent artist reached its zenith.

NOTES

1. Max Martersteig, *Das deutsche Theater im 19. Jahrhundert* (Leipzig: Breitkopf & Härtel, 1904), 632.

2. Adolf L'Arronge, *Deutsches Theater und deutsche Schauspielkunst* (Berlin: Concordia, 1896), 28.

3. Emanuel Reicher quoted in Heinrich Braulich, *Max Reinhardt* (Berlin: Henschel, 1969), 22.

4. Max Grube, *Adalbert Matkowsky* (Berlin: Paetel, 1909), 13.

5. Ludwig Barnay, *Erinnerungen* (Berlin: Henschel, 1951), 369.

6. Eugen Zabel, "Adalbert Matkowsky," *Bühne und Welt* I, 1 (1898), 560.

7. Maximilian Harden, *Köpfe*, 22d ed. (Berlin: Reiss, 1910), 455.

8. Julius Bab, *Matkowsky* (Berlin: Oesterheld, 1932), 11.

9. Theodore Fontane, *Schriften und Glossen zur Europäischen Literatur*, ed. Werner Weber, Klassik der Kritik (Zurich & Stuttgart, 1965), I, 267.

10. Otto Brahm, *Theater, Dramatiker, Schauspieler*, ed. Hugo Fetting (Berlin: Henschel, 1961), 139.

11. Paul Schlenther, *Theater im 19. Jahrhundert,* ed. Hans Knudsen, SGT 40 (Berlin: VGT, 1930), 151.

12. Kuhnhold Wahr, *Josef Kainz: Kritische Blitze eines forschenden Zuschauers* (Berlin: Hettler, 1887), 37.

13. Erich Kober, *Josef Kainz: Mensch unter Masken* (Vienna: Neff, 1948), 227.

14. Ernst Stahl, *Shakespeare und das deutsche Theater* (Stuttgart: Kohlhammer, 1947), 525.

15. *Kainz: Ein Brevier,* ed. Marie Mautner-Kahlbeck (Vienna: Österreichische Staatsdruckerei, 1953), 46.

16. Felix Salten, *Gestalten und Erscheinungen* (Berlin: Fischer, 1913), 151.

17. Quoted in Hermann Bahr, *Essays,* ed. Heinz Kindermann (Vienna: Bauer, 1962), 305.

18. Oscar Maurus Fontana, *Wiener Schauspieler* (Vienna: Amandus, 1948), 45.

19. Hermann Bang, *Josef Kainz* (Berlin: Bondy, 1910), 8.

20. Joseph Handl, *Schauspieler des Burgtheaters* (Vienna & Frankfurt-am-Main: Humboldt, 1955), 101.

21. Alfred Kerr, *Das Welt in Drama,* ed. Gerhard F. Hering, 2d ed. (Cologne: Kiepenhauer & Witsch, 1964), 359.

22. Julius Bab, *Was ist uns Kainz?* (Berlin & Leipzig: Saemann, n.d.), 10.

23. Hugo von Hofmannsthal, "Verse zum Gedächtnis des Schauspielers Josef Kainz," *Gedichte und lyrische Dramen in Gesammelte Werke in zwölf Einzelausgaben* (Stockholm: Bermann-Fischer, 1946), 48.

24. Helene Richter, *Schauspieler-Charakteristiken,* TF 27 (Leipzig & Hamburg: Voss, 1914), 61.

25. Ferdinand Gregori, "Josef Kainz: Romeo," *Jahrbuch der deutschen Shakespeare-Gesellschaft* 40 (1904), 90.

26. A. Lindner quoted in Norbert Fuerst, *Grillparzer auf der Bühne* (Vienna & Munich: Manutius, 1958), 215.

27. Helene Richter, *Kainz* (Vienna & Leipzig: Speidel, 1931), 127.

28. Konrad Falke, *Kainz als Hamlet: Ein Abend im Theater* (Zurich: Rascher, 1911).

29. Ludwig Speidel in *Kainz: Gedenkbuch,* ed. Benno Deutsch (Vienna: Frisch, n.d.[1924]), 38.

30. *Die Schaubühne,* 5, 1 (1909), 164.

Chapter 7

INTO THE TWENTIETH CENTURY

Two days before he died, Kainz was appointed *Regisseur* in the Burg-theater. It was a position he had been coveting for several years and one he could never fill. Kainz's desire gradually to shift from performance to stage direction was a recognition of fundamental changes in the structure by which artistic decisions in the theatre were being made. In the nineteenth century, those actors not in the few companies that cultivated the ensemble were normally free to give the roles in the way they chose, with the *Regisseur* serving mainly as coordinator for the physical arrangements of the performance. The rise of the professional stage director toward the end of the nineteenth century challenged the actor's preeminence, and did so successfully. Although the actor did not lose the interest of audiences, the most prominent creative artists in the German theatre in the first half of the twentieth century have been directors—Max Reinhardt, Leopold Jessner, Bertolt Brecht, Erwin Piscator. Actors have most frequently earned their reputation as members of a director's ensemble, less as artists in their own right. So, while Kainz on stage appeared to his contemporaries as the embodiment of "modern man," his professional and artistic status was of a passing age.

The shifting of artistic responsibility to the stage director has tended to deprive the polarity described in this book of much of its potency. Directors on the whole like to see a sameness of approach among their actors, both within a production and from one production to another. But it has not entirely disappeared. The extreme emotionalism of expressionist acting can be seen as an extension of the romantic-realistic approach to acting, while Brecht's "alienated" acting, cultivated between the 1920s and 1950s, can be regarded either as a continuation of the idealist tradition or, more interestingly, especially in the light of one of those actors between the schools, Karl Seydelmann, as an attempt to combine the two poles. In Brecht's theory, the actor is expected both to realize the role and to stand outside it. The widespread influence of Brecht's ideas about acting and theatre in general has led to a conception of theatre radically different from that by which actors from Ekhof to Kainz performed. No longer does the theatre just reflect life in a more or less heightened style, it also keeps the audience aware of the very means of reflection. In this self-conscious theatre, acting becomes self-conscious, and the actor uses not only the role but style itself as his subject matter.

This can lead to exciting theatre, as was demonstrated, for example, in a recent production of *Othello* at the Schillertheater in Berlin, first staged in June 1982. In set design, costume, and direction the production was entirely presentational, no specific time or period being established. A particular contrast was established in the two lead actors' interpretations of their roles. Iago, played by Boy Gobert, who spent several years at the Burgtheater, was a model of negligent elegance, a thoroughly charming, just slightly unsavory philanderer. Little in his appearance or character would seem to justify a close bond between him and Othello, played by Peter Roggisch as a very dark-skinned black, at times a clown, at times proletarian, rarely capable of understanding himself or of controlling the powerful promptings of his instinct. The severe contrast between the two actors was unsettling, as the natural flow of trust that extends from Othello to Iago and generates the action was difficult for an audience member to feel. The two men appeared worlds unto themselves. However, a surrogate tension grew between them as compelling as that suggested by Shakespeare's text. In the place of men with conflicting or complementary values and personalities emerged actors with contradictory styles. The nonchalant, raffish Iago was a barely travestied version of the elegant man-of-the-world of the nineteenth-century stage, a Sonnenthal *manqué,* while Othello, whose paroxysms with Desdemona reached peaks of excruciating pain, was one totally bewildered. This rendering of Othello was strikingly reminiscent of the non-idealist acting of an earlier period. The context of the actors' performances and the artifice with which the contrast was established, pointing clearly to the actors themselves as objects of interest, created a rich ambiguity that then could be read back into the text. After all, Iago is conventionally thought of as the "demonic" figure, while Othello, despite his wildness, normally begins and ends a man self-possessed and noble. By making acting style the subject of interest, new perspectives were thrown upon the play and textual ambiguities highlighted.

Of course not all theatre in Germany is as self-conscious as that influenced by the ideas of Brecht and, more recently, of Peter Handke. More traditional production approaches, growing from the illusionism of the nineteenth century, can still be seen. Although few actors stand out as prominently as the nineteenth-century virtuoso, ensemble work being almost universally assumed, vestiges of the old polarity can still be seen. Some modern actors have been directly linked to past traditions. The most famous of all, Gustav Gründgens, has frequently been described as the continuer of the idealist school, comparisons being drawn above all to Iffland. Meanwhile, cinema-goers who have seen the films of Werner Herzog might, in the haunted stare of Klaus Kinski, be reminded of the equally haunted Ludwig Devrient. At the Burgtheater, tradition is far from dead. The uniformity of approach that Laube first introduced into the company has survived, despite considerable modifications brought about in the interests of deeper characterization, introduced partly through the contributions of Mitterwurzer and Kainz. And in Vienna the spirit of Kainz is still potent, as talk can be heard of this or that actor being the latest purveyor of his particular style of acting.

Despite the changes brought about in the twentieth century, the polarity of the nineteenth can still be observed.

BIBLIOGRAPHIC ESSAY

Of all historians of the fine arts, the writer on acting is most dependent on secondary sources, due to the necessary absence of the primary source, the living actor on stage. In the descriptive passages of this book especially, almost every sentence could be referred back to one or several secondary sources. In order to avoid overloading the text with notes, I have acknowledged my sources in most cases only when quoting from them. In this essay, I outline the principle sources to which I have been indebted. I hope it will also provide those who wish to read further with a preliminary guide to the voluminous literature on German acting.

GENERAL

All historians of the German theatre are indebted to three standard works, W. H. Bruford's *Theatre, Drama, and Audience in Goethe's Germany* (London: Routledge & Kegan Paul, 1950), Heinz Kindermann's monumental *Theatergeschichte der Goethezeit* (Vienna: Bauer, 1948), and Max Martersteig's equally monumental *Deutsche Theater im 19. Jahrhundert* (Berlin: Breitkopf & Härtel, 1904). I have relied substantially on these books for background and in my discussion of the actors. An excellent, recent survey of the eighteenth-century theatre, Sybille Maurer-Schmoock, *Deutsches Theater im 18. Jahrhundert,* Studien zur deutschen Literatur 71 (Tübingen: Niemeyer, 1982), contains sections not only on theatrical life and conditions, but also on acting. Reference has also been made to the relevant volumes of Kindermann, *Theatergeschichte Europas* (Salzburg: Müller, 1957-1974) and to Marvin Carlson, *The German Stage in the Nineteenth Century* (Metuchen, N.J.: Scarecrow, 1972). In the absence of a comprehensive bibliography on the periods in question, bibliographies in Kindermann and Carlson are the most complete, though they are not exhaustive.

There are several general histories of acting. Among these, pride of place

must still go to Eduard Devrient's *Geschichte der deutschen Schauspielkunst.*
This has appeared in several editions, the later ones including material on actors
who lived after Devrient's death in 1876. The most recent edition came out in
1970 (Munich: Langen/Müller). I have used the 1905 edition (Berlin: Elsner).
No good modern history of acting exists, but reference has been made to Adolf
Winds's rather complex categorization of acting styles in *Der Schauspieler in
seiner Entwicklung vom Mysterien zum Kammerspiel* (Berlin: Schuster & Loeffler, 1919). Toby Cole and Helen Krich Chinoy include valuable material on
the eighteenth-century German actor in *Actors on Acting,* new rev. ed. (New
York: Crown, 1970), but unaccountably fail to do justice to the nineteenth-
century actor. Seydelmann, Mitterwurzer, and Kainz all wrote important essays;
without these, Cole and Chinoy's otherwise comprehensive anthology is incomplete. Concise biographies and pertinent comments on many important
actors can be found in the following volumes: Paul Landau, *Mimen: historische
Miniaturen* (Berlin: Reiss, 1912), Julius Bab, *Kränze der Mimen* (Emsdetten:
Lechte, 1954), Wolfgang Drews, *Die grossen Zauberer* (Vienna & Munich:
Donau, 1953), Friedrich Rosenthal, *Schauspieler aus deutscher Vergangenheit*
(Zurich: Amalthea, 1919), and Oskar Maurus Fontana, *Wiener Schauspieler*
(Vienna: Amandus, 1948). Monty Jacobs's superb anthology of reviews, *Deutsche
Schauspielkunst,* new ed., rev. Eva Stahl (Berlin: Henschel, 1954) has been an
indispensable source, providing a generous selection of descriptions of actors
in major classical roles. Good reference books on acting include Ludwig Eisenberg, *Grosses biographisches Lexikon der deutschen Bühne im
19. Jahrhundert* (Leipzig: List, 1903), Werner's *Gallerie von teutschen Schaus-
pielern und Schauspielerinnen nebst Johann Friedrich Schinks Zusätzen und
Berichtigungen,* ed. Richard Maria Werner, SGT 13 (Berlin: VGT, 1910), and
Philipp Stein, *Deutsche Schauspieler: Eine Bildnissammlung,* 2 vols. SGT 9
& 11 (Berlin: VGT, 1906 & 1908).

The newspaper and periodical literature is vast and would take a lifetime's
research to cover properly. The *Bibliographie der Zeitschriften des deutschen
Sprachgebiets bis 1900,* 3 vols. (Stuttgart: Hiersemann, 1969-1977) lists over
400 periodicals devoted to theatre alone, ranging from those that had a single
issue to such important series as Adolf Bäuerle's *Wiener Theaterzeitung* that
appeared regularly from 1806 to 1856, as did the later *Wiener Theater-Chronik*
from 1859 to 1884. The writings of the most important chroniclers and critics
of the theatre have been collected in various editions. These include Ludwig
Tieck, *Kritische Schriften,* 4 vols. (Leipzig: Brockhaus, 1848-1852), and his
Phantasus, 2 vols., in *Schriften,* 20 vols. (Berlin: Reimer, 1828), which has
much on Schröder and Fleck; Karl Frenzel, *Berliner Dramaturgie* (Erfurt: Bar-
tholomäus, 1877); Ludwig Speidel, *Kritische Schriften,* Klassiker der Kritik
(Zurich: Artemis, 1963), Berthold Auerbach, *Dramatische Eindrücke,* ed. Otto
Neumann-Hofer (Stuttgart: Cotta, 1893); Otto Brahm, *Theater, Dramatiker,
Schauspieler,* ed. Hugo Fetting (Berlin: Henschel, 1961) and *Kritiken und*

Essays, Klassiker der Kritik (Zurich: Artemis, 1964); Theodore Fontane, *Schriften und Glossen zur Europäischen Literatur,* vol. 1, Klassiker der Kritik (Zurich: Artemis, 1965); Helene Richter, *Schauspieler-Charakteristiken,* TF 27 (Leipzig & Hamburg: Voss, 1914), and Hermann Bahr, *Kritiken,* ed. Heinz Kindermann (Vienna: Bauer, 1963).

Memoirs are always a valuable source for the theatre historian, and Germany is especially fortunate in having a rich literature in this area. Three classics of the eighteenth-century theatre are Josef Anton Christ, *Schauspielerleben: Erinnerungen* (Berlin: Henschel, n.d. [1949]), Johann Christian Brandes, *Meine Lebensgeschichte,* 3 vols. (Berlin: Maurer, 1799-1800), and J. H. F. Müller, *Abschied von der k. k. Hof- und Nationalschaubühne* (Vienna: Wallishausser, 1802). Among the several nineteenth-century memoirs, I have found the following informative and, not infrequently, highly entertaining: Heinrich Anschütz, *Erinnerungen aus dessen Leben und Wirken* (Leipzig: Reklam, n.d. [1900]); Ludwig Barnay, *Erinnerungen* (Berlin: Henschel, 1951); August Haake, *Theater-Memoiren* (Mainz: Kunze, 1866); Karl von Holtei, *Vierzig Jahre,* ed. Max Grube, 4th ed., 2 vols. (Schweidnitz: Heege, n.d.); Ernst von Possart, *Erstrebtes und Erlebtes* (Berlin: Mittler, 1916); Friedrich Ludwig Schmidt, *Denkwürdigkeiten des Schauspielers, Schauspieldichters und Schauspieldirektors,* ed. Hermann Uhde, 2 vols. (Hamburg: Mauke, 1875); Heinrich Schmidt, *Erinnerungen eines weimarischen Veteranen* (Leipzig: Brockhaus, 1856); Carl Sontag, *Von Nachtwachter zum türkischen Kaiser!* (New York: Lauter, 1880), and Rudolf Tyrolt, *Allerlei von Theater und Kunst* (Vienna: Braumüller, 1909), and *Aus Lebenswege eines alten Schauspielers* (Vienna: Schworella & Heick, 1914). Diaries are equally as valuable a source as memoirs. I have profited especially from Carl L. Costenoble, *Tagebücher von seiner Jugend bis zur Übersiedlung nach Wien (1818),* SGT 18 & 19, ed. Alexander von Weilen, 2 vols. (Berlin: SVGT, 1912), and *Aus dem Burgtheater, 1818-1837* (Vienna: Konegen, 1889), from August Klingemann, *Kunst und Natur: Blätter aus meinem Reisetagebuche,* 3 vols. (Brunswick: Meyer, 1819-1828), from Eduard Devrient's fascinating *Aus seinem Tagebüchern, 1836-1870,* ed. Rolf Kabel, 2 vols. (Weimar: Bohlau, 1964), and Eduard Genast, *Aus dem Tagebuche eines alten Schauspielers,* 2d ed., 2 vols. (Leipzig: Voigt & Gunther, 1862).

Histories of plays in performance are always of value, especially in tracing how each period's conception of roles changed. Especially useful in this regard have been Alexander von Weilen, *Hamlet auf der deutschen Bühne* (Berlin: Reimer, 1908), Adolf Winds, *Hamlet auf der deutschen Bühne bis zur Gegenwart,* SGT 12 (Berlin: VGT, 1909), Wilhelm Widmann, *Hamlets Bühnenlaufbahn, 1601-1877,* ed. Joseph Schick & Werner Deetjen, Schriften der deutschen Shakespeare-Gesellschaft, new ser. 1 (Leipzig: Tauschnitz, 1931), and Wolfgang Drews, *König Lear auf der deutschen Bühne,* Germanische Studien 114 (Berlin: n.p., 1932). Ernst Leopold Stahl, *Shakespeare und das deutsche Theater* (Stuttgart: Kohlhammer, 1947) is a fund of information.

Goethe's *Faust* has also been well covered in Wilhelm Creizenach, *Die Bühnen-geschichte des Goetheschen Faust* (Frankfurt-am-Main: Rutten & Loening, 1881), Eugen Kilian, *Goethes Faust auf der Bühne* (Munich: Muller, 1907), and Julius Petersen, *Goethes Faust auf der deutschen Bühne* (Leipzig: Quelle & Meyer, 1929). Brief mention should also be made here of city theatre histories. Each major city has several histories written about its theatres. Particularly helpful are Gustav Wahnrau, *Berlin Stadt der Theater* (Berlin: Henschel, 1957), and, from the *embarasse des riches* on Vienna, Felix Salten's essay, "Wiener Theater (1848-1898)" in *Die Pflege der Kunst in Österreich, 1848-1898* (Vienna: Perles, 1900), as well as Oscar Fontana's suggestive opening chapter in *Wiener Schauspieler*.

CHAPTER 1

The literature of and on the eighteenth-century German theatre is dauntingly vast. General histories have already been mentioned. More specifically, use has been made of Rudolph Genée, *Lehr- und Wanderjahre des deutschen Schauspiels* (Berlin: Hofmann, 1882), Julius Petersen, *Das deutsche Nationaltheater*, Zeitschrift für den deutschen Unterricht 14 (Leipzig & Berlin: Teubner, 1919), and Rudolf Schlosser, *Von Hamburger Nationaltheater zur Gothaer Hofbühne, 1767-1779*, TF 13 (Leipzig & Hamburg: Voss, 1895). The complex area of theory has been well expounded in Hans Oberländer, *Die geistige Entwickelung der deutschen Schauspielkunst im 18. Jahrhundert*, TF 15 (Leipzig & Hamburg: Voss, 1898) and more recently in a broader survey relating to the whole theatre in Alberto Martini, *Geschichte der dramatische Theorien in Deutschland im 18. Jahrhundert*, Studien zur deutschen Literatur 32 (Tübingen: Niemeyer, 1972). A valuable anthology of writings is available in *Dramaturgische Schriften des 18. Jahrhunderts*, ed. Klaus Hammer, Geschichte des deutschen Theaters, Section B, vol. 1. (Berlin: Henschel, 1968). An interesting survey of theories of acting, with particular attention to its mental and physical dangers, has recently been published by Gloria Flaherty, "The Dangers of the New Sensibilities in Eighteenth Century German Acting," *Theatre Research International*, 8, no. 2 (Winter 1982/83), 95-109. The influence of costuming on acting style is clearly explained in Winifried Klara, *Schauspielkostüm und Schauspieldarstellung*, SGT 43 (Berlin: VGT, 1931), as is the complex issue of the *Fach* system in Bernhard Diebold, *Das Rollenfach im deutschen Theaterbetrieb des 18. Jahrhunderts*, TF 25 (Leipzig & Hamburg: Voss, 1913). Discussion of the social status of the actor is included in Leo Schidrowitz, *Sittengeschichte des Theaters* (Vienna & Leipzig: Verlag für Kulturforschung, n.d.).

Biographies of early actors are hard to come by; the only two readily available are Carl Heine, *Johannes Velten* (Halle: Karras, 1887) and Friedrich von Reden-Esbeck, *Caroline Neuber und ihre Zeitgenossen* (Leipzig: Barth, 1881). Interesting documents relating to the Neubers can be found in *Die Neuberin: Ma-*

terialen zur Theatergeschichte des 18. Jahrhunderts (Berlin: Ministerium für Kultur, 1956). Two of the early actor-managers have been well covered in Hans Devrient, *Johann Friedrich Schönemann und seine Schauspielergesellschaft,* TF 11 (Leipzig & Hamburg: Voss, 1895) and, in a fine piece of modern scholarship, Herbert Eichhorn, *Konrad Ernst Ackermann: Ein deutscher Theaterprinzipal,* Die Schaubühne 64 (Emsdetten: Lechte, 1965). There are three brief biographies on Ekhof: Joseph Kurschner, *Conrad Ekhofs Leben und Wirken* (Vienna: Hartleben, 1872), Hermann Uhde, "Konrad Ekhof," *Der neue Plutarch,* vol. 4 of 12 vols. (Leipzig: Brockhaus, 1876), and Hugo Fetting, *Conrad Ekhof: Ein Schauspieler des achtzehnten Jahrhunderts* (Berlin: Henschel, 1954). The last of these is especially useful as it includes letters, eye-witness reports, documents on the Schönemann Academy, etc. These documents are also available *in toto* in Heinz Kindermann, *Conrad Ekhofs Schauspielerakademie,* Österreichische Akademie der Wissenschaften, Philosophisch-historische Klasse, 230, vol. 2 (Vienna: Rohrer, 1956), and some have been translated by John Terfloth in "The Pre-Meiningen Rise of the Director," *Theatre Quarterly,* 6, no. 21 (Spring, 1976), 65-86. An exhaustive discussion of the academy and its relationship to contemporary theories about acting is conducted in Gerhard Piens, *Conrad Ekhof und die erste deutsche Schauspielerakademie* (Berlin: Studien für die künstlerische Lehranstalten, 1956).

CHAPTER 2

Few actors have been such prolific writers as Iffland. His autobiography, *Meine theatralische Laufbahn,* ed. Oscar Fambach (Stuttgart: Reklam, 1976) is a wonderfully informative work, catching well the theatrical atmosphere of the time. His early writings on acting are included in Wilhelm Koffka, *Iffland und Dalberg* (Leipzig: Weber, 1865), while the later essays that appeared in the *Berlin Almanach* are available in *Iffland in seine Schriften als Künstler, Lehrer, und Direktor der Berliner Bühne,* ed. Carl Duncker (Berlin: Duncker & Humblot, 1859). A more recent collection of Iffland's essays can be found in *Über Schauspieler und Schauspielkunst: Ausgewählte Abhandlungen von August Wilhelm Iffland und Johann Gottfried Seume,* ed. Kurt Böwe, Studienmaterial für die künstlerische Lehranstalten, Theater und Tanz 5 (Berlin: Ministerium für Kultur, 1954). Of the several eye-witness accounts, the best is probably Karl Böttiger's detailed *Entwickelung des Ifflandschen Spiels in vierzehn Darstellungen auf dem Weimarischen Hoftheater im Aprillmonath 1796* (Leipzig: Goschen, 1796), which, incidentally, gives a good idea of Engel's ideas in practice. Modern biographies are Erwin Kliewer's perhaps over enthusiastic *A. W. Iffland: Ein Wegbereiter in der deutschen Schauspielkunst,* Germanische Studien 195 (Berlin: Ebering, 1937) and Wilhelm Hermann, *Thaliens liebster Sohn: Iffland und Mannheim* (Mannheim: Gesellschaft der Freunde des Mannheimer Nationaltheater, 1960). The Henschel brothers' sketches are reproduced and commented on in Heinrich Härle, *Ifflands Schauspielkunst*, SGT 34 (Berlin: VGT, 1926).

Goethe's theatre at Weimar has, of course, attracted several writers. Two recent books in English have been most helpful; Marvin Carlson's informative and engrossing *Goethe and the Weimar Theatre* (Ithaca, N.Y.: Cornell University Press, 1979) and T. J. Reed, *The Classical Centre: Goethe and Weimar, 1775-1832* (New York: Barnes & Noble, 1980), which examines more than just theatre. Among the several books available in German on the subject, three in particular are of great use: Julius Wahle, *Das Weimarer Hoftheater unter Goethes Leitung*, Schriften der Goethe Gesellschaft 6 (Weimar: Goethe-Gesellschaft, 1892), Hans Knudsen, *Goethes Welt des Theaters* (Berlin: Tempelhof, 1949), and Willi Flemming's fine and exhaustive discussion in *Goethe und das Theater seiner Zeit* (Stuttgart, Berlin, Cologne & Mainz: Kohlhammer, 1968). *Wilhelm Meisters Lehrjahre* is, of course, standard reading both as background for the eighteenth-century theatre and for Goethe's ideas on theatre. The standard English translation by Thomas Carlyle is available (New York: Collier, 1962), but a new translation by Eric A. Blackall is forthcoming in a new series, *Goethe in English* (Boston: Suhrkamp Insel). The one full-length study of Wolff, which includes interesting essays that define in length aspects of the Weimar style, is Max Martersteig, *Pius Alexander Wolff* (Leipzig: Fernau, 1879).

CHAPTER 3

A most helpful introduction to the Romantic theatre is offered by Edgar Gross, *Die ältere Romantik und das Theater*, TF 22 (Leipzig & Hamburg: Voss, 1910). Gross is also responsible for the only biography of Fleck, *Johann Friedrich Ferdinand Fleck*, SGT 22 (Berlin: VGT, 1914). There is, of course, an exhaustive literature on Schröder. Most important is F. L. W. Meyer's compendious two-volume biography, *Friedrich Ludwig Schröder*, new ed. (Hamburg: Campe, 1823). Of later biographies, the best is Berthold Litzmann, *F. L. Schröder*, 2 vols. (Leipzig & Hamburg: Voss, 1890-1894), while Schröder's connection with the Burgtheater is thoroughly explored in Dieter Hadamzcik, *F. L. Schröder und das Burgtheater*, SGT 60 (Berlin: VGT, 1961). As with Iffland, there are several eye-witness accounts of Schröder's acting. The best of these by far, both because of its vigorous writing and the inclusion of many telling details, is J. F. Schink, *Friedrich Ludwig Schröders Charakteristik als Bühnenführer, mimischer Künstler, dramatischer Dichter und Mensch* (n.p., n.d.). Karl August Böttiger, *Friedrich Ludwig Schröder in Hamburg im Sommer 1795* (n.p., n.d.) gives much interesting information on how he ran the company and on the impressive physical stock acquired by the Hamburg City Theatre under his direction.

Naturally, Ludwig Devrient has exercised the imagination of many writers, not always in the interests of strict, historical accuracy. The standard critical biography, which is reliable and informative, is Georg Altman, *Ludwig Devrient: Leben und Werke eines Schauspielers* (Berlin: Ullstein, 1926). Heinrich Smidt's *Devrient-Novellen* (Berlin: Duncker, 1852) is unsound, but his memorial piece, *Ludwig Devrient* (Berlin: Bechtold & Hartje, 1833) can be trusted. Ludwig Rellstab's essay, "Ludwig Devrient," in vol. 9 of *Gesammelte Schriften* (Leipzig: Brockhaus, 1860) vividly recreates the man and his roles and has strongly influenced later writers such as Carl Gerold, *Ludwig Devrient* (Berlin: n.d. [1869]). Two accounts of his performances in Vienna, full of insights, can be found in the *Allgemeine Zeitung* (November 11-December 18, 1828) and in Franz Ermin, *Devrient in Wien* (Vienna: Adolph, 1829). Hermann Ulrici's reconstruction of Devrient's Lear in "Ludwig Devrient als König Lear," *Jahrbuch der deutschen Shakespeare-Gesellschaft* 2 (1867) captures well the quieter quality of Devrient's acting. Julius Bab, *Die Devrients: Geschichte einer deutschen Theaterfamilie* (Berlin: Stilke, 1932) treats Carl, Eduard, and Emil as well as Ludwig.

CHAPTER 4

As can be expected, the contemporary literature on Seydelmann was considerable. The standard biography, which includes generous extracts from his letters, is Theodore Rötscher, *Seydelmanns Leben und Wirken* (Berlin: Duncker, 1845), while the only modern study, S. Troizkij, *Karl Seydelmann: Die Anfänge der realistischen Schauspielkunst* (Berlin: Henschel, 1949) relies very heavily on Rötscher. Among the writings of Seydelmann's contemporaries, the following are most helpful, not only for pure description but also for establishing the importance he had in the theatre of his time: August Lewald, *Seydelmann und das deutsche Schauspiel* (Stuttgart: Liesching, 1835); Heinrich Laube, "Seydelmann und die deutsche Schauspieler," *Moderne Charakteristiken* I (Mannheim: Löwenthal, 1835); D. R. K., "Seydelmann und die letzte Entwicklung der deutschen Schauspielkunst," *Hallische Jahrbüher*, 44-50 (1838); Karl Gutzkow, "Erinnerungen an Karl Seydelmann," *Aus der Zeit und dem Leben* (Leipzig: Brockhaus, 1844), and Karl Reinhold, "Erinnerung an Seydelmann," *Jahrbuch der Gegenwart* (Tübingen: 1845). Seydelmann's letters and promptbooks are also invaluable sources. They are most readily available in *Rollenhefte Karl Seydelmanns*, ed. Max Grube, SGT 25 (Berlin: VGT, 1915) and in Karl Seydelmann, *Aus seinen Rollenheften und Briefen*, Studienmaterial für die künstlerischen Lehranstalten 2 (Berlin: Ministerium für Kultur, 1955).

The most extensive study of Emil Devrient is available in Heinrich Hubert Houben, *Emil Devrient: sein Leben, sein Wirken, sein Nachlass* (Frankfurt-am-Main: Rutten & Loening, 1903). Somewhat uncritical laudations are offered in Emil Kneschke, *Emil Devrient* (Dresden: Meinhold, 1868) and Rudolf Gottschall, "Emil Devrient," *Literarische Charakterköpfe* in vol. 6 of *Porträts und*

Studien (Leipzig: Brockhaus, 1876). Paul Legband provides an appreciative, relatively sane assessment in "Emil Devrient," *Bühne und Welt*, 6, 1 (1903). Of all the actors written about in this book, only one has been the subject of a recent biography, Dawison. Peter Kollek's scholarly and meticulously researched *Bogumil Dawison: Porträt und Deutung eines genialen Schauspielers*, Die Schaubühne 70 (Kastellaun: Henn, 1978) provides both a full assessment of Dawison's work and painstakingly detailed reconstructions of his major roles. There are three contemporary biographies, all of interest: Theodore Fasoldt, *Bogumil Dawison* (Dresden: Teubner, 1857); Adolf von Hirsch, *Bogumil Dawison* (Leipzig: 1866), and Alfred von Würzbach, *Bohumil Dawison, Zeitgenossen* 11 (Vienna: Hartleben, 1871). Gustav Freytag's essays on both Dawison and Emil Devrient in *Aufsätze zur Geschichte, Literatur, und Kunst,* vol. 8 of lst ser. of *Gesammelte Werke* (Leipzig: Hirzel, n.d.) are most suggestive.

CHAPTER 5

With the exception of the Comédie Française, no single theatre can have been quite so widely written about as the Burgtheater. Among the several dozens of books available, the following are the most useful: Rudolf Lothar, *Das Wiener Burgtheater: Dichter und Darsteller* (Leipzig, Berlin & Vienna: Seemann, 1899); Franz Herterich, *Das Burgtheater und seine Sendung* (Vienna: Neff, n.d.); Emil Haeussermann, *Die Burg: Rundhorizont eines Welttheaters* (Vienna: Deutsch, 1964), and Friedrich Schreyvogl, *Das Burgtheater: Wirklichkeit und Illusion* (Vienna: Speidel, 1965). A recent publication, edited by Margret Dietrich, *Das Burgtheater und sein Publikum,* Philosophische-historische Klasse 305 (Vienna: Der Österreichischen Akademie der Wissenschaften, 1976) is highly recommended for the breadth and depth various scholars of Viennese theatre bring to their analysis of the social milieu of the Burgtheater and the importance of the actor within it. Josef Schreyvogel's *Tagebücher, 1810-1823,* ed. Karl Glossy, SGT 2 & 3 (Berlin: SVGT, 1903) are an important source for the founding of the ensemble, as is Heinrich Laube's history and memoir, *Das Burgtheater*, most easily available in Laube, *Schriften über das Theater,* ed. Eva Stahl-Wisten (Berlin: Henschel, 1955), an anthology of Laube's writings that includes many of his essays on the history of German theatre in general. One of the best books on Laube as *Regisseur* is Georg Altman, *Heinrich Laubes Prinzip der Theaterleitung,* Schriften der literarhistorischen Gesellschaft V (Dortmund: Ruhfus, 1908). Alexander von Weilen wrote a concise summary of his importance in "Heinrich Laube und das Burgtheater," *Bühne und Welt* 6, no. 2 (1905), and a substantial part of *Maske und Kothurn* 2, nos. 3/4 (1956) is devoted to Laube's work.

Sonnenthal, being the subject of great public interest, had much written about him. The standard work is Ludwig Eisenberg, *Adolf Sonnenthal* (Dresden: Pierson, 1900), but Rudolf Lothar's attractive essay, *Sonnenthal,* Das Theater

7 (Berlin: Schuster & Loeffler, n.d. [1904]) also catches the man's appeal accurately. Herman Bartsch's heralding of the actor to the United States in *Adolf Sonnenthal* (New York: Bartsch, 1885) is less trustworthy.

While the periodical and newspaper literature on Mitterwurzer is extensive, few books have been written on him. There are three fairly brief biographical and critical studies: Eugene Guglia, *Friedrich Mitterwurzer* (Vienna: Gerold, 1896); J. J. David, *Mitterwurzer*, Das Theater 13 (Berlin: Schuster & Loeffler, n.d. [1905]), and Max Burckhard, *Anton Friedrich Mitterwurzer* (Vienna: Wiener, 1906). Hugo von Hofmannsthal's review of Guglia's book, "Eine Monographie," in *Prosa* I, *Gesammelte Werke* (Frankfurt-am-Main: Fischer, 1950) includes an important assessment of Mitterwurzer's position vis-à-vis the Burgtheater. Maximilian Harden's essay on him in *Köpfe* I, 22d ed. (Berlin: Reiss, 1910) is both perceptive and moving.

Jakob Minor's book of essays on Burgtheater actors, *Aus dem alten und neuen Burgtheaters* (Zurich: Amalthea, 1920) is an invaluable source, while Joseph Handl's history, *Schauspieler des Burgtheaters* (Vienna & Frankfurt-am-Main: Humboldt, 1955) includes much pertinent information.

CHAPTER 6

The rise of the director in the late nineteenth century has been the subject of some interest recently; Michael Hays, *The Public and Performance: Essays in the History of French and German Theater, 1871-1900,* Theater and Dramatic Studies 6 (Ann Arbor, Mich.: UMI Press, 1982) offers a very stimulating analysis of this phenomenon that challenges the general perception that the director was automatically the savior of a declining theatre. John Osborne, *The Naturalist Drama in Germany* (Totowa, N.J.: Rowman & Littlefield, 1971) also provides an excellent survey and analysis of the Berlin theatre late in the nineteenth century. For a contemporary discussion of the broader theatre world, seen from the viewpoint of a concerned practitioner, Adolf L'Arronge, *Deutsches Theater und deutsche Schauspielkunst* (Berlin: Concordia, 1896) is full of pertinent information. The Deutsches Theater, an institution whose importance has possibly been underestimated by recent theatre historians, interested many critics and scholars. Of the many publications, the best on the pre-Reinhardt years of the Deutsches Theater is Kurt Raeck, *Das Deutsche Theater zu Berlin unter der Direktion von Adolphe L'Arronge* (Berlin: Verein für die Geschichte Berlins, 1928).

As Julius Bab observed, few people wrote about Matkowsky, as there was so little actually to write about. The standard work is Bab's adulatory biography, *Adalbert Matkowsky* (Berlin: Oesterfeld, 1932), but Max Grube, *Adalbert Matkowsky* (Berlin: Paetel, 1909) and Philipp Stein, *Matkowsky,* Das Theater 6 (Berlin & Leipzig: Schuster & Loeffler, 1904) also give a clear idea of the

man, as does Eugen Zabel, "Berliner Bühnenkunstler VIII: Adalbert Matkowsky," *Bühne und Welt* 1, no. 1 (1898).

In comparison to Matkowsky, Kainz gave rise to an utter deluge of literature,
and he is still, in comparison to almost all the other actors in this book, the
subject of some interest today. The best biography is undoubtedly Helene
Richter, *Kainz* (Vienna & Leipzig: Speidel, 1931), which incorporates many
of the unusually vivid reconstructions of roles she had written at the start of
the century when Kainz was still alive; Richter's contribution to the history of
acting is here, as elsewhere, invaluable. Hermann Bang, *Josef Kainz* (Berlin:
Bondy, 1910) is of major importance in coming to an understanding of this
difficult actor. Other biographies are also of use; Eugen Isolani, *Joseph Kainz:
Ein Lebensbild* (Berlin: Pulvermacher, 1910); Ferdinand Gregori, *Kainz* (Berlin
& Leipzig: Schuster & Loeffler, 1904); Paul Wiegler, *Josef Kainz: Ein Genius
in seinen Verwandlungen* (Berlin: Deutscher, 1941), and Erich Kober, *Josef
Kainz: Mensch unter Masken* (Vienna: Neff, 1948). Especially stimulating are
the relevant passages of Felix Salten, *Gestalten und Erscheinungen* (Berlin:
Fischer, 1913). Konrad Falke, *Kainz als Hamlet: Ein Abend im Theater* (Zurich:
Rascher, 1911), while utterly exhaustive, is of limited value as at times one
fails to see the wood for the trees of detail. An appreciative summary of Kainz's
importance, which includes substantial extracts from many of the above writers
and from other Kainz enthusiasts, such as Hermann Bahr, can be found in
Huldigung für Josef Kainz (Vienna: Wiener Bibliophilen-Gesellschaft, 1958).
Kainz himself was no mean writer, and a selection of his letters and essays can
be found in *Kainz: Ein Brevier,* ed. Marie Mautner-Kahlbeck (Vienna: Österreichische Staatsdruckerei, 1953). One of the finest collections of letters ever
written by a single actor is available in Josef Kainz, *Briefe,* ed. Wolfgang Noa
(Berlin: Henschel, 1966).

INDEX

About the Author

Simon Williams is Associate Professor of Theatre History at the University of California, Santa Barbara. His articles have appeared in *Theatre Research International*, *Shakespeare Survey*, *New German Critique*, and *The Romantic Century*.

Recent Titles in
Contributions in Drama and Theatre Studies
Series Editor: Joseph Donohue

American Popular Entertainment: Papers and Proceedings of the Conference on
the History of American Popular Entertainment
Myron Matlaw, editor

George Frederick Cooke: Machiavel of the Stage
Don B. Wilmeth

Greek Theatre Practice
J. Michael Walton

Gordon Craig's Moscow *Hamlet*: A Reconstruction
Laurence Senelick

Theatrical Touring and Founding in North America
L. W. Conolly, editor

Bernhardt and the Theatre of Her Time
Eric Salmon, editor

Revolution in the Theatre: French Romantic Theories of Drama
Barry V. Daniels

Serf Actor: The Life and Career of Mikhail Shchepkin
Laurence Senelick

Musical Theatre in America: Papers and Proceedings of the Conference on the
Musical Theatre in America
Glenn Loney, editor
*The American Society for Theatre Research, The Sonneck Society, and the
Theatre Library Association, joint sponsors*

Garrick Claims the Stage: Acting as Social Emblem in Eighteenth-Century
England
Leigh Woods

A Whirlwind in Dublin: *The Plough and the Stars* Riots
Robert G. Lowery, editor